DISCOVER
CHINA

To Wah and Ken

DISCOVER
CHINA

Sophia M.R. Leung

ISBN 0-88839-141-2
Copyright © 1982 Sophia M.R. Leung

Cataloging in Publication Data
Leung, Sophia M.R. (Sophia Ming Ren), date.
Discover China

Guidebook ISBN 0-88839-141-2

1. China — Description and travel — 1976
—Guidebooks.   I. Title.
DS705.L48   915.1'0457   C82-091108-9

Edited by Nancy Flight & Elizabeth McLenehan
Typeset in Garamond on a Comp/Edit Varityper by
Lisa Smedman
Design and layout by Peter Burakoff

Printed in Canada by Friesen Printers

Published by
HANCOCK HOUSE PUBLISHERS LTD.
19313 Zero Avenue, Surrey, B.C., Canada V3S 5J9
HANCOCK HOUSE PUBLISHERS
1431 Harrison Avenue, Blaine, WA 98230

TABLE OF CONTENTS

Part 3: Cities and Sites

PREFACE

Because I was born and raised in China, I have a special attachment for this country. In recent decades, China has gone through an incredible change. For me and for many others, a trip to the People's Republic of China is a discovering of the new China.

During four recent visits to China, I met and interviewed many Chinese peasants and workers, as well as scholars, artists, and officials, about different aspects of the new China. Thus, in addition to describing places to see in China, this book attempts to present the attitudes and mores of the Chinese people.

Discover China is divided into three parts. Part I gives the practical information you need for your trip and includes a special section for businessmen on conducting business in China. Part II provides background information on China's history and political system, various aspects of life in China today, and the major museums in China. In Part III sixty cities or significant sites and their main points of interest are described. At the end of the book there are lists of useful Chinese terms and phrases and suggested books and periodicals for the interested reader. The appendix contains tables and maps. Throughout the book I have used the Hanyu pinyin system of spelling.

For their help in putting this book together, I would like to express special thanks to David Hancock, Nancy Flight, Elizabeth McLenehan, Peter Burakoff, and Lisa Smedman of Hancock House. I would also like to thank Ian Gray, Jack Webb, Clare Ash, and Douglas Hollingworth of CP Air for their support. I am indebted to Consul General Zhu Yi, Consul General Chen Liang, and Consul Sang Sung-sen, all of the People's Republic of China; the Xinhua News Agency and the China News Agency; Ditu Chubanshe of Beijing; Marwyn Samuels; and Howard Lo for their valuable advice, maps, and photographs. I am grateful to C.C. Wang, the renowned scholar and artist, for rendering the title of this book in Chinese calligraphy. For their encouragement and support, I thank my dear friends Kay and Max Walters, Margaret and Winston Lee, Doreen and Rod Macdonald, Peggey and Lum Lai, David M.Y. Liang, and Milton and Harriet Miller. Finally, I would like to express my appreciation to my family—Mary and Walter Clyde, my mother, and my son Ken, for their endless support, and my loving husband, So Wah, who has been a most valuable consultant and supporter.

Sophia Ming Ren Leung
Vancouver, British Columbia
March 1982

PART 1

PRACTICAL INFORMATION

Boarding the CAAC plane.

Planning for Your Trip

Because tourism is still a very young industry in China, the simplest way to visit China at present is to join a tour group offered by the major airlines and private travel agencies. In North America, Europe, and the Mideast, Canadian Pacific Airlines, Pan Am, Japan Air Lines, China's national airline (Civic Aviation Administration of China, or CAAC), Swissair, Air France, Iranair, and a number of selected travel agencies have recently been granted the right to organize tours to China throughout the year. Generally, they offer a wide selection of times, duration, and itineraries. Each group is accompanied by a tour manager who takes the responsibility of handling your visa application, as well as making all the arrangements for your tour programs and entertainment.

If you have a specific professional or academic interest in China, you may wish to meet with your Chinese counterparts and organize your own group of colleagues for that purpose. Under these circumstances you should contact the Chinese consulate or the China International Travel Services (*Luxingshe* or CITS) in Beijing directly. Information to be provided includes the professional nature of your group, the number in the group, your choice of itineraries and cities, the length of your stay, the places of entry and exit, the preferable means of transportation, and the language spoken by your group. You should submit your request six months to a year in advance to CITS, 6 Dong Changan Avenue, Beijing.

Occasionally the Chinese government issues special invitations to individuals and groups to visit China for the purpose of reciprocating trade or exchanging ideas on education, the arts, science, and foreign policy. These visits are usually initiated by the Chinese counterpart organization. For example, the Chinese Ministry of Education may host a group of educators, the Chinese Medical Association may sponsor a group of physicians and medical personnel, or a Chinese music academy may coordinate a Western artist's visit.

With an official invitation an individual or group may approach the Chinese consulate in San Francisco, Houston, or New York in the United States or Vancouver in Canada, or contact the consular office of the Chinese embassy in Washington, D.C., or in Ottawa.

In North America and Europe, China Friendship Associations regularly sponsor group tours to China in order to promote understanding and friendship between China and their own countries. These tours are open to the association members and to individuals with a special interest in China's social, economic, and political development. As a private delegation, the group meets members of the Chinese People's Association for Friendship in China.

Overseas Chinese—either native-born Chinese who have taken foreign citizenship, or those of Chinese ancestry living abroad—can contact the Chinese consulate or China Travel Services in Hong Kong or Beijing to arrange their trip to China. Overseas Chinese are also generally given permission to travel singly as well as in groups and may be granted longer visits. In many of the major Western cities Chinese community organizations sponsor tours especially for Chinese-speaking travelers who wish to visit relatives in China.

All tour groups are met and welcomed by the representatives of the China Travel Services when they reach China. These representatives accompany the group throughout their tour of China, acting as guides and translators for the group. In each city, the group is further assisted by local representatives of China Travel Services.

Passport and Visa

If you travel on your own or with a small group, you must submit your passport for visa application to the nearest Chinese consulate. If you are with a tour group, your travel agent or tour manager will handle your passport and visa application. If your itinerary includes stopovers in other countries, you should look into the visa requirements for these countries. American and Canadian citizens do not require a visa for brief stops in Japan and Hong Kong.

Customs Requirements

Upon entry into China, visitors must complete a "Baggage Declaration for Inward Passengers" form, listing accompanied and unaccompanied baggage, jewelry, watches, cameras, radios, tape recorders, and the amount of currency and traveler's checks carried into China. This important document is in duplicate; one is to be carried by the visitor while in China, and the other is retained by Chinese customs for clearance when the visitor leaves China. It is extremely important not to lose this form.

For personal use each visitor may bring in, duty free, four bottles of liquor, three cartons of cigarettes, a watch, a radio, cameras and accessories, a movie camera not exceeding 8 mm, a tape recorder, films, and calculators. These items may not be transferred but must be taken out of China on departure. There are some gift items that visitors may import duty free in accordance with Chinese government regulations. Duty must be paid on other items. The Chinese consulate can provide a current list of these items. It is prohibited to import arms and ammunition, wireless receivers and transmitters, narcotics and drugs, and printed material detrimental to China's morals, ethics, culture, politics, and economy. There are export restrictions on Chinese currency, currency drafts or securities, and antiques unless approved for export as indicated by a red seal attached to the item by the Chinese government. All invoices, sales slips, and currency exchange memos should be kept and, if requested, shown to customs at the point of exit.

Health Regulations

Visitors from Canada and the United States do not require innoculation. Appropriate vaccination is required, however, if you visit infected areas. Generally, travel in China involves considerable walking, frequent climbing, and a full schedule of daily activities, so you should be in good health and freely mobile. If you require emergency medical attention, you should advise your *Luxingshe* guide, your hotel, or the local CITS office. In such a case, Western-trained physicians and local hospitals will be able to accommodate you. It is recommended that you take with you any minor personal medications you may need while traveling, such as prescribed drugs and cold and digestive remedies, since most Western medications are not available in China.

Nanjing Station.

Currency, Exchange, and Traveler's Checks

换款和支票

There is no limit on the amount of foreign currency and traveler's checks that visitors may bring into China. However, all foreign money must be declared and recorded on a "Declaration of Foreign Currencies and Bills" form upon entry and endorsed by the customs office. Foreign exchange counters, where visitors can convert their traveler's checks into either Chinese currency or Foreign Exchange Certificates, are located at banks, airports, railway stations, and hotels throughout China.

The currency used by the Chinese is the *renminbi* (RMB), which is based on the decimal system and issued by the People's Bank of China. The basic unit of the RMB is the *yuan* (dollar), which is divided into smaller units, the *jiao* and *fen* (cent). Thus, a *yuan* is divided into ten *jiao*, and each *jiao* is equal to ten *fen*. *Yuan* and *jiao* are issued in notes and *fen* in coins. *Yuan* are available in denominations of one, two, five, and ten, while *jiao* notes and *fen* coins occur in denominations of one, two, and five.

Since April 1980, all foreign visitors have been required to use Foreign Exchange Certificates, instead of RMB, in such places as the Friendship Stores, hotels, and trade centers, and in paying for transportation, telecommunication, and postage. Prior to departure, visitors must convert any unused Chinese currency or Foreign Exchange Certificates back into foreign currency at the Bank of China or an exchange agency, as it is forbidden to take *renminbi* out of China.

Credit cards are not generally used in China, although there are a few exceptions. VISA is accepted in Guangzhou at the Dongfang Hotel, the Guangzhou International Trade Center, the Bank of China, and the airport to a limit of $1,000.00 (US). However, a 4 percent service charge is added to each transaction. DINERS CLUB is accepted in Shanghai at the Jinjiang Hotel, the Bank of China, and the Friendship Store. MASTERCARD is accepted at the Jinjiang Club in Shanghai. Broader acceptance of credit cards at other locations in China is currently under consideration.

MONEY CONVERSION CHART

US DOLLARS	CANADIAN DOLLARS	RMB (*YUAN*)
$ 1.00	$ 1.21	Y 1.49
5.00	6.05	7.46
10.00	12.10	14.93
15.00	18.15	22.39
25.00	30.15	37.31
50.00	60.15	74.63
75.00	90.75	111.75
100.00	121.00	149.25

Canadian $1.00 = Y1.23   (Exchange rate subject to change.)

Overseas Chinese Hotel, Guangzhou.

Transportation and Travel Arrangements

Canadian Pacific Airlines, Pan Am, and Japan Air Lines are among the several major international airlines that have regular flights to China. From North America, one can easily fly to Beijing and Shanghai via Tokyo, or one can enter Guangzhou from Hong Kong by air, hovercraft, or Kowloon's express train. Although the route through Tokyo is faster and more direct, the latter has the obvious advantage that you may enjoy a view of the countryside of South China. Upon arrival, Chinese guide-interpreters assist you to and from the hotels and arrange for all sightseeing trips.

Within China, the domestic airline operated by the Civil Aviation Administration of China (CAAC) has regular internal flights between eighty major cities. Fares are comparable to the international air rates. Because of the great demand and limited number of flights, travelers should make airline reservations well in advance of the date of travel. Each passenger on the domestic airline is allowed twenty kilos of baggage and a five-kilo carry-on bag free of charge. Children between two and twelve years of age are charged 50 percent of the adult fare. A child under two without a separate seat pays 10 percent of the adult fare. A fee is charged for any cancellations.

Trains link all the major cities in China. The trains are clean, comfortable, and economical, and, for those who have more time, they are a good way to see the vast landscape of China. Trains generally run on schedule and travelers tend to receive a lot of attention and care from train attendants, conductors, and chefs. Your Chinese guide or the desk clerk at the hotel lobby can assist you in arranging your train trip. Tickets should be obtained in advance.

For sightseeing and shopping, taxis are generally available at the hotel. The hotel clerk may have to help you give directions to the driver, since the majority of taxi drivers do not speak foreign languages. Return taxi transportation should be arranged at the same time. It is also possible to request your driver to wait for a short time in order to avoid the difficulty of locating a taxi later.

Beijing Hotel, Beijing.

Hotel Services

旅
館
情
況

The China Travel Services (*Luxingshe*) provides first class hotel accommodation to visitors. The hotel facilities are generally adequate and clean but not luxurious. In big cities like Shanghai and Beijing, hotels tend to be more modern and comfortable. In small towns and rural areas, be prepared for a simpler style of accommodation.

Rooms are generally simple and comfortable, usually with two single beds to each room. The room may or may not include a bathroom. Most of the hotels have bathtubs but not showers. They may, however, have hand-held shower sprays. Towels, tissue paper, and soap are usually provided by the hotel.

The voltage in China is 220V AC. Therefore, if you take any personal electrical items with you, it is advisable to take those which have built-in transformers. You will also need a few adapters to fit the different outlets. Alternatively, it might be useful to take along a Franzus converter kit, which contains a transformer and several adapter plugs.

If you need an iron and an ironing board, the service clerk on your floor will provide them for you. Keep in mind, however, that the laundry services in most hotels are quick and inexpensive.

You will always find in your room a tin of fine Chinese tea, a full thermos of boiled water, and cups with lids. Following the Chinese tradition, you may make tea any time you wish. If you prefer coffee, you might like to take you own favorite brand of instant coffee along or else you can try the Chinese coffee, which is quite palatable. In the hot summer of 1978, the clerk noticed that I preferred to drink the thermos water after it had cooled in my cup, and he thoughtfully provided me with a thermos of ice water each day. So I could have iced coffee too. Room service for ice, drinks, or mixes may also be requested through your floor clerk. These items are usually to be paid for on receipt.

Radio and television are commonly not included in your room, but hotel guests may share a color televsion set in a common room. There are several

16

other services and facilities in most of the big hotels, such as hair salons, which are adequate and inexpensive.

Hotel clerks are most cordial and helpful when one, in turn, is polite and pleasant. In fact, the young clerks set up a special Chinese class for my son, while he taught them English in exchange. At six o'clock in the morning, they even played badminton with him.

Climate

Most of China lies in the temperate zone, which has four seasons. The climate is suitable for traveling all year round, but there is considerable variation in temperature from the north to the south. Thus, while northern China is dry with cold winters, southern China, which lies in the subtropical zone, experiences warmer winters and hot and humid summers.

The following table lists the average monthly temperatures for the major cities in China:

Approximate Monthly Temperatures

	BEIJING		CHENGDU		GUANGZHOU		GUILIN		HANGZHOU		HARBIN		KUNMING		NANJING		SHANGHAI		WUHAN		XI'AN	
	F	C	F	C	F	C	F	C	F	C	F	C	F	C	F	C	F	C	F	C	F	C
JANUARY																						
Average	24	-4	42	6	57	14	46	8	38	3	3	-20	46	8	35	2	38	3	37	3	30	-3
High	51	11	64	18	82	28	82	28	75	24	40	4	72	22	67	20	68	20	70	21	61	16
Low	-9	-23	24	-4	32	0	23	-5	18	-8	-37	-39	22	-6	7	-14	15	-10	1	-17	-5	-21
FEBRUARY																						
Average	28	-2	46	8	58	15	48	9	41	5	4	-16	50	10	39	4	40	4	41	5	36	2
High	65	18	69	21	83	29	84	29	83	29	52	11	76	25	74	24	74	24	77	25	70	21
Low	-17	-27	26	-3	32	0	26	-3	15	-10	-27	-33	29	-2	9	-13	18	-8	5	-15	-2	-19
MARCH																						
Average	40.	4	54	12	64	18	56	13	49	10	23	-5	56	13	47	8	47	8	50	10	46	8
High	74	24	85	30	88	31	89	32	85	30	63	17	82	28	83	29	82	28	85	30	82	28
Low	10	-12	31	-1	38	3	32	0	26	-3	-20	-29	27	-3	19	-7	22	-6	23	-5	18	-8
APRIL																						
Average	56	13	63	17	71	22	65	18	59	15	43	6	62	17	58	15	57	14	61	16	57	14
High	86	30	89	32	91	33	96	36	93	34	82	28	87	31	93	34	92	34	92	34	92	34
Low	27	-3	37	3	46	8	39	4	33	1	9	-13	33	1	32	0	32	0	31	-1	25	-4
MAY																						
Average	68	20	70	21	78	26	74	24	69	21	58	15	67	20	68	20	66	19	70	21	67	20
High	99	38	97	36	97	36	95	35	98	37	96	36	89	32	97	36	92	34	97	36	100	38
Low	37	3	48	9	58	15	52	11	45	7	26	-3	43	6	41	5	44	7	45	7	38	3
JUNE																						
Average	76	25	75	24	81	27	79	26	76	25	68	20	67	20	76	25	74	24	78	26	78	26
High	103	40	96	36	98	37	99	38	103	40	97	36	88	31	101	39	98	37	100	38	107	42
Low	50	10	58	15	66	19	55	13	57	14	41	5	49	10	53	12	54	12	58	15	49	10
JULY																						
Average	79	26	78	26	83	29	83	29	84	29	73	23	68	20	83	29	82	28	84	29	80	27
High	101	39	97	36	100	38	101	39	102	39	98	37	84	29	100	38	101	39	101	39	106	41
Low	60	16	63	17	71	22	70	21	67	20	52	11	54	12	62	17	66	19	63	17	59	15
AUGUST																						
Average	76	25	77	25	83	29	82	28	83	29	71	22	67	20	82	28	82	28	83	29	78	26
High	97	36	99	38	102	39	103	40	103	40	96	36	85	30	105	41	102	39	103	40	103	40
Low	54	12	60	16	72	22	65	18	65	18	47	8	48	9	63	17	67	20	64	18	54	12
SEPTEMBER																						
Average	67	20	71	22	81	27	78	26	74	24	58	15	64	18	73	23	75	24	74	24	67	20
High	89	32	95	35	100	38	101	39	97	36	87	31	83	29	102	39	99	38	98	40	94	35
Low	39	4	53	12	60	16	55	13	54	12	30	-1	43	6	49	10	54	12	50	10	41	5
OCTOBER																						
Average	55	13	62	17	75	24	69	21	63	17	43	6	59	15	62	17	64	18	64	18	56	13
High	85	32	86	30	92	34	95	35	90	32	80	27	79	26	92	34	88	31	94	35	91	33
Low	26	-3	43	6	52	11	46	8	34	1	10	-12	36	2	32	0	35	2	35	2	31	-1
NOVEMBER																						
Average	39	4	54	12	67	20	59	15	54	12	22	-6	53	12	51	11	55	13	51	11	44	7
High	76	25	75	24	90	32	87	31	88	31	59	15	77	25	80	27	83	29	83	29	71	22
Low	10	-12	33	1	42	6	37	3	26	-3	-15	-26	33	1	21	-6	25	4	23	-5	2	-17
DECEMBER																						
Average	27	-3	45	7	59	15	50	10	43	6	4	-16	47	8	40	4	43	6	42	6	33	1
High	55	13	69	21	85	30	82	28	80	27	43	6	70	21	74	24	74	24	74	24	64	18
Low	-1	-18	27	-3	35	2	29	2	20	-7	-32	-36	24	4	11	-12	17	-8	16	-9	-3	-20

Telecommunications and Postal Services

In all major cities hotel rooms have extension telephones, and local calls may be made by dialing 0 and the number. To place long distance calls from your hotel room you must request assistance from the personnel at the front desk. Telegrams are classified as (1) urgent, (2) ordinary, and (3) letter-telegrams. The telegraph office in Beijing is on Xi Changan Street. Phone: 668531.

Post offices are usually located in hotels. Letters and postcards sent air mail generally take five to ten days to reach destinations outside of China.

Time

When it is 12 noon in Beijing, Guangzhou, and Shanghai, the standard time in other cities of the world is:

CITY	TIME	CITY	TIME
Bangkok	11:00	Paris	05:00
Bombay	09:30	Rome	05:00
Cape Town	06:00	San Francisco	20:00*
Chicago	22:00*	Singapore	11:30
Delphi	09:30	Tokyo	13:00
Geneva	05:00	Toronto	23:00*
Hong Kong	12:00	Vancouver	20:00*
London	04:00	Vienna	05:00
Manila	12:00	Washington, D.C.	23:00*
Melbourne	14:00	Wellington	16:00
Mexico City	22:00*		
Moscow	07:00		
New York	23:00*		
Osaka	13:00	* previous day	

Note: Although China spans four time zones, the entire country is considered to be a single zone. Thus, time changes do not occur within the country.

Clothing and Packing

衣服和行装

Spring and fall are the best seasons for traveling in China. Visitors can simply wear sweaters, jackets, and light raincoats. In the winter a warm coat, heavy clothing and underwear, gloves, and a hat are necessary. In the humid and hot summer light cotton clothing is most suitable.

In China, clothes tend to be less colorful and varied than in the West. Fancy dresses, jewelry, and high heels are not only unnecessary but also inappropriate in China. Men will find a sports jacket or one suit with or without tie adequate for official functions. Scant clothing such as beach wear and night attire are not considered suitable in public places other than at beaches or public swimming facilities. Basically your attire ought to be simple, comfortable, and in good taste during your stay in China. Try to pack lightly, using one medium suitcase and a small overnight bag, so that you will have room for Chinese handicrafts and souvenirs when you return home. All luggage should be locked before you enter China and in airports and railway stations in China.

Chinese Guide-Interpreters

旅行社代表

When you arrive in China, you will be welcomed by Chinese guides who are familiar with your language. They are generally university educated, young or middle-aged men and women who are knowledgeable about travel in China and about China in general. They are assigned to your group to serve as hosts, interpreters, guides, and friends throughout your travels, and you are invited to exchange ideas, discuss issues, and share toasts with them. They may become your teachers and your special friends. How well they serve you depends in part on how you relate to them and in part on the luck of the draw. One young male guide discussed Chinese poetry and Shakespeare with me, and another young woman played Chopin for our group. The guides are specially selected, since they not only must act as public relations personnel and educators about China but also must assist with luggage, accommodation, travel, sightseeing, and personal gripes. They will be of most help to you when you are aware of their abilities and sympathetic with their problems in trying to help you. Mutual appreciation can easily be established. On one of my trips to China, I asked the head guide to arrange a special dinner for my group. He insisted that I obtain the group's consent before he made the necessary arrangements. In his eyes I was acting like a dictator. So the guides are aware of democratic procedures in China too. The point is, once you have gained their confidence, the guides are generally quite open and frank in their conversation with you.

General Conduct

At receptions and official functions, Chinese hosts and guides usually arrive before the appointed time. You should be punctual for all appointments, as it is considered extremely rude to be late.

Don't be upset if people on the streets stare at you. It is an expression of natural interest about your general appearance and clothing. Many Chinese cyclists would turn their heads to look at me and my family, even while they were pedaling in traffic!

Visitors should address the host country as the People's Republic of China, or China, not as Communist China, Red China, or Mainland China. Also, you must always refer to the country's leaders with respect. It is considered poor taste to make jokes and silly remarks about Chinese leaders as well as foreign leaders.

The Chinese are always eager to share information and are open to discussion with foreign visitors. Visitors, however, must avoid open confrontations and arguments. In a tour group you may present your problems to your tour manager or your leader, who will discuss it with your guides to resolve any difficulties.

At a banquet the leading host customarily makes a cordial welcome speech and proposes a toast to the guests. It is expected that the leader of the guest group will graciously respond and offer a toast in return. Throughout the dinner the hosts and the guests may lift their wine glasses to drink with each other and express good wishes at the same time. This pleasant, mutual exchange of informal toasts with friends at dinner is in keeping with Chinese tradition.

It would greatly please your Chinese hosts if you made an effort to learn some simple phrases such as "how are you?" (*ni hao?*), "thank you" (*xie xie*), and "goodbye" (*zaijian*). (A glossary of useful Chinese phrases is provided at the back of this guide.)

Tipping for services is prohibited. Suggestive remarks or expressed sexual interest towards the opposite sex is not tolerated. And in public or at the hotel, excessive noise and loud conversation are considered rude and impolite.

Photographing and Filming

It is a courtesy to ask permission before you take a photograph of someone. If he or she refuses, you should accept the refusal graciously. Areas of national defense and security are not permitted to be photographed or filmed. Filming at airports or out of airplanes is also forbidden. To avoid any embarrassment it is often best to consult your travel guide. You can now buy film in many of the major hotels and retail stores in China. However, since it is not always available everywhere in the country, you might want to carry a supply of your favorite kind with you.

Food and Drink

Chinese cuisine is among the best and most diverse in the world. With such varying geography and climatic conditions, many areas of China have developed their own specialty dishes and cooking techniques.

The climate and geography of the northern provinces are favorable for growing wheat. As a result, northern cuisine relies heavily on wheat and flour. Meals frequently consist of fried or grilled meats accompanied by small wheat cakes and fritters. Because of the cold weather in the North and the absence of central heating, the "hotpot" style of cooking meats and vegetables in a broth is very popular. Genuine Beijing food is little known in the West, where Chinese food is mainly of the Cantonese and, more recently, of the Shanghai and Sichuan type. When in Beijing, you must try one of the three famous "Peking duck" restaurants, where bite-sized pieces of crispy duck skin are served with fresh green onion and a sweet plum sauce and wrapped in a thin pancake. The meat is served separately. Dishes consisting of other parts of the duck, such as liver, tongue, webbed feet, and wings, are also available on request.

The cuisine of Shanghai, Nanjing, Suzhou, and Wuxi is sweeter and more delicate in taste and appearance. The dishes can literally be works of art. Suzhou is famous for its handmade delicate pastries. The dinner dishes are beautifully decorated with colorful miniature animal figures cut from vegetables, such as carrots and bamboo shoots, and some molded out of pastry. They are a feast for the eyes and almost too lovely to eat.

Cantonese cooking is the best-known and most popular Chinese food in the West. However, you might be pleasantly surprised by the much greater variety of dishes available in Guangzhou (Canton). Besides the excellent duck and chicken dishes, the Cantonese specialties are turtle, bear, snake, and a variety of wild game dishes.

The provinces of Sichuan and Hunan are noted for hot, spicy food. Pimento, chili peppers, red pepper, and black pepper are used liberally. Tea-smoked duck and chicken, hot pepper fish, spicy chicken, and beancake dishes are specialties of these provinces.

From Mongolia to Xinjiang the Moslem tradition influences the food. Specialties are grilled mutton and Mongolian hotpot. Pork, of course, is totally excluded. The mutton is usually cut into fine thin strips, soaked with herbs, dipped in egg yolk, and then grilled on a large, hot iron sheet over charcoal. The Mongolian hotpot is prepared in a big, round copper pot heated by a coal fire. The pot is filled with delicious boiling soup, and the diners cook thin sliced beef and mutton by dipping them into the soup, much as one does with fondue. Different sauces are used to flavor the meat.

Throughout China, visitors may have the chance to try the "Monks' Feast," which is essentially the Chinese vegetarian food (usually made from soybeans into different forms with the look and taste of meats) served in the specialty restaurants. There is a popular one in Shanghai near the International Hotel.

It is a great mistake to think Chinese drink only tea. Although tea is the most popular beverage, China also produces a wide range of wines, whiskey, brandy, and beer. The Chinese do not have the habit of the cocktail hour; alcoholic beverages are usually served with meals. Popular drinks are the sweet red wine, called *shao-xing*, and the medium sweet, rather sharp yellow wine, called *huang-chiu*, which are served warm. Their alcoholic content is 6 percent by volume. *Mao tai*, a strong spirit distilled from sorghum produced in Guizhou, is usually served at banquets. Visitors must be cautious, since *mao tai* is over 100 proof. Consequently, it is usually served in tiny glasses. The red and white wines are much sweeter. Sparkling wine is almost like cider and quite pleasing. Chinese brandies and liqueurs are relatively unknown to the West, but they are very good in quality and taste. The brandies are similar to French cognac. Beijing *ginseng* brandy is said to have a rich content of vitamins.

Many Chinese towns and cities produce their own wines and spirits. You might be amazed at the wide range of the liquor available in the department stores. Among liqueurs, the light, clear *chu yeh qing* (Bamboo Leaf Green) and *mao tai* are favorites with the Chinese. Chinese beer, which is similar to German beer, is light and excellent. At the hotels, you will be served beer or orange soda as part of the meal. Mineral waters are readily available at the dining room.

Most of the hotels offer Western food as well as excellent Chinese meals. At the Beijing Hotel, coffee and yogurt are served at breakfast. However, you should try the authentic Chinese breakfast at least once. The typical breakfast offers a variety of *dim sum*, roasted meats and cold cuts, spiced peanuts, hard-boiled salted duck eggs, spiced beancakes, and light rice congee. You might also try a typical worker's breakfast of soybean milk and Chinese salty long-john, *yui-tiao*. Because the hotel chefs do not expect foreign visitors to have a Chinese worker's taste, you may have to specially request such a breakfast. If you don't like the Chinese breakfast, you can always switch the next day to ham and eggs, toast, and coffee without any problem. But be sure to inform your waiter in advance.

Although tipping is not proper in China, a word of thanks to the waiters and clerks is greatly appreciated. After many good meals, I usually requested the chef's presence to meet my group, so that we could express our thanks for the delicious food.

Entertainment

In each city visitors will have a chance to attend evening performances of ballet, musicals, drama, opera, circus, and acrobatics. Sports are another popular form of entertainment in China and provide an opportunity to see the Chinese people and their public stadiums.

Some major hotels have cocktail lounges and music for dancing. Visitors may also be invited to special dinners or banquets. Since it is a Chinese tradition to reciprocate hospitality, it would be a courtesy to thank your Chinese guides with a farewell dinner at the end of your journey.

娱
乐

The Beijing ballet.

Play depicting the life of Zhou Enlai.

Working on embroidery.

Papercutting by a Shanghai master.

Shopping for Gifts and Souvenirs

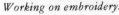

Most stores in China are state owned. The prices are fixed and clearly stated by the store clerks. The Chinese are scrupulously honest so that any bargaining or haggling over the price of the merchandise may be taken as a sign of mistrust or as an insult to the clerks. Despite their limited ability to speak and understand English, the clerks are usually friendly, courteous, and eager to assist you.

Most of the large cities have Friendship Stores, which are mainly for the benefit of foreign visitors and offer better quality and selections than many of the other local shops. They carry everything from jade carvings to television sets to candies, as well as a wide range of gift items produced throughout China. The prices are fixed and the same as in the public stores.

If you have time, you also should go to the local People's Department Stores for local crafts, wines, and folk souvenirs. Because your purchases will be wrapped and tied with string, you might want to take along one of your own shopping bags. These stores do not carry imported goods; such items may be purchased at the Friendship Stores. The shops and department stores are usually open from 8:00 a.m. to 8:30 p.m.

During your shopping adventures you might be interested in some of the local Chinese shops and markets. At the People's Markets, for example, you can observe not only the great variety but also the quantity and quality of food, some of which you may never have seen before. Even if you do not intend to purchase anything, the experience of seeing a local market is worthwhile.

Following is a list of popular items and the best places to purchase them.

Antiques — Wen-wu stores of the major cities in China.

Chinese paintings — Wen-wu stores in major cities, specialty stores in the Liulichang section of Beijing (e.g., Rong Bao Zhai), and To Yun Shuan (422 Nanjing Road) and the Friendship Store in Shanghai.

Ceramics — Beijing, Changsha, Chengdu, Datong, Foshan, Fuzhou, Guangzhou, Jingdezhen, Nanchang, Shanghai, Xiamen.

Clay Figurines — Beijing, Changsha, Shanghai, Wuxi, Xiamen, Xi'an.

Cloisonné and lacquerware — Beijing, Fuzhou, Shanghai, Tianjin.

Embroidery — Changsha, Chengdu, Hangzhou, Suzhou.

Furniture — Beijing, Guangzhou, Shanghai, Tianjin.

Furs and suedes — Beijing, Shenyang.

Ivory carvings — Beijing, Guangzhou, Shanghai. (It is illegal to bring ivory into the United States and Canada.)

Jade carvings — Beijing, Guangzhou, Shanghai.

Jewelry — Beijing, Guangzhou, Shanghai.

Papercuts — all cities in China.

Rugs and weavings — Beijing, Datong, Hangzhou, Lhasa, Shanghai, Tianjin.

Silk — Beijing, Chengdu, Hangzhou, Shanghai, Suzhou.

Stone rubbings — Beijing, Datong, Guangzhou, Luoyang, Shanghai, Xi'an

Wood-block prints — major cities in China.

Potter in Jingdezhen.

Figurines from Foshan.

Artistic repair on old calligraphy.

27

Conducting Business and Foreign Trade in China

外
贸
和
商
讨

In the past few years there has been a notable increase in international business exchanges with China. It has been estimated that 50 percent of Western visitors to China since 1978 have been there for trade purposes. Most of China's export trade business originates from the Trade Fair held twice annually in Guangzhou (Canton). Attendance at this fair is by invitation only. Official invitations are usually issued by the major foreign trade corporations of China and have proved to be the most effective method of encouraging the international export of China's many products. Generally, these invitations are sent to representatives of major Western industries that already have established trade relations with China, although the Chinese are always ready to welcome new foreign trade associations. If your firm is interested in establishing trade business with China and wishes to obtain business contacts as well as an invitation to one of the trade fairs, you can either approach the nearest Chinese embassy or consulate or write directly to the Chinese Export Commodities Fair, Pearl River Square, Guangzhou, People's Republic of China. Whether you write or express your interests in person, you should discuss not only your business intentions but also your firm's references.

The Chinese Export Commodities Fair or the Guangzhou Trade Fair was first held in October 1957 for the benefit of foreign businessmen to view some twelve thousand Chinese products available for export trade. The Trade Fair is held in the spring from April 15 through May 15, and from October 15 through November 15 in the fall. Recently attendance of foreign businessmen at the trade fairs has increased to over thirty thousand from 110 different countries. In April 1974 a new Trade Fair complex opened in Guangzhou. Much larger than the original complex, it covers sixty thousand square meters of display space, which is divided into twelve exhibition halls housing over forty thousand Chinese products for foreign export trade.

Although the Chinese trade representatives are eager to do trade with the Western businessmen, smooth negotiations depend on the establishment of a trusting and friendly relationship. Maintaining the traditional cultural approach, Chinese trade representatives tend to be polite and passive, rather than aggressive. However, they are interested in obtaining detailed order specifications from their invited guests. With your business card in hand you should approach the appropriate Chinese trade representatives in the products section featuring your business line. You will then be able to make an appointment in order to discuss your specific buying interests. Since such a large number of Western businessmen are invited to the Trade Fair, you should arrange an appointment as soon as you arrive in Guangzhou. Cancellations and late arrivals for appointments are considered thoughtlessly rude. During your initial discussion you must appreciate the patience and politeness of your Chinese hosts in order to win their trust and confidence and reach a final contract agreement. As the

Chinese put a lot of emphasis on contract negotiations, it is important to have specific terms and conditions, including requirements for export documentation, insurance, claims settlement, arbitration, and arrangements for inspection. Chinese export products are usually delivered by ship directly from the PRC by its merchant fleet. You can, of course, present your own preference in the shipping arrangements. Chinese insurance coverage is regulated through the Ocean Marine Cargo and Ocean Marine Cargo War Clauses of the People's Insurance Company of China. China also has agents in most international ports to handle claims and arising business.

Western buyers of Chinese commodities are required to have an irrevocable letter of credit payable to the Bank of China, which has established business relationships with the following banks in the United States and Canada:

In Canada

Bank of British Columbia
Bank of Montreal
Bank of Nova Scotia
Canadian Imperial Bank of Commerce
Royal Bank of Canada
Provincial Bank
Toronto Dominion Bank

In the United States

American Express International Banking Corporation
American Security Bank, N.A. (District of Columbia)
Bank of America
Bankers Trust Company
Chase Manhattan Bank, N.A.
Chemical Bank (New York)
Citibank, N.A.
Commerce Union Bank
First National Bank of Boston and Chicago
Manufacturer's Hanover Trust Company
Manufacturer's National Bank of Detroit
Michigan National Bank of Detroit
Morgan Guaranty Trust Company of New York
Rainier National Bank of Seattle
United California Bank of Los Angeles
Wells Fargo Bank, N.A.

If you are interested in establishing trade and business relations with China, usually the first step is to contact the nearest Chinese embassy or consulate, or to write to the Trade Fair in Guangzhou. However, another channel for making contact with your Chinese counterparts is to present your business interests directly, in writing, to the head office of the related foreign trade corporation in China (see appendix). The latter course often prompts the

Chinese corporation to extend an invitation to the Trade Fair for one of your firm's representatives.

Alternatively, special exchange of business delegations can be arranged through the China Council for the Promotion of International Trade (4 Tai Ping Chiao Street, Beijing, PRC). Its counterpart in the United States is the National Council for US-China Trade (1050 17th Street, N.W., Washington, D.C. 20036). In Canada, one may approach the Canada-China Trade Council (199 Bay Street, Suite 900, Toronto, Ontario M5J 1L4), for information and assistance.

There is a new law in China to regulate foreign investment. Foreign investors and firms should be fully aware of this new regulation as well as any others that pertain to doing business in China. If you wish to have additional information, you can contact either the Canada-China Trade Council or the National Council for US-China Trade. The latter organization publishes a bimonthly magazine entitled "China Business Review," which is a valuable source providing current reports and news on China's trade and economy. The Chinese also publish a magazine, "China's Foreign Trade," as well as numerous guides, which are produced in several languages and are available at any Chinese embassy.

PART 2

THE LAND, HISTORY, AND PEOPLE

地史與人民

Brief History of China

THE DYNASTIES

China is thought to be the world's oldest civilization. For over four thousand years, from 2205 B.C. until the revolution of 1911, China was ruled by dynasties (see table). Under the earliest dynasties, China was a collection of slave-owning principalities. During the period of the Warring States (476-221 B.C.), these principalities were transformed into a feudal system of states, and during the Qin dynasty (221-206 B.C.), China finally became a unified country. Thereafter, China was repeatedly divided and then unified again under the various dynasties.

In 1280, China fell to the Mongols, marking the beginning of the Yuan dynasty (A.D. 1280-1368). This was the first time China came under foreign rule. In 1368, the Hans regained control of China, and the Ming dynasty (A.D. 1368-1644) was established. When peasant uprisings and internal rebellion caused the last Ming emperor's suicide, the Manchus invaded Beijing from northeastern China, overthrew the Ming dynasty, and founded the Qing dynasty (A.D. 1644-1911).

In the early part of the nineteenth century, foreign powers began to exert control over Chinese ports and trade. The Opium War (1839-1842) marked the

中国简史

Pinyin	Wade-Giles	Dates
Xia	Hsia	2205-1766 B.C.
Shang	Shang	1766-1122 B.C.
Zhou	Chou	1122-770 B.C.
Spring and Autumn Period	Spring and Autumn Period	770-476 B.C.
Warring States	Warring States	476-221 B.C.
Qin	Chin	221-206 B.C.
Han	Han	206 B.C.-A.D. 220
Three Kingdoms	Three Kingdoms	A.D. 220-265
Jin	Tsin	A.D. 265-420
Southern and Northern Dynasties	Southern and Northern Dynasties	A.D. 420-589
Sui	Sui	A.D. 589-618
Tang	Tang	A.D. 618-907
Five Dynasties	Five Dynasties	A.D. 907-960
Song	Sung	A.D. 960-1280
Yuan	Yuan	A.D. 1280-1368
Ming	Ming	A.D. 1368-1644
Qing	Qing	A.D. 1644-1911

beginning of foreign concessions and occupation in China. By the end of the nineteenth century, China had become the helpless prey of world powers, which controlled Chinese trade, customhouses, ports, and concessions in major cities. The injustice of the foreign powers created deep resentment toward foreigners. In 1900 a group of peasants and secret societies dedicated to the expulsion of foreigners organized the Boxer Rebellion, which, although it failed, was a direct reaction to the aggressiveness of the outside powers. The decay and the reactionary control of the Empress Xi Ci and her corrupt court led to revolutionary movements and the downfall of the Qing dynasty.

The Great Wall.

MODERN CHINA (1911-1949)

The Chinese patriotic revolution of 1911 finally overthrew the ineffectual Qing dynasty and abolished the Chinese monarchical system. Dr. Sun Zhong Shan (Sun Yat-sen), the founder of the Republic of China, was elected president of a provisional government in Nanjing. Dr. Sun had planned to unify China by eliminating the regional control of warlords, but he died in 1925. From 1926 to 1928, Chiang Kai-shek led the northern military expedition to dissolve the warlords' government. China was finally unified under the Nationalist government with the capital in Nanjing.

In 1930, Mao Zedong established a revolutionary party in Jiangxi Province, and the first units of the Red Army, or the People's Liberation Army (PLA), were formed. In 1934, the Nationalists pushed the Communists out of their home base. The PLA started the Long March from the west to Yan'an, Shaanxi Province, in October 1935.

During the Sino-Japanese war and the Second World War, the Nationalists moved to Chongqing, Sichuan Province, to establish a war capital. In August 1945, China regained control of the nation, including Manchuria and Taiwan, following the surrender of Japan.

After these wars had ended, conflict between the Nationalists and the Communists was renewed. Internal warfare between these two parties persisted until October 1949, when the Communist Army took over China completely. The Nationalists retreated to Taiwan, where they established their government in Taipei.

Silver jar from the Tang dynasty.

Jade horse from the Han dynasty.

Gold bowl from the Tang dynasty.

Celadon vase from the Song dynasty.

Carved lacquerware from the Ming dynasty.

Neolithic pottery basin, Banpo Museum.

Neolithic pottery jar, Lotu,
Qinghai.

Bronze Kuei-vessel, Zhou dynasty.

Bronze Bo-vessel, Zhou dynasty.

THE PEOPLE'S REPUBLIC OF CHINA

In Beijing, on October 1, 1949, Mao Zedong proclaimed the formation of the People's Republic of China. Agrarian reform permitted a better distribution of land and helped the peasants in the countryside. The Marriage Law, passed on April 30, 1950, assured the legal right to marital selection of one's mate.

The first Five-Year Plan (1953-1957) was launched to build heavy industry with Russian help. In 1958, the second Five-Year Plan began another stage in agrarian and industrial development. This phase was popularly known as the "Great Leap Forward." The cooperative farms were combined into large units, called People's Production Communes, in order to achieve the benefits of organized cooperative farming. By 1962, there were 70,000 communes established.

The division of China into military administrative zones and the establishment of higher education centers occurred in the mid-1960s. The Great Proletarian Cultural Revolution (from 1966 to 1968) brought chaos and change to China. In 1970 Canada recognized China diplomatically, and once again, China established official contact with the West. In the winter of 1972, China invited Richard Nixon to visit, and he was followed by Gerald Ford.

In 1973, the People's Republic of China and the United States established liaison offices in Beijing and Washington, D.C. Following Chairman Mao's death in September 1976, Hua Guofeng succeeded as Chairman of the Central Committee and Premier of the State Council of China. In January 1979, after a lapse of thirty years, the People's Republic of China and the United States re-established their diplomatic relations. A new era of travel to China has begun.

Oil painting of Chairman Mao Zedong.

The Great Hall of the People, Beijing.

China's Political System and Government

改治系統及政府

In 1949 the Communist Party came into power in China. Although other political parties exist, they have limited influence on the nation's politics. Membership in the Communist Party numbers about 30 to 35 million, or 3 percent of the national population. Generally, leading positions in the army, ministries, bureaus, schools, and communes are held by party members.

The Central Committee of the Communist Party is the most important and powerful organ in China's political hierarchy. The chairman and the four vice-chairmen of the committee are the top political leaders. Power within the Central Committee resides in the Politburo, which includes twenty-three full members and three alternate members. The Central Committee of the Politburo has five members and is the most powerful group of all; the chairman and the four vice-chairmen are the leaders of both the party and the nation.

The Central Committee of the party is elected by the National Party Congress, which meets about every five years and is composed of 1,500 delegates selected from the provincial parties and the military service. The National Party Congress elects the members of the Central Committee and its chairman, and the four vice-chairmen.

The chief lawmaking body in China is the National People's Congress, which is made up of 3,497 deputies elected by the people's congresses of the provinces, municipalities, and autonomous regions, and by the People's Liberation Army. Each deputy is elected for a term of five years. The congress is convened at least once annually. The functions and powers of the People's Congress are mainly to amend the constitution and laws, to choose the premier of the State Council based on the recommendation of the Central Committee of the Communist Party of China, to elect the president of the Supreme People's Court, and to examine and approve the national economic plan, the state budget, and so on.

The Premier and the State Council are responsible for the administration and implementation of national policy and law. The State Council includes the heads of all major ministries in the central government, such as Foreign Affairs, National Defense, Education, Foreign Trade, Culture, and Public Health. The State Council is headed by a premier and fourteen vice-premiers

The army plays an important role in China's government. The leading military organization is the People's Liberation Army (PLA). About three million men and women, drawn mainly from the peasants and working classes, serve the PLA. Besides being responsible for national defense, the PLA also participates in highway and railway construction, and assists the farmers with their tasks.

The legislative power in China lies with the National People's Congress. Deputies to the People's Congress of Counties are directly elected by the voters for a term of three years. People's congresses at the provincial and county levels hold at least one session annually. These congresses exercise power on important administrative issues and elect and recall members of the standing committees, the presidents of the people's courts, and the leading members of the people's government at the provincial and county levels. The people's congress at the provincial level has the power to act and promulgate local statutes. All the leading members of the people's governments are chosen by the people's congresses, and the people's governments, and are responsible and accountable to the people's congresses at the same levels.

In 1949, China began to develop a classless society. The purpose of life is to "serve the people." Men and women serve the people and the country equally in their various roles as peasants, workers, and soldiers. The abolition of elitism encourages respect for menial work. Special recognition and privileges are given to the working classes instead of the educated elites. Individualism as the precursor to self-centeredness is strongly repudiated. Within the last three decades, China's independence, international power, and pride have been restored. China has made tremendous progress in cultural developments, technical support to the developing countries, and the basic improvement in the people's daily life.

Tianan Men, Beijing.

China's Political Structure (Simplified)

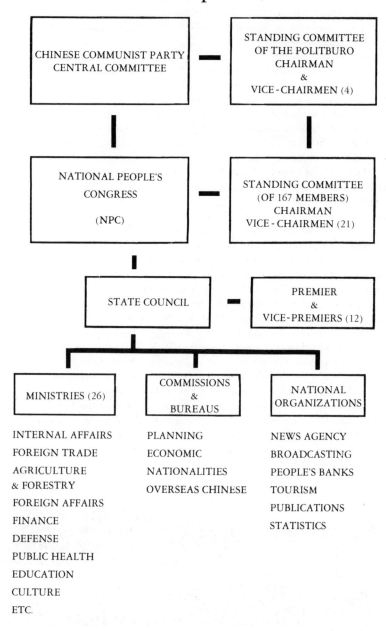

CHINESE COMMUNIST PARTY CENTRAL COMMITTEE	STANDING COMMITTEE OF THE POLITBURO CHAIRMAN & VICE-CHAIRMEN (4)
NATIONAL PEOPLE'S CONGRESS (NPC)	STANDING COMMITTEE (OF 167 MEMBERS) CHAIRMAN VICE-CHAIRMEN (21)
STATE COUNCIL	PREMIER & VICE-PREMIERS (12)

MINISTRIES (26)	COMMISSIONS & BUREAUS	NATIONAL ORGANIZATIONS
INTERNAL AFFAIRS	PLANNING	NEWS AGENCY
FOREIGN TRADE	ECONOMIC	BROADCASTING
AGRICULTURE & FORESTRY	NATIONALITIES	PEOPLE'S BANKS
FOREIGN AFFAIRS	OVERSEAS CHINESE	TOURISM
FINANCE		PUBLICATIONS
DEFENSE		STATISTICS
PUBLIC HEALTH		
EDUCATION		
CULTURE		
ETC.		

Yungang Grottoes, Datong, Shanxi Province.

The Geography, Climate, and People

China is situated in eastern Asia on the western coast of the Pacific Ocean. Its vast territory of 9.6 million square kilometers makes China the third largest country in the world, after the U.S.S.R. and Canada. China extends over 5,000 kilometers, both east to west and north to south, and spans four time zones. It ranges in altitude from 8,922 meters on Mt. Everest, which it shares with Nepal, to 154 meters below sea level in the Turpan Depression.

China has common borders with many countries—Korea to the east; Afghanistan, Pakistan, India, Nepal, Sikkim, and Bhutan to the west and southwest; Laos and Vietnam to the south; the Soviet Union to the northeast and northwest; and Mongolia to the north. Off the mainland across the East and South China Seas, are the islands of Japan, the Philippines, Malaysia, and Indonesia.

There are twenty-two provinces, five autonomous regions, and three municipalities in China, all of which fall directly under the administration of the central government. Beijing, Tianjin, and Shanghai are the three municipalities. The first two are situated north of the Huang He (Yellow River), the cradle of Chinese civilization. The provinces around these two cities, north of the river, are considered part of North China. Shanghai is situated on the estuary south of the Yangtze River (Chang Jiang). This is China's largest river and drains a huge basin of 1.8 million square kilometers (19 percent of China's total area), which is inhabited by 250 million people. The southern provinces have been greatly enriched by the Yangtze River and favored by mild weather and rich farmland. In contrast, the provinces north of the Huang He are less desirable for farming but are rich in minerals and oil. Southwest China consists of numerous hills and valleys and, being near the Tropic of Cancer, has a semitropical climate. The area is well known for its natural scenic beauty and for several minority nationalities indigenous to this region.

地理与人民

Because China covers such a vast territory, the climate varies considerably from one part of the country to another. Climatic conditions are further influenced by the complex terrain of China.

Most of the country lies in the north temperate and monsoon zones, yet only the southwest experiences hot, wet monsoonal weather. In summer, the north, south, and midwest are all quite warm. In winter, however, the north of China is totally covered with ice and snow.

The provinces of Yunnan, Guangxi, and Guangdong and the island of Taiwan in south China are all located in the subtropical zone. Consequently, most of the time the days are sunny and warm, as in Hawaii and Florida. In winter, the south remains comfortably warm not only because of the low latitude but also because the mountain ranges, which run in an east-west direction, block the icy winds from the north.

The population of China is made up of many different cultures. Since the Han people are in the majority, others are referred to as the minority nationalities. There are fifty minority nationalities who have the right to national regional autonomy. The minority nationalities inhabit various parts of China, including Xinjiang, Inner Mongolia, Xizang (Tibet), and many southwestern provinces. They make up 6 percent of the total Chinese population and are mainly Mongolian, Hui, Tibetan, Uighur, Miao, Yi, Chuang, Puyi, Korean, Manchu, and Kaoshan. Each minority group has a population of over a million, and each has its own culture and tradition.

The policy of the central government is to recognize the cultural differences among these different nationalities instead of exercising the supremacy of the majority Chinese, the Han. Thus, many minority nationality areas have been provided with education, medical care, and an adequate standard of living. The Beijing Minority Nationality Institute is an educational institution dedicated to the preservation and propagation of the social and cultural traditions of the minorities. Over 1,700 students from forty-seven nationalities study in the Institute. Its special role is to educate the future leaders of the minority nationalities.

Li River in Guilin, Guangxi Province.

Logan Commune, Guangdong Province.

From Family Units
to Communal Living

The concept of the family is deeply rooted in Chinese culture. Through the family each individual acquires his sense of propriety, responsibility, and loyalty to others, to his society, and to his country. China is an agrarian society, and production depends on intensive use of manpower on the land. Family members, including children, become the most dependable and available resource in producing food for survival.

THE NEW CHINESE MAN AND WOMAN

For centuries, the ultimate goal for a Chinese man, as suggested by the Chinese proverb, was "having a family, establishing a career, then serving the people and the world." In order to produce more progeny, a man could rightfully have more than one wife. Chinese women had to be submissive and endured much social injustice and maltreatment from the male-oriented family. This was the tradition for many centuries. Although the revolution of 1949 did much to bring about social reform, the nuclear and extended family units continued to exist and today play an important role in the changing society of China. In new China, the conceptual roles of the individual have altered as a result of changes in social and political orientation.

Over the past three decades, Chinese women have been emancipated from their former passive and subservient role and have attained equality with men. By demonstrating their ability to hold demanding jobs as steel workers, pilots, and mining engineers, which were traditionally held only by men, women in China have achieved recognition and acceptance. In turn, men now share household tasks and responsibilities with their wives.

Under the new political ideology, the ancient tradition of "having a family, establishing a career, then serving the people and the world" has given way to "love and serve your people, establish your career, and then have a family." Today young people usually work for the state for several years. Then, when a man is about twenty-eight and a woman is around twenty-five, they may be married in a simple civic ceremony with the approval and blessing of the state.

After marriage, both men and women continue to work and to "serve the people." Because of effective public education on family planning, couples tend to have only one or two children. With both parents working, the children are generally cared for by their grandmothers or at day-care centers. Family life has changed radically from prerevolutionary days.

You will seldom see overt displays of affection in public by either young or old couples. Such displays are considered improper and in poor taste. The current Chinese attitude toward sex is rather puritanical. Illegitimate births are so rare as to be almost unheard of. Unless mutually agreed to, divorce could meet with public objection and court disapproval, especially if there are children in the family. Divorces may be granted, however, on the grounds of unresolved differences if there is mutual consent. In general, individual choice and personal wishes are subjugated to majority opinion.

Before 1949, many marriages were arranged by the parents. Today, both women and men are educated and have their own jobs. Their personal freedom gives them greater opportunities to meet and select a suitable mate. The old-fashioned "matchmaker" role has been discarded as a part of social reform. Nevertheless, marriage is still largely the result of contacts made through friends or the family. Although courtship and dating in China may not follow the romantic ritual of the West, with its pattern of "falling in and out of love," I have seen young couples holding hands or sitting closely with heads on each other's shoulders in movie theaters. While outward expressions of love between unmarried couples were frowned on before 1976, there have recently been some changes in this attitude. In addition, open discussions of love and marriage are now becoming regular features in China's newspapers and journals.

In today's Chinese family, domination by the elders, the worship of ancestors, and superstitious practices have been replaced by a pragmatic, nonreligious, and socialist attitude. Also, a new relationship has evolved among

Sugarcane fields of Koozen Commune, Zhongshan, Guangdong Province.

High school students of Guangzhou.

the generations. Although the elders no longer hold their traditional authoritative positions within the family, they are still respected and cared for by the younger generation. Today, however, the older generation of new China is far more involved outside the family. As contributing members of the larger community, the old grandparents and uneducated peasants now have some purpose beyond their productive years. In particular, they provide much help to the young, assisting in child care and imparting their knowledge and wisdom as teachers and counsellors. Within the extended family, many working parents are fortunate to have grandparents to look after their young children at home. Thus, the older generation has become helpful in different roles. At the same time, the parent-child relationship is no longer based on blind obedience and unquestioned filial piety. There is more sharing of opinions and discussion, and decisions are reached on a more democratic basis. Young people are astonishingly frank and vocal about their ideas and opinions. From university students to hotel employees, they are well informed about China's social and political issues. As a result, conversations with the old and the young in China can be a rewarding experience.

LIFE ON THE COMMUNES

"Urban neighborhoods" or "workers' villages" are organized social and political districts comparable to the rural communes. Beijing, for example, is divided into nine neighborhood districts, each district covering an area with a resident population of fifty thousand or over. Each neighborhood district has an administrative body, the Neighborhood Party Committee, which is responsible for organizing the social, political, educational, and health programs for the residents. The committee also operates stores, day-care centers, schools, and hospitals for the neighborhood members. The twenty or more members of each party committee are elected mainly from the district residents, usually on the basis of their community interests and experience, with representation from different age groups, both sexes, and various occupations. Each neighborhood district is in turn divided into a number of residential areas, with about two to three thousand residents in each area. A Residents' Committee of fifteen to twenty-five members is the self-governing body that sets policy and runs day-to-day affairs for the local residents.

In the autumn of 1958, rural communes were introduced throughout China as a new social, political, and economic development. These communes, serving over 80 percent of the country's population, are owned by their members. The typical commune not only is involved in agriculture, light industry, and trade but also provides educational, health, and social programs. As a basic unit of China's socialist society, the commune is organized administratively by the party cadres and local leaders. The people's commune has three levels of organization. Each commune consists of a number of production brigades; under each production brigade are several production teams, and usually a number of family units make up a production team. Collective responsibility and ownership runs through each of these three levels, but the production team is the basic accounting unit. Each team is responsible for its own farm, output and home-industry production as the basic source of their income. This income is then distributed among the members according to the number of work units earned. Besides sharing in the profit, the team has to bear any financial losses.

When projects are beyond the ability of a production team to manage or undertake, the production brigade is called in for consultation or assistance, as for example in the building of small reservoirs or irrigation canals, the processing of farm products, or the management of schools and health clinics. When the brigades have difficult projects, they turn to the commune. The commune is responsible for such major undertakings as power generation and the distribution of extensive irrigation and drainage work, farm machinery repairs, manufacturing products, the building of schools, and the operation of hospitals. It also provides the social and economic leadership for its large membership.

Income distribution is carried out at the production team level. Management and production costs are deducted from the team's gross annual income, as well as a small sum for state tax and another for the team's reserve and welfare funds. The remaining income is distributed among the members of the team. This distribution is based on the principle "from each according to his ability, to each according to his work, more income for those who work more." Thus, each

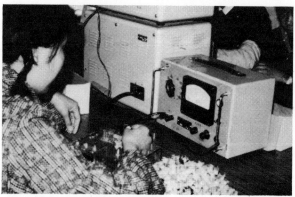

Woman worker at Wuhan Commune, Hubei Province.

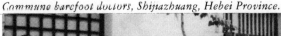
Commune barefoot doctors, Shijiazhuang, Hebei Province.

member receives income based on the number of work points (units of payment for work) he or she earned. Produce grown in private plots may also bring in a small additional income. Housing, education, and health care are all provided for the commune. General stores are operated by the commune for its members, and state banks are available for savings accounts, which offer a small interest for the depositors.

The team's reserve funds are used to buy farm machinery and other equipment, and the welfare fund covers any additional expenses for culture and education, aid to the sick, and pensions for retired members. It also subsidizes the cooperative medical system for which the members pay only about one *yuan* (approximately 60¢ U.S. and 80¢ Canadian) a year for complete medical coverage.

The standard of living in a commune naturally reflects the commune's productivity and net income. A few communes, especially in the northern provinces, where the land and the cold climate are not advantageous, provide only a simple and austere standard of living. In contrast, a well-to-do Wuxi commune operates many light industries, including fish farming, silk-worm raising, and the growing of fresh-water cultured pearls from giant clams. However, an advantage of this commune is that it is in the "land of plentiful fish and rice," in the Jiangsu Province of South China. In such communes as this, the members have a relatively high standard of living, with plentiful food and extra income from their various industries.

Women health workers, Fengsheng District, Beijing.

Women and Their Role in the New Society

Historically, Chinese women have had an extremely low position both socially and politically. Even recently, up until 1949, women were treated more often than not as a mere commodity or as slaves to be bartered or sold. According to Chinese tradition, the female is the *Yin* in cosmology. The *Yin* represents the passive, the dark, and the weak, in contrast to the *Yang*, the male, which is the positive, the bright, and the strong. Thus, it is not surprising that Chinese philosophers, scholars, and even the gods have traditionally been male. Foot binding in China was an outrageously dehumanizing custom that suppressed the freedom of women in the name of vanity; deformed feet of a few inches in size were glorified by Chinese men as "golden lilies." I learned of this degrading and painful fate of Chinese women from my maternal grandmother when I was a little girl. My grandmother was fortunate in that she came from a more liberated family. She ended up with only half-bound feet because her family could not stand to witness the continual pain and suffering she had to endure. When she became a mother, she determined to spare her daughters the cruel and senseless custom. Although foot binding has been completely abolished in China, one can still see many women with pitifully deformed feet who have difficulty moving about. They are the last victims of a demeaning tradition that began in the tenth century.

Traditionally the married woman's major role in life was the bearing of male children for the family. In addition, she had to devote herself wholly to the welfare of her husband's family, submissively serving her in-laws, her husband, and other male members of the household. If a woman failed to bear male heirs to continue the family's name, she was in disgrace and was ostracized by her relatives and neighbors. The husband was then permitted to take other wives to replace her. Polygamy and infidelity were tolerated in males, but even Chinese widows were not permitted to remarry. Marriage was not based on mutual consent and personal love but on the wishes of the families. Commonly, women had to endure a life of suffering and frustrations, with slim hopes of changes for the better. Of course there were some exceptions; daughters of officials and scholars had the opportunity to obtain an education and to become poetesses, painters, and writers. However, in general, whether rich or poor, women had limited opportunity for self-expression and personal growth.

In 1950, a new marriage law was passed by the Communist government as one of the first major laws of the new regime. This important law abolished arranged marriages, polygamy, and child marriages, and guaranteed the wife's right to divorce, and the widow's right to remarry. From 1950 to 1953, a mass campaign was launched to enforce the new marriage laws. This new concept of women's equality, of course, met resistance. A tradition that has been in existence for centuries, especially in the rural areas, dies hard. However, the women's liberation movement was strongly reinforced by special programs to educate women and to ensure equal pay for women's work. The provision of child-care facilities in factories and communes freed women to work outside the home.

The emancipation of women was strongly supported by Chairman Mao Zedong, who, in 1955, stated that "in order to build a great Socialist Society, it is of the utmost importance to arouse the broad masses of women to join in productive activity. Men and women must receive equal pay for equal work in production. Genuine equality between the sexes can only be realized in the process of the Socialist transformation of society as a whole."

Today, Chinese women have achieved equal status with men and are involved in a multitude of jobs. Since 1971, 90 percent of the women in China have been working outside the home. No longer barred from the traditional male roles, they now work as airplane pilots, steel mill controllers, teachers, police officers, construction laborers, doctors, administrators, cab drivers, and bus drivers. Women are also pursuing higher education. Half of the medical students in China are female, with the majority entering the fields of pediatrics, internal medicine, psychiatry, obstetrics and gynecology, and dentistry. Most of the barefoot doctors, who are public health workers with minimum medical training, are also women. Since Chinese women are now working to a far greater extent within the public sphere, household duties are no longer the sole concern of the female. At home, husbands now readily share in domestic responsibilities.

Women have also gained political recognition at the local level, although not to quite the same extent as at the national level. Many women are leading figures in the neighborhood districts, people's communes, and citizens' committees. They are not necessarily the young and the educated; some are simply old-fashioned housewives dedicated to serving their neighbors.

One must not overlook the supportive facilities and services that the state provides for the working mother. In each factory, neighborhood district, and communal village, there are nurseries and day-care or residential care for preschoolers. Women are given a standard maternity leave of fifty-eight days, with pay. Once they have returned to work, mothers may nurse their babies at the nurseries during their breaks or lunch hours. The maternal care of young children is a high priority. In the industrialized and advanced West, we have not done much for working mothers at all. Unfortunately, they have to suffer and struggle to care for their families and to maintain their work, with limited support.

Lian Jujie, silver medalist of the International Women's Fencing Competition, 1978.

Yungang Grottoes, Shanxi Province.

Ling Yin Temple, Hangzhou.

China's Religions and Philosophy

The major religions in China are Buddhism, Daoism (Taoism), Islam, Catholicism, and Protestantism. The first three have a long history in China and have had great influence on Chinese tradition and cultural development.

Buddhism reached China's northwest from India in the third century B.C. It became popular after the fourth century, with the support of emperors and devotees, and reached its peak during the sixth to tenth century. Although many Chinese followed Buddhism prior to 1949, activity declined as a result of political and social changes. However, in 1953 the first Buddhist Congress was held, and the China Buddhist Association was founded. Since then many famous Buddhist temples and shrines have been put under the protection of the government. Recently, Chinese Buddhists have established relations with Buddhists and fellow organizations in more than twenty countries in the world. Chinese delegations also attend world conferences on religion.

Daoism was founded around the second century A.D. by Zhang Daoling. In feudal China, Daoism developed into a strong religious force equivalent to Buddhism. It began to decline during the Ming dynasty (1368-1644). By 1949 there were about twenty thousand Daoist temples and forty thousand believers. In April 1957 the China Daoist Association was founded in Beijing to bring all the Daoist schools together. For the past three decades official efforts have been made to preserve and protect the major Daoist temples in the Qingcheng Mountains of Sichuan Province and the Wudang Mountains of Hubei Province.

Islam was transmitted to China around A.D. 651 through Islamic scholars, disciples, and merchants who came from West Asia and North Africa. They propagated Islam and built mosques in Chinese cities. Islam was popular with the Hui, Uighur, Kazakh, and other minority nationalities. In 1949 it was estimated that there were about ten million Moslems in China. In May 1953 the first Islamic Congress was held in Beijing, and the China Islamic Association was formed. The Association has organized eleven pilgrimages to Mecca and has sent delegates to world conferences on religion.

Catholicism was first introduced in China in 1582 during the Ming dynasty. Its popularity grew considerably after the Opium War and by 1949 there were about three million Catholics in China. In July 1957 the China Patriotic Catholic Association and the Catholic Congress were founded in

宗教与哲学

Beijing. However, resolutions adopted at the Congress stipulated that the Chinese Catholic Church sever its ties with the Vatican by managing the church independently.

Protestantism was introduced to China in 1807. During the 1830s, following the Opium War, many missionaries came to China. By 1949 there were about seven hundred thousand Protestants in China. In July 1950 active Protestant individuals joined together with Chinese Protestant organizations in openly opposing the foreign control of church affairs. A national Protestant Congress was held in July 1954. Recently the Chinese Protestants have re-established contacts with Christians and fellow church organizations in the West.

The philosophy of *Confucianism* has long been the fundamental ethical system of the Chinese. Founded in the sixth century B.C. by Confucious (551-479 B.C.), who was the leading philosopher and political thinker of China at the time, it was not so much a religion as a code of morality and personal conduct. Confucious stressed that every man should know his duty and act according to his responsibilities. He believed that if filial piety and fraternal love were practiced at home, they would extend to the larger community and nation, thus securing moral order and social stability. Although the philosophical principles of Confucianism had an enormous effect on the social structure of Chinese society for centuries, it was severely criticized during the Cultural Revolution (1966-1968). Today, however, it has regained its importance as one of the moral bases for the ordering of social and family relationships.

Pagoda of Six Harmonies, Hangzhou.

Courtyard Pagoda, Lingyin Temple, Hangzhou.

Barefoot doctor.

Health Care

The health care system within China has changed dramatically over the past decades. During the 1930s the leading causes of death were infectious and parasitic diseases and starvation. Health services were inadequate, and medical personnel were insufficient. The majority of the population simply could not afford the medical costs. Most of the medical resources were concentrated in a few big cities, and the rural population was totally without medical attention. Sick children and ailing adults were a common sight in China.

Today, as a result of the "mass movement" approach to health care, initiated in 1950, the Chinese people are in good health. Through public health education, improvements in personal hygiene and public sanitation, and mass immunization, many common infectious diseases have been eradicated. Venereal disease, a serious problem in prerevolutionary China, is now virtually nonexistent. Immunization against such common diseases as measles, polio, diphtheria, and encephalitis among Chinese children has reached 90 to 100 percent. These are spectacular medical and public health successes in a developing country with one billion people.

Although China is a country with a strong central government, administration of health care is directed primarily at the provincial, county, and commune levels. Health clinics and health stations operate to serve the factories and commune brigades and are administered by the local committee. Financing of health care in the communes, factories, and institutions is on a cooperative system. Each individual usually contributes a small amount annually to the cooperative medical fund. For this the member receives free medical care, including hospitalization at the commune hospital. When hospitalization at the county or provincial level is needed, the cooperative medical fund covers part or all of the costs, depending on the individual's circumstances.

Trained physicians are assisted by health workers in the factories and neighborhood districts and by barefoot doctors in the communes. The health workers and barefoot doctors treat mainly common, uncomplicated diseases, and teach about family planning, nutrition, immunization, and environmental sanitation. Usually they visit patients at work or at home.

衛生保健

Education in a New Society

新
中
国
教
育

     Before 1949 over 80 percent of the Chinese population could neither read nor write. Today, China provides universal education for children in day-care centers, kindergartens, and primary and secondary schools. Young adults, too, now have the opportunity to further their training or education at vocational institutes, colleges, and universities, while the older generation has been encouraged to participate in continuing education programs provided by communities. Consequently, illiteracy has been drastically reduced and replaced with a national interest in learning and education. The young and old are eager to learn from each other and to share knowledge with their fellow countrymen. The old illiterate peasants are frequently invited to the schools to tell of their "bitter past." Grandmothers pass on their skills and knowledge of child rearing, and the barefoot doctors and health workers teach family planning and personal hygiene.

     Early education of Chinese children has also changed as a result of the tremendous increase of working mothers in the new society. Children of three to seven years usually attend kindergartens or day-care centers near their home, either as day pupils or weekday boarders. Chinese kindergarten is divided into three grades according to the children's age: groups of three- to four-year-olds, four- to six-year-olds, and six- to seven-year-olds. The program includes lessons in Chinese, arithmetic, music, physical training, fine arts, games, songs, and dances. Most of the songs and dances emphasize contemporary accepted social values and political themes.

     Children begin primary school at age seven and continue for five years. School is in session for nine and a half months each year. Emphasis is put on the basic subjects of Chinese, arithmetic, natural sciences, English, politics, physical education, music, and the arts. School discipline is strict. In addition to school work the children are expected to participate in working projects in the local factories or nearby farms in order to have closer contact with the workers and peasants.

Secondary education in the middle school starts at age twelve. During the five-year period, children attend three years of junior high and two years of senior high school. The basic subjects covered in middle school are politics, Chinese language, mathematics, physics, chemistry, biology, foreign language (English or others), history, geography, basic farm skills, physical education, music, and the arts. In the last few years, additional technical courses in farm skills and mechanics and specific vocational training courses have been added to the regular secondary school curriculum as a result of the need in China for more vocationally trained individuals The middle school system is gradually putting more emphasis on vocational training than on general secondary education. Workers can enroll for part-time study.

Seven million high school students graduate in China each year. Approximately 3 to 4 percent of these graduates are eligible for admission to schools of higher education providing they pass the national entrance examination, instituted in 1977, which all middle school graduates are required to write. Students' admission to higher education is based on merit rather than on political and social standing, which were the criteria during the Cultural Revolution. Students may indicate their desire for admission to science and arts and name one to three choices in specific universities. Tuition is free, and students live in rent-free dormitories and are covered by free medical service. The technical institutes require four years of training in science, engineering, political theory, mathematics, foreign language, and physical education. Students are required to obtain practical training in factories and plants related to their field for about ten months. Colleges and universities provide four years of training in the arts and science faculties. Medical and dental education includes six years of basic training and additional training in specializations.

Today a small number of foreign students attend universities and colleges in China. Those from the developing third world countries take mainly professional or technical training, such as medicine or agricultural science. For students from the West, Chinese history, language, and literature are popular choices. In addition, a small number of foreign teachers may be found in Chinese colleges and institutes, especially in the foreign language institutes. Like their Chinese counterparts, foreign teachers and students have to adjust to the spartan life of the Chinese campus. Also, quite often the lack of active social contacts with other Westerners, the absence of Western entertainment, and few social exchanges with the Chinese people tend to aggravate feelings of isolation and frustration.

Elementary school students.

Lacquer carver.

Potter at Jingdezhen.

Arts and Crafts

艺术和工艺

The folk arts and modern crafts of China are as diverse and colorful as its land and people. A country as vast as China naturally has many forms of artistic expression. China's artists work in a variety of mediums creating art forms that reflect the style of a particular community and the specific skills of the artists.

POTTERY

For centuries pottery has been one of China's leading crafts. During the second century A.D. the discovery of *pai-tun-ci* (a hard crystal composed of quartz and feldspar) and Kaolin (a white clay found at a hillside district of Jingdezhen, the "capital of Chinese ceramics") in Jingdezhen, Jiangxi Province, led to the making of the first porcelain in the world. Although in the early decades of this century both the quantity and the quality of Chinese ceramics declined, many of the traditional ceramic centers have gradually been revived in recent years.

Finely crafted black and painted pottery was produced in China as early as the Neolithic age. Glazed pottery, however, did not appear until the Shang dynasty (the sixteenth through the eleventh century B.C.). Eventually, Chinese potters developed more sophisticated methods and artistic skill in creating unique glazes and designs, as is evident in the lively three-colored glazes of blue, brown, and green produced in the Tang dynasty (A.D. 618-907). During the Song dynasty (A.D. 960-1280), porcelain attained a high level of quality and artistry. The porcelain of this period is characterized by the shadowy blue and white *qingbai* and the gray-green celadon glazes. Multicolored ceramics were really developed during the Ming (A.D. 1348-1644) and Qing (A.D. 1644-1911) dynasties in the form of glazed wares and enamel overglazes. Today Chinese potters still produce traditional wares while also creating modern designs.

Jingdezhen has been the major center of the pottery industry of China since the tenth century and continues to produce some of the finest porcelain in China today. A creamy white porcelain, Blanc de Chine, is produced from the Dehua kilns in Fujian Province. At Liling, Hunan Province, a colorfully underglazed porcelain can be found.

Dark brown stoneware teapots, fashioned in various folk styles, are well-known forms of pottery from Yixing, Jiangsu Province. The pottery of Shihwan, Guangdong Province, is characterized by its vigorous shapes, simple lines, and appealing combination of different-colored glazes. One also finds attractive pottery and porcelain made in northern China in the provinces of Hebei, Shandong, Shanxi, and in the southwest provinces of Sichuan, Guangxi, and Yunnan.

EMBROIDERY

Embroidery has been a highly treasured art form for many centuries. Today, however, it has reached a level of beauty and perfection previously unknown. The four distinctive types of Chinese embroidery come from Suzhou, Hunan, Guangdong, and Sichuan. Over the last decades, skilled workers have developed many ingenious techniques to produce special effects, such as the use of straight stitches of irregular lengths to create a textured surface resembling an oil painting. The Embroidery Research Institute of Suzhou has perfected the "reversible embroidery" technique, in which vivid and delicate embroidery is perfectly presented on both sides of transparent fabric. Through the use of silk threads finer than human hair, swimming goldfish or several playful kittens are portrayed so realistically that they seem to come alive. Amazingly, each thread is split into forty-eight separate strands, and the embroidery is done on a delicate transparent nylon or silk fabric. It takes many months to complete such a piece of reversible embroidery, which is then displayed in a glass frame in order to show the identical images on both sides. Traditional embroidery with detailed, delicate stitches depicting ancient themes, figures, and landscapes is found throughout China. Landscape embroidery that combines traditional water-color painting with simple, accented outline stitches to highlight the scenes is available for a reasonable price.

Embroidery design based on themes drawn from modern China is also much in vogue. This is quite a departure from the traditional decorative art prevalent in former days. Embroidery is used chiefly for wall hangings, decorative screens in public buildings, and, in very large sizes, as gifts to other nations. Tourists may, of course, obtain smaller embroideries from the stores.

Several famous silk tapestry and brocade centers are located in the provinces of Jiangsu, Zhejiang, and Sichuan. *Keszu* of Suzhou, Jiangsu Province, is a special type of silk tapestry in which the raw silk is used mainly for the warp. The skillful craftsmen here created a special method, "broken weft," in which different colors and shades of the pattern are worked with a separate shuttle to produce a perfectly identical tapestry on both sides. These prized silk tapestries are treasured by the Chinese. A high degree of craftsmanship is required to execute the complicated, intricate designs for this special method of weaving.

Many fine silk tapestries and brocades are made in Hangzhou, Zhejiang Province. The tapestries offer a wide range of subjects and designs in figures, landscapes, and reproductions of masters' paintings as well as modern China themes. When one visits Hangzhou, it is difficult to resist the rich and colorful brocades of fine silk fabric. Because they are attractive, inexpensive, and light and easy to carry, they make practical and popular gifts. In Chengdu, Sichuan Province, a special brocade is produced, known as *shu jin* in ancient times. This Sichuan brocade uses geometric or lineal patterns in its design.

Intricate Chinese needlepoint and woolwork are also highly admired for their fine craftsmanship. The woolwork of Shanghai and Shandong has gained international recognition and is used in the huge artistic murals presented by the Chinese government as special gifts to other countries.

Modern Chinese carpets are also known for their fine quality and distinctive style. Their most appealing characteristics are their subtle and harmonious colors and refined designs. You may visit a carpet factory in North China to observe the interesting but laborious process.

The loom used for knotting rugs was originally a strong, wooden frame of four beams set at right angles to each other. Today the loom is arranged so that the vertical beams are anchored to the floor and the horizontal beams are movable. Several carpet workers sit on narrow wooden planks in front of the warp, working all at once. Balls of hanging wool are used to make the required knots for each carpet. The outline of the carpet design is drawn onto the warp threads for the weavers to follow. Embossing and incising are techniques commonly used to accent the carpets. Traditional designs with symbolic meanings based on mythology and folktales are often used on carpets. Upon completion on the looms, there follows a process of shearing, washing, drying, and final inspection for quality control. Then the carpets are ready for the international market. The modern carpets are finer in texture, improved in color, and larger in size than the old, traditional ones. There are four carpet centers in China: Beijing, Tianjin, Shanghai, and Qingdao.

PAPERCUTS

It was recorded that an emperor of the Tang Dynasty (A.D. 618-908) was the first to give his guests a silk flag decorated with papercuts during the Spring Festival. Through the centuries, papercuts became the traditional and favorite decorations for Chinese families at New Year and at festivals. Intricate and delicate patterns cut from tissue-thin white or colored paper are pasted on walls, windows, or door panels as well as on lanterns, mirrors, and fans for decorative purposes. Papercuts have also been used, for many years, as patterns for embroidery on clothing and shoes for women and children. The papercuts are probably the most popular folk art throughout China and each province has its own favorite designs. For instance, the provinces of Jiangxi and Zhejiang in South China are known for their motifs of animals, natural scenes, flowers, and figures. Papercuts of theatrical characters usually come from the northern provinces, Hebei and Shandong. The rich and colorful silver and gold papercuts of exquisite court ladies, playful children, and flowers are generally made in Fushan. From Henan come special flower designs for the ceiling, called ceiling flowers. The most delicate figure and flower cuts of all are undoubtedly from Jiangsu Province in southern China. These papercuts are usually carefully painted in different colors.

Papercuts are made using two basic techniques, knife cuts and scissor cuts. Each technique requires a pattern. However, an experienced master can make a unique design quickly and freely by using small sharp scissors. Today the themes of modern China are commonly used as the subjects for papercuts. Perhaps the most charming designs are of playful children and the Chinese minority nationalities because they convey so vividly the joyful expression of the people.

CARVING

Ivory and jade carvings excavated from the ancient tombs of the Shang dynasty (the sixteenth through the eleventh century B.C.) in China, provide evidence that carving has had a long and illustrious role in Chinese art history. Through the centuries, Chinese craftsmen have created various types of sculptures and carvings in ivory, jade, wood, clay, and semiprecious stones, thus developing one of China's traditional art forms.

Today Guangzhou, Beijing, and Shanghai are noted for their fine ivory carvings. Guangzhou is well known for delicate openwork and intricately carved ivory balls. A large ivory ball may have as many as thirty smaller movable balls, each inside of the other. It is simply astonishing when you consider the time and skill required to make such an object. Shanghai is internationally renowned for its complicated and exquisite ivory carvings. Beijing is known for detailed landscapes, figures, and colored ivory carvings.

The carving of jade has had a longer history than that of ivory, dating back to the Neolithic age. Chinese refer to jade as *yu* or *pi-yu* to designate nephrite, and *fei-tsui* to designate jadeite.

Nephrite, a silicate of calcium and magnesium, is found in the mountains and river beds of eastern Turkestan (near Khotan and Yarkand) and Lake Baikal in Siberia. The Chinese have treasured nephrite, with its wide range of color in browns, grays, and greens, since ancient times. *Pi-yu* is a dark green variety of nephrite jade that has been found abundantly in Taiwan and, more recently, in western Canada. Both nephrite and jadeite are lustrous white when they are free of impurities. Mutton-fat jade, *yang-zhi-yu*, is pure white nephrite and is especially treasured by collectors.

Jadeite, a silicate of sodium and aluminum, is a harder, glossier stone than nephrite and has a higher specific gravity. Originally found in the valleys of the Uru River near Mogaung, Burma, it was first carved by Chinese craftsmen around the eighteenth century. Jadeite is generally bright, translucent, and more vivid in color than nephrite. It may be of many colors: white, greens, blues, lavender, browns, or a mixture of these colors. Emerald green jadeite is of fine quality and has been widely prized for jewelry. It is in great demand today and is very expensive.

Jade has been treasured by the Chinese throughout the centuries. Since Confucius' time, it has been favored by the scholars because it is considered to represent the basic virtues of brilliance, loyalty, and rarity. Jade pieces found by archaeologists in excavations of ancient tombs indicate that the stone not only was used in making decorative objects but also was important in Chinese ritual and symbolism. Found in their original context, these pieces provide the archaeologists with a better understanding of the history of Chinese civilization.

Jade is harder than many metals and most stones except diamond and quartz. As a result, the process of grinding and polishing jade for carving is long and laborious. A master jade carver may take many months and even years to complete a single piece. Today the master craftsmen use high-precision instruments and modern electric tools to work the semiprecious stone, creating exquisite designs in traditional motifs, human figures, animals, flowers, and decorative objects for export purposes.

Sculptures carved out of soapstone from Qingtien and Shoushan may be very attractive and cost much less than jade. These stone carvings are as gracefully and skillfully done as the jade carvings. Fine wood carvings are made in many places in China. The richly decorated wooden vessels from Dongyang, Zhejiang Province, and the delicately carved miniature landscape motifs from Yangzhou, Jiangsu Province, offer good examples of fine craftsmanship in this medium.

Ivory carving from Fujian Province.

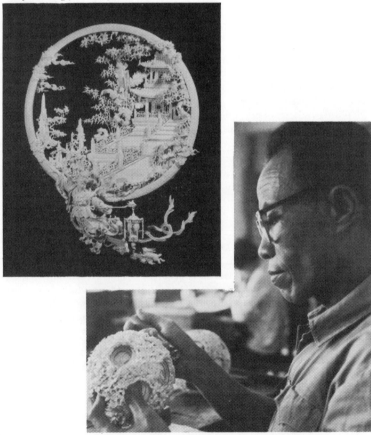

Guangzhou master carver working on ivory ball.

"Ta Yu Harnessing the River" jade carving from Qianlong period, Palace Museum, Beijing.

Five hundred-year-old bell, Yongle Bell Temple, Beijing.

Major Museums in China

PALACE MUSEUM, BEIJING

The Forbidden City is now known as the Palace Museum of China. The main attractions of this vast national museum are the Museums of Treasures, Ceramics, Bronzes, and Paintings, the Sculpture Exhibition of the Rent Collection Courtyard, the Museum Workshops of Repair and Reproduction, and the Exhibition of the Archaeological Findings.

The Museum of Treasures This museum is well known to the Chinese as *Chen Pao Kuan*, which means the Gallery of Precious Treasures. This extraordinary collection of the Qing rulers is housed in the former palaces of Emperor Qianlong in three separate pavilions: (1) the Hall of Cultivation of Character, (2) the Hall of Pleasure and Longevity, and (3) the Pavilion of Peace and Happiness. They are located at the northern corner of the palace complex.

The first pavilion displays numerous sets of jade musical instruments. Throughout Chinese history, nephrite jade has been used to make a stone chime called a *qing*. One of the traditional eight musical instruments, the *qing* is in the shape of a mason's square, an upside-down L, with a hole pierced near the angle for suspension from a decorated frame. A beautiful set of sixteen stone chimes, or *bian qing*, can be seen in the display.

The second pavilion contains clocks, cups, bowls, and washbasins made of solid gold, all of which were used in the imperial household. There are also sets of "golden pages" the size of present-day paperback books, which were imperial wedding gifts for a bride or a favorite concubine. In the central hall of the second pavilion, jeweled royal crowns and fancy armors inlaid with precious stones are displayed. In the side hall are exquisite jeweled pagodas and stupas (miniature towers) made of gold and precious stones.

The third pavilion is entirely devoted to exhibits of semiprecious stone carvings, jeweled trees, and miniature landscapes made of precious stones. Many outstanding nephrite jade objects from the Zhou, Han, and Song dynasties are on display. The most impressive exhibit is the huge nephrite mountain deeply carved with the scene of "Ta Yu Harnessing the River." Created by the finest jade carvers of Qianlong's reign and completed in A.D. 1788, it is the largest and finest nephrite carving in existence. Many lovely lacquerware pieces and wood carvings are also to be found in the collection.

The Museum of Ceramics   This museum contains the imperial collection of the Qing emperors from 1644 to 1912. It is attractively situated in the Palace of Heavenly Favor (*Zheng Qian Gong*) and the Palace of Eternal Harmony (*Yong He Gong*), both of which are located in the northern area of the palace complex and to the east of the main axis. The ceramic displays are skillfully arranged in chronological order.

Earthenware of the fourth millennium B.C. through the Ming dynasty is exhibited in the Palace of Heavenly Favor. Fine funerary stoneware of the Shang and Zhou periods and three-color Tang pottery is also well represented in the displays. The finest Song ceramics and the colorful *junyao* vases are a visual feast for pottery lovers. The misty bluish white qingbai wares and the blue and white bowls and plates of the Yuan dynasty (1280 - 1368) are the fine creations of the kilns of Jingdezhen.

The second pavilion of the Palace of Heavenly Favor contains underglazed red Ming ceramics of the Yongle period (1403-1424) and Wanli (1573-1620) and Jiaqing (1522-1566) three- and five-color porcelains. The famous white *dehua* wares of Fujian, known in the West as Blanc de Chine, and the finest variety of Ming blue and white wares are also attractively displayed. Kangxi (1622-1722) wares of famille noire, famille verte, and famille rose types, and interesting overglazed and underglazed examples of the Yongzheng (1723-1735) and Qianlong (1736-1795) periods are well presented in the collection. The graceful monochromes of Kangxi have a prominent place in the museum.

The Museum of Bronzes   This collection is housed in the Palace of Delights (*Zhai Gong*) and the Palace of Prosperity (*Qian Fen Gong*), which are next to the Museum of Ceramics. These palaces formerly housed the royal concubines.

Palace Museum, Beijing.

Two-thousand-year-old pottery horse. *Pottery pot of the Spring and Autumn period.*

The Palace of Prosperity was the residence of the Pearl Concubine, who was thrown down a palace well for her rebellious remarks to the Dowager Empress Ci Xi. Each palace has two pavilions containing the finest bronze objects, which are displayed according to type and function—for example, whether it is a ritual or utilitarian vessel. The methods of production of the bronzes are also well illustrated.

The Museum of Paintings   The collection is displayed in two wings of the Qianlong palaces, located in the northeastern area of the Palace Museum. The paintings are outstanding for their quality and abundance. The display frequently changes according to the season. In spring and summer, the focus is usually on the paintings from the Ming to the Qing dynasties. Selected paintings of the Tang, Song, and Yuan dynasties are generally on display in autumn and winter.

The Museum Workshops of Repair and Reproduction   These workshops, which unfortunately are not open to the public, are located at the northwestern corner of the Palace Museum. Here the museum staff work at artistic restoration and antique reproduction. Six divisions in this organization are devoted to the repair of precious clocks, bronzes, ceramics, sculptures, paintings, and furniture.

One well-known painter has worked for over forty years in the painting division. For the past three years, she has been working on a reproduction of the Song dynasty painting by Chang Tse-tuan, "Life along the River on the Eve of the Qing-ming Festival." The original is a world-famous horizontal hand scroll, many fine copies of which are on exhibit in museums in Taiwan and the West. Working from the original painting, this artist expects to take four years to complete the reproduction, a task requiring undivided concentration and meticulous artistic skill. The finished reproduction will be displayed in other provincial museums.

In the workshop there is also a special training class where young artisans learn the techniques of restoration and reproduction of works of antiquity. The trainees come from many different museums throughout China, and after a year of training, they return to their posts better able to carry out new tasks in art restoration.

The Sculpture Exhibition of the Rent Collection Courtyard   Because this exhibition has recently been moved to the palace from faraway Sichuan

Province, it may easily be missed. It is now housed in the Chapel of Imperial Ancestors (*Feng Xian Dian*), which is near the Nine Dragon Wall and the Museum of Paintings.

Over one hundred life-size figures depict the story of rent collection as a typical case of oppression and class struggle between the landlords and the peasants in Tayi County, Sichuan Province, during the pre-1949 period. The angular and powerful sculptures were created by a group of artists skilled at expressing the sorrow and despair of peasants in China before the present regime. The same artists later created similar tableaux with Tibetan peasants as the subject.

The Exhibition of the Archaeological Findings In the past few decades, a national policy has been established to protect all antiques and historical relics found in China. The State Administrative Bureau of Museums and Historical Relics has subsequently succeeded in its attempts to find, collect, and maintain the many historical relics scattered throughout the nation. These artifacts have now been brought together as representative archaeological collections in many of the provincial museums across China. Housed in the Hall of Preserving Harmony (*Bao He Dian*) in the Palace Museum is one of the finest national archaeological collections. The pieces in this collection are presented in a regularly rotating exhibition and include the ceramics, bronzes, and relics from the "Silk Road" and from the tomb of Emperor Qin (221-206 B.C.).

SHANGHAI MUSEUM

The Shanghai Museum was established in 1952, following a long period of preparation and gathering of the museum collections. The museum is housed in a huge structure that was formerly a bank owned by Tu Yueh-sheng. The collection consists of archaeological finds from the Jiangsu Province and special gifts of antiques from local citizens. The museum, which employs a staff of approximately two hundred, has its own archaeological team as well as departments of display, education, restoration, printing, mounting, and reproduction. Each department holds its own study groups and education courses for the staff. Consequently the staff are fully conversant with Chinese history and recent archaeological finds. In addition to the regular staff, a group of academicians is associated with the museum for consultation and teaching purposes.

The three major collections exhibited in this museum are the internationally famed bronze collection, the painting collection, and the unique collection of Chinese ceramics. The bronze collection comprises about eight hundred pieces, systematically displayed to show the four different stages of the Bronze Culture in China. The first stage presents the "Inter-relationship Between Early Bronzes and the Slave Society" and consists of a fine collection of bronzes from the Shang dynasty (1600-1027 B.C.) and Zhou dynasty (1027-771 B.C.). The second stage is titled the "Early Development and Technique of Bronze-making in China." In 1954, many pottery molds were excavated from the site of a bronze foundry at Houma, Shanxi, proving that direct casting was the main method used in the production of bronze about three thousand years ago. The

third section presents the "Development of Chinese Bronzes," with a display of the graceful bronze vessels of the Shang and Zhou dynasties. And the last section of the bronze exhibit examines the "Bronze Representation from the Minority Nationalities" in China.

The painting section consists of classical paintings from the Song and Tang dynasties.

The ceramics collection of the Shanghai museum is arranged in chronological order to show the development of Chinese pottery and ceramics from the Neolithic period through the present. Included in the display are the prototype celadons, a selection of Sui and Tang pottery, and a representative collection of the refined Song wares.

BANPO MUSEUM

In 1953, during highway construction in Shaanxi Province, the remains of an eight-thousand-year-old Neolithic village that belonged to the Yangshao culture of Chinese primitive societies were discovered. The Banpo village, located in the eastern suburbs of Xi'an, covers an area of approximately fifty thousand square meters. At the site one can see three types of dwellings: small, low underground mud houses; rounded upright structures supported by columns with a roof; and column-supported mud houses with triangular roofs.

The museum, which was constructed on the village site, houses many of the remains found in the excavation. Bone needles and stone wheels suggest that the Banpo dwellers had mastered spinning, weaving, and sewing. Also on display are various vessels.

The public cemetery indicates that men and women were not buried together. The Banpo people loved their children dearly and so buried them close to their homes in funerary urns with a hole in the bottom. It was believed that the child's immortal soul would be released from the opening after death. Three uniform pieces of pottery were buried with every deceased individual, without any class distinction. It has been suggested that Banpo villagers existed in a classless, collective, matriarchal society.

SHAANXI PROVINCIAL MUSEUM IN XI'AN

This museum is internationally renowned for its collection of the ancient sculptures of the Han and Tang dynasties from the third century to the tenth century. A beautiful life-size stone stallion was one of the eighteen tomb guards for General Hui Ju-Bin of the Han dynasty. This forceful and handsomely carved stone horse was produced in 174 B.C. and is held to be one of the earliest stone sculptures in China. The tomb of the second emperor of the Tang dynasty, Li Sze-ming, is famous for the life-size "Six Finest Stallions" exquisitely carved on the wall. Today they are mounted in a display case at the museum. Four of the stallions are in poor condition, but the fourth and fifth are in perfect condition. Apparently these two sculptures were stolen from the site and sold to a Westerner in 1914. Now the museum displays perfect copies of the two stallions. The two originals are presently in the museum collection at the University of Pennsylvania, Philadelphia.

The Forest of Calligraphy Tablets is the most famous collection of Chinese calligraphy tablets, dating from the Han dynasty to the Qing dynasty (the third century to the twentieth century). The calligraphy tablet is a dark gray stone block, approximately two meters by one meter, carved with various styles of Chinese calligraphy. The carved tablets served the multiple purpose of recording knowledge, historical events, and the official styles of Chinese calligraphy for scholars prior to the invention of printing. *Zhao Zhun Bai*, a historical record of Eastern Han dynasty made in A.D. 135, can be found here. During the Tang dynasty, Emperor Wen-Zhong commissioned three scholars to record the complete set of *Shi San Qing* (the Thirteen Books) on 114 tablets in A.D. 837. It took three years to accomplish this monumental task. One of the Tang tablets was discovered during the Ming dynasty. It contains the historical record of the first Christian missionary from Persia to China in A.D. 635, including a description of the geography of Persia and the regulations of the church.

The different schools of Chinese calligraphy in Liu, Zhao, and Yan styles are well illustrated on the tablets for young learners. In the Tang dynasty, Monk Wai-su of Henan was outstanding for his creative style in calligraphy. Chairman Mao was a devotee of his fluid style. Two Song scholars in the eleventh century, the poets Su Dong-po (1036-1101) and Mi Fei (1051-1107), were both famous for the unique strength and control in their calligraphy.

Besides calligraphy, landscape and figure paintings are inscribed on the stone tablets. A lovely Guanyin, the Goddess of Mercy, attributed to the Tang painter Wu Daozi, is in the collection. The famous Buddhist theologian Xuan Shang traveled to India and brought the texts of Mehayova back to his Tang emperor, Taizhong. This extraordinary event is recorded on tablets in the collection. The romantic Xing-Qing Palace of Tang Ming Huang (A.D. 731-756) and his beloved wife Yang Guifei was also depicted on one of the Song tablets. During the reign of Kangxi (1662-1723), eight outstanding scenic spots of interior China were beautifully carved in the traditional style of landscape painting.

Cizhou vase from the Song dynasty, Shanghai Museum.

Three colored glazed porcelain pillow from the Song dynasty, Shanghai Museum.

QIN SHI HUANG SOLDIER AND HORSE FIGURE MUSEUM

During an irrigation project in 1974 the Yanzhai Commune of Lintong discovered the burial ground of the pottery soldiers and horses of Qin Shi Huang, the first emperor of Qin (221-209 B.C.). An archaeological team was formed to conduct an extensive excavation on the site. A long tunnel containing massive life-size terra-cotta soldiers and horses and metal weapons was unearthed; it was one of the most spectacular finds in archaeological history. In 1975, the construction of a large exhibition hall was begun to shelter the special findings. Two more tunnels containing military figures were found during the construction. On October 1, 1979, this museum was officially opened to the public as the Qin Shi Huang Soldier and Horse Figure Museum.

Qin Shi Huang was born in 259 B.C. He conquered the Warring States and unified China in 221 B.C. at the age of thirty-nine. Calling himself the First Emperor of China, he created a centralized government, and unified writings, measurements, codes, and currencies in China. He also extended the Great Wall along the northern border. Over two thousand years ago, Emperor Qin established an outstandingly proficient political and military state. The forceful and detailed life-size terra-cotta soldiers and horses are the legacy of this powerful and creative empire.

HUNAN PROVINCIAL MUSEUM

This provincial museum is located in the northeastern section of Changsha and houses the unearthed finds from the Han (206 B.C.-A.D. 220) tombs No. 1-3 at Mawangdui in the city. Included in the display is a well-preserved two-thousand-year-old body of a noblewoman who was the wife of the Marquis of Dai. She lived around 193-141 B.C. The three decorative inner and outer coffins were encased in thick layers of charcoal and white peat. Over twenty layers of silk encased the woman's body, whose organs and tissues are in remarkable condition. Medical examination has shown that the woman suffered from tuberculosis, heart trouble, and a gallstone condition. She died suddenly at the age of fifty. The thousands of funerary objects, including silk gowns, grains, fruits, medicinal herbs, lacquerwares, figurines, and musical instruments, are also on display. The silk painting draped over the inner coffin, depicting heaven, earth, and human figures, retains its brilliant colors. The painting, which is two hundred centimeters long by eighty centimeters wide and in a T shape, is a masterpiece of detailed subjects and attractive colors. In the No. 3 tomb, the woman's son and burial objects, including a seven-string zither, and a chess game, were found and are on display. From these Han tombs many elegantly painted lacquer containers, jars, and baskets are exhibited, reflecting the advanced crafts and artistry in ancient China.

HENAN PROVINCIAL MUSEUM

This museum is located in the new section of Zhengzhou, Henan Province. It contains special artifacts from the Neolithic period through modern times. On display you will see ancient tools from the Yangshao culture, bronzes from the Shang and Zhou dynasties, and figurines, lacquerwares, ceramics, and textiles from the Han, Tang, Song, and Yuan dynasties.

Some of the most interesting artifacts include the Shang dynasty (1766-1122 B.C.) porcelain wine vessel, which is one of the earliest ever to be found in China so far, and the musical instruments that date from the Spring and Autumn Period (770-476 B.C.). In addition to the archaeological collection, the Henan Museum contains a small exhibit tracing the development of Modern China from the beginning of this century, and a painting collection.

Celadon lion-shaped water pot from the Jin dynasty, Shanghai Museum.

PART 3

CITIES AND SITES

Steel plant, Anshan.

ANSHAN (Anshan)　　　Liaoning Province

鞍
山

Anshan, the steel and iron capital of China, is situated in southeastern Liaoning Province about 90 kilometers southwest of Shenyang. The iron mining and smelting industry began around 100 B.C. and expanded during the tenth and eleventh centuries A.D. The rich deposits of iron and coal around this city provide a natural site for industry. Although the many factories dominate Anshan, the city is well planned and has wide streets attractively bordered with greenery and flowers.

With a population of 900,000, Anshan also produces construction materials, chemicals, agricultural tools, and consumer goods. In addition, there are many metallurgical institutes in the city.

PLACES TO SEE

Tang Gang Zi　　This hot spring is located 9.6 kilometers southeast of the city and includes bath facilities for visitors.

Home of Zhang Zuo-lin　　Zhang was a warlord of this region in the early 1900s. His son was the chief instigator of the "Xi'an Incident"—in 1936, Chiang Kaishek was imprisoned here, and Zhou Enlai negotiated his release in exchange for an agreement that the Nationalists and the Communists would unite to fight against the Japanese invasion.

Thousand Lotus Hill (Qianshan)　　This former Buddhist retreat is a place of great natural beauty not far from Shenyang.

Arts and crafts workshop, Anyang.

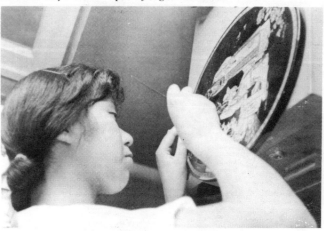

ANYANG (Anyang)   Henan Province

Situated in the northern Henan Province, Anyang is the gateway to the Red Flag Canal of Linxian County. It has an area of 240 square kilometers and a population of 430,000. On the Beijing-Guangzhou railway line it is about eight hours from Beijing.

Anyang is the cradle of Chinese civilization. It was the capital of the Shang dynasty (1766-1122 B.C.) for 273 years. Numerous oracle bones with inscriptions, Shang bronzes, pottery, jade, and gold pieces have been discovered here. In 1951, an archaeological station was set up for excavation and research work. Today Anyang is a modern industrial city with iron and steel plants, a carpet factory, a straw-ware factory, and jade carving and pottery workshops.

PLACES TO SEE

Wenfeng Pagoda   Located at the Tianning Temple, which is over a thousand years old, the pagoda was built in A.D. 952 during the Five Dynasties Period. With a lotus-shaped base, the octagonal pagoda is thirty-eight meters high and has five stories. From the top of the pagoda, one can see the entire city of Anyang.

People's Park   This peaceful and scenic park is a favorite spot for the local people as well as for visitors. The elegant Jade Belt Bridge and Mid-Lake Pavilion are the two main attractions.

The Yin Ruins   The remains of the Shang dynasty capital were accidentally uncovered in 1899 near the village of Xiaotun Cun about two kilometers northwest of Anyang. Wan Yirong (1845-1900), a Qing official and scholar, discovered the ancient oracle bones covered with ideographic writing, also known as *Jiagu wen*, at the Shang site. Excavation did not begin, however, until a few decades later. The site of the Yin Ruins covers an area of six kilometers from east to west, and four kilometers from south to north. It consists of the palace foundation, imperial tombs, and shops. The excavation of the imperial tombs showed that the Shang rulers were traditionally buried with live slaves, animals, food, tools, and bronzes. The oracle inscriptions confirm the presence of the last nine kings of the Shang dynasty. In 1976, the undisturbed tomb of Lady Fu Hao, a woman general and Royal Consort of the fourth Shang king, Wu Ding, was discovered. From her tomb were taken two hundred bronze vessels, two hundred bronze weapons and tools, six hundred sculptures and ritual objects of jade and stone, and five hundred objects of carved bone. It was one of the most remarkable archaeological discoveries in Anyang. On the Yin Ruins site, a museum containing many Shang objects is open to the public.

ACCOMMODATION

Taihang Guesthouse   This modern inn was built in 1978 and is located on Dengta Road, on the eastern side of the city.

Anyang Guesthouse   This older hotel is located on Jiefang Road in the center of Anyang.

Shang bronze wine vessels.

Ivory cup excavated from the Shang tombs.

Beidaihe.

BEIDAIHE (Peitahe)   Hebei Province

北戴河

Beidaihe is a lovely seaside resort on the Gulf of Bohai in Hebei Province. Located southwest of Qinghuang Dao, it is about six hours from Beijing by train.

Beidaihe was established in the early 1900s when Western residents of Beijing and Tianjin began building fashionable villas and spending the summers there. Today Beidaihe is still a popular summer resort for Western diplomats, but increasing numbers of Chinese use it as well. The resort includes a children's holiday camp, scenic parks, and historical monuments. In the town of Beidaihe, which is about fifteen kilometers southeast of the resort, there are several restaurants, a bread and cake shop, and a public park.

BEIJING (Peking)

Beijing, capital of the People's Republic of China, is known as the "Northern Capital" in Chinese. Situated at Taku, in the southwestern region of the great North China Plain near the gateway to Mongolia, it is about 152 kilometers inland at an altitude of 135 meters and occupies 17,800 square kilometers of land area. It has been the capital of the nation for the last seven centuries. Today, with a population of eight million, it is the political, cultural, and administrative center of the People's Republic of China.

Beijing was originally a walled city built by Kublai Khan, the Yuan emperor in 1260. The Inner City is the site of the Forbidden City (now the Palace Museum) and the headquarters of the central government. The Outer City is the commercial sector on Beijing's south side. Most of the old walls and gates have been demolished for new construction and roads. However, you may sense the historical grandeur when you visit the Tianan Men Square, the Palace Museum, the Temple of Heaven, and Bei Hai Park. Changan Boulevard, running east-west through the center of Beijing, is an attractive six-lane avenue lined with trees and modern buildings. You can take a leisurely stroll from the Beijing Hotel to Tianan Men Square along the Changan Boulevard, where you will see masses of people clad in somber blue-gray Mao suits or white sports shirts in summer, and thousands on bicycles, riding the crowded buses, or walking in a peaceful, orderly manner. In contrast, children are dressed in colorful jackets and are lively and talkative. While you are walking you may attract a lot of curious stares. You may feel uneasy at first, but you will quickly sense the people's friendliness.

HISTORY

About three thousand years ago human settlement was established in the Beijing Basin. The earliest site of Beijing was the hamlet of Yan, which was established in the principality of Chi during the Shang dynasty (1766-1122 B.C.). During the Qin dynasty (221-206 B.C.), Yan became a provincial capital as it gained economical and military importance. For several dynasties it was the defensive base for military expeditions against the nomads in the north.

During the Tang dynasty (A.D. 618-907) Yuzhou was developed and then destroyed in 986 by the Liao. A new city called Nanjing (the Southern Capital) was then established by the Liao invaders. After the Jin defeated the Liao in 1135, the city's name was changed to Zhongdu (the Middle Capital). As the capital of the Jin dynasty, Zhongdu was the beginning of an outstanding imperial city. In 1260, Kublai Khan, emperor of the Yuan dynasty (A.D. 1280-1368), built a new city outside the old Zhongdu called Dadu (the Grand Capital). During the Ming dynasty (A.D. 1368-1644) the city was expanded and named Beijing, and became the national capital.

The construction of the Forbidden City began in 1406 under Emperor Yongle and later became the home for twenty-four rulers of the Ming and Qing dynasties. It took fourteen years of mass labor to complete the major palaces, which cover 72,000 square meters. The entrance to these palaces of the Forbidden City is Tianan Men Gate, which has been a backdrop to Beijing's major political movements. On May 4, 1919, Beijing students held a rally in front of Tianan Men to protest against the feudal controls. In 1935 the December Movement broke out in Beijing as students and workers demonstrated in front of Tianan Men against Japanese imperialism. On May 20, 1947, Beijing students held a mass parade there in protest against hunger and the civil war. On October 1, 1949, Chairman Mao Zedong declared the founding of the People's Republic of China at Tianan Men Square. It is here that the demise of old powers and the celebration of the new regime took place.

When the Qing dynasty fell in 1911, the Nationalist government moved the capital to Nanjing and renamed the city Beiping ("Northern Peace"). About two decades later, on January 31, 1949, the Chinese Communists took over the city. Thus it became the national capital of the People's Republic of China. Today Beijing has much to offer in science, agriculture, education, and the arts. It is known for its ancient historical sites as well as for its modern communes, the Workers' Neighborhood District, art centers, and universities.

PLACES TO SEE

Tianan Men Square   *Tianan Men* means "Heavenly Peace Gate," which is the name of the famous gate located in this vast square. Tianan Men Square is the historical and political center of Beijing. With an enormous area of about forty hectares, the square includes the Great Hall of the People, the museums of the Chinese Revolution and Chinese History, and Chairman Mao Zedong's Memorial Hall. There are permanent reviewing stands on the Tianan Men where China's leaders preside over the mass rallies and parades in the square. It was here that Chairman Mao proclaimed the birth of the People's Republic of China in 1949.

Great Hall of the People   This is a huge modern structure located on the west side of the Tianan Men Square. It is the home of China's parliament, the National People's Congress. The Great Hall is an enormous building consisting of numerous conference rooms, banquet halls, and reception areas. The main conference hall seats ten thousand people, and the banquet hall can accommodate five thousand. In spite of its immense size, the Great Hall was completed in ten months during 1958 and 1959.

The Museum of the Chinese Revolution   Located on the east side of the square, it has an excellent display of the history of China and its revolutions. The Memorial Hall of Zhou Enlai contains many personal and historical documents.

Museum of Chinese History   This imposing building was constructed in 1959 and is located on the east side of Tianan Men Square next to the Museum of the Chinese Revolution. The museum exhibition covers the primitive period one million years ago to the May Fourth Movement of 1919. It is divided into four parts: Primitive Society, Slave Society, Feudal Society, and Semi-Colonial and Semi-Feudal Society. It was closed during the Cultural Revolution and reopened in 1976.

Chairman Mao Zedong Memorial Hall   This impressive and relatively new structure is a twin-roofed building supported by massive granite pillars. The building was completed in November 1977, after ten months under construction. A wide stairway leads you to the first hall, where there is an enormous seated figure of Chairman Mao in white marble. In the next hall the Chairman's body is preserved in a crystal coffin and draped with the red flag of the People's Republic of China. The sarcophagus rests on a bier surrounded by fresh flowers. In the third hall, a large marble screen bears a poem by Chairman Mao in his own handsome calligraphy.

South Gate (Qianmen)   On leaving the Chairman Mao Zedong Memorial Hall you get a fine view of the South Gate, located on the south side of the square. As one of the few remaining gates of the Imperial City Wall constructed under Emperor Yongle (1403-1425) of the Ming dynasty, this gate was reserved for imperial use.

The Monument to the People's Heroes   This 36-meter-high granite obelisk on a raised platform is located in the center of the square. The obelisk is inscribed with writings of Mao Zedong and Zhou Enlai, and its base has carvings of revolutionary themes.

The Palace Museum   From Tianan Men you go through the Meridian Gate (Wu Men), which is the front entrance to the Forbidden City, now the Palace Museum. In 1406, under Emperor Yongle, the construction of the palace began. He instructed his architects to build "in Harmony with the Universe and to obey the Laws of Space and Discretion." Following the instruction, the vast construction of imperial palaces (known as Zi Jin Cheng in Chinese) was undertaken over a period of fourteen years. The purple color of the palace's tiled roof is associated with the North Star, which is the prominent symbol of the imperial residence. The Forbidden City was the home of twenty-four rulers of the Ming and Qing dynasties. It covers 72,000 square meters and is surrounded

Chairman Mao Zedong Memorial Hall.

Temple of Heaven.

Great Hall of the People.

by a wall 10 meters high and a moat 52 meters wide. The imperial rulers rarely ventured outside of the Forbidden City, where they controlled China from the Dragon Throne until the fall of Qing dynasty in 1911.

Over the years, the palaces suffered neglect and damage, but restoration work was done by Emperor Wanli (A.D. 1573-1620), Emperor Qianlong (A.D. 1736-1796), and Dowager Empress Ci Xi (A.D. 1835-1908). The grand scale of the palace architecture is remarkable for its harmony and serenity; no structure exceeds two stories and they all face spacious courtyards. The main axis of the Forbidden City consists of three major palaces strictly reserved for official functions. To either side are other palaces where the emperors and their families lived.

The Meridian Gate (Wu Men) is the entrance to the imperial palaces. It was constructed in 1420 and restored in 1647 and 1801. From here the emperor used to preside over parades and ceremonies. Beyond the gateway you will cross one of the five elegantly carved marble bridges over the Golden Water Stream to reach the wide open courtyard and the Gate of Supreme Harmony (Tai He Men). This gate is the entrance to the immense stone-flagged court of the Three Great Halls, which stand on an H-shaped platform.

The first hall, the Hall of Supreme Harmony (Tai He Dian), is a huge, impressive timber structure, supported by eighty-four elaborate cedar pillars. This hall was built in 1420 and was reconstructed in 1441, 1557, 1562, 1627, and 1692 because of damage caused by fires. On its triple-decked terrace stand large bronze herons and tortoises and four giant gilded bowls that were formerly filled with oil and floating wicks and used as lamps. A gilded throne, called the Dragon Throne, is raised on a six-foot-high balustraded platform made of gilded carved woodwork and reached by five elaborate staircases. Pairs of cloisonné elephants and cranes stand to either side of the throne, which is backed by a carved and gilded screen. From the throne the emperor presided over such ceremonies as the nomination of military officers, the announcement of scholars who had passed the imperial examination, coronations, and New Year celebrations. The emperor would also receive foreign envoys from the throne while officials formed processional lines in the courtyard.

Behind this hall is the Hall of Perfect Harmony (Zhong He Dian). Here the emperor used to inspect the agricultural instruments before the ploughing ceremony each spring, and he would rest here before ceremonies in the Hall of Supreme Harmony. There is a raised throne and a sedan chair on either side in the Hall of Perfect Harmony. This palace was built in 1420 and was restored in 1627, 1690, and 1978.

The Hall of Preserving Harmony (Bao He Dian) is the next palace. It was used for the reception of princes and ambassadors and for the imperial examination of scholars applying for the highest literary ranks. Today this palace is a museum displaying a fine collection of archaeological findings, including the life-size pottery figures from the tomb site of Qin Shi Huang Di (221-206 B.C.)

Descending the steps of the Hall of Preserving Harmony you will see the Dragon Pavement, the largest sculptural ramp leading down to the courtyard of the Gate of Heavenly Purity (Qian Qing Men), the oldest monument of the Forbidden City. This fantastic ramp was first carved in the Ming dynasty and recarved in 1726. It is a single block of stone almost seventeen meters long, about three meters wide, and almost two meters thick, weighing 245 tonnes. This huge stone piece came from a quarry fifty kilometers away from Beijing. Ten thousand laborers transported it in winter over roads frozen with ice by pouring water over the stone at regular intervals.

After passing through the Gate of Heavenly Purity, you will enter another courtyard, which leads to the Palace of Heavenly Purity (Qian Qing Gong). This palace was used as a private residence in the Ming dynasty and as a chamber for private audiences in the Qing dynasty. Today it houses the Museum Collection of Paintings.

Behind this palace is the Hall of Union (Jiao Tai Dian), which has a modest-sized throne surrounded by twenty-five imperial seals. A large hydraulic clock on the left side of the throne was made in the eighteenth century for Emperor Qianlong, who had a special interest in Chinese artifacts.

Behind the Hall of Union is the Palace of Earthly Tranquility (Kun Ning Gong), which was used as the residence for Ming empresses and later as a nuptial chamber for the last Qing emperor and his bride. Alongside the main halls are six eastern and six western palaces, known as the East and West Palaces, which served as living quarters for the imperial family.

Beyond the Hall of Union is the lovely Imperial Garden (Yu Hua Yuan), which contains a variety of flowers, rock gardens, and graceful cypress and pine trees. Leaving the garden you will pass through the Shun Zhen Men and the Gate of Divine Pride (Shen Wu Men). Then you have made a quick tour of the major palaces of the Forbidden City.

In addition to these palaces, the Palace Museum includes the Museums of Treasures, Ceramics, and Paintings and Bronzes, the Sculpture Exhibition of the Rent Collection Courtyard, the Museum Workshops of Repair and Reproduction, and the Exhibition of Archaeological Findings. Detailed information about these museums is given in the section entitled "Major Museums of China."

Hall of Supreme Harmony (Tai He Dian).

The Seventeen-Arch Bridge, Summer Palace (Yi Yuan).

PLAN OF PALACE MUSEUM

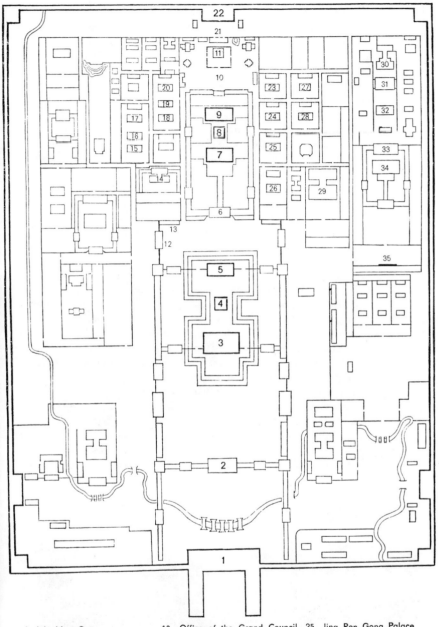

1. Wu Men Gate
2. Tai He Men Gate
3. Tai He Dian Hall
4. Zhong He Dian Hall
5. Bao He Dian Hall
6. Qian Qing Men Gate
7. Qian Qing Gong Palace
8. Jiao Tai Dian Hall
9. Kun Ning Gong Palace
10. Imperial Garden
11. Qin An Dian Hall
12. Long Zong Men Gate
13. Office of the Grand Council
14. Yang Xin Dian Hall
15. Tai Ji Dian Hall
16. Ti Yuan Dian Hall
17. Chang Chun Gong Palace
18. Yi Kun Gong Palace
19. Ti He Dian Hall
20. Chu Xiu Gong Palace
21. Shun Zhen Men Gate
22. Shen Wu Men Gate
23. Zhong Cui Gong Palace
24. Cheng Qian Gong Palace
25. Jing Ren Gong Palace
26. Zhai Gong Palace
27. Jing Yang Gong Palace
28. Yong He Gong Palace
29. Feng Xian Dian Hall
30. Yi He Xuan Hall
31. Le Shou Tang Hall
32. Yang Xing Dian Hall
33. Ning Shou Gong Palace
34. Huang Ji Dian Hall
35. Nine-Dragon Screen

Summer Palace (Yi He Yuan) About thirty minutes by bus to the northwest side of Beijing you will find the imperial Summer Palace. Surrounded by trees, lakes, and islands, the palace was built in 1751 by Emperor Qianlong for his mother, the Dowager Empress Nihulu. He also named the palace site Wan Shou Shan, "the Mountain of the Ten Thousand Years of Longevity," to celebrate the dowager's birthday.

After her death, the palace was not maintained until Empress Ci Xi enlarged it in 1893, using China's military and naval fund. At the flamboyant entrance to the palace is a huge pair of bronze lions. The empress had an official palace for her public audiences and an elegant palace and pavilions for her private residence, called the Hall of Happiness and Longevity (Le Shou Tang); both have retained Empress Ci Xi's original style. In her living quarters there are sitting rooms and hallways where she usually displayed her collection of ceramics, calligraphy, furniture, clocks, jade, and precious stone carvings. The Empress's bedchambers are done in the imperial color of yellow.

In the adjoining Hall of Jade Ripples (Yu Lan Tang), Emperor Guangxu (1875-1908) spent the last ten years of his young life as the political prisoner of his Aunt Ci Xi. One can easily imagine how sad and desolated Guangxu was by looking at the lonely garden of his former residence.

A covered corridor winds alongside the palaces and the beautiful manmade Kunming Lake. This 728-meter-long corridor, called the Long Corridor (Changlang), is decorated with handsome paintings of historical legends. At the entrance to the temples built by Qianlong on the sixteenth anniversary of his mother's death, a handsome marble gate bears the inscribed poetry and calligraphy of the literary Emperor Qianlong. Climbing up Longevity Hill to the Temple of the Ten Thousand Buddhas (Fo Xiang Ge), you can enjoy a panoramic view of the Kunming Lake, pavilions, islands, and the lovely Girdle of Jade Bridge. Visitors can also enjoy Chinese culinary art in the splendid Summer Palace by having a special lunch at Ting Li Guan, which was the pavilion of performing arts for the enjoyment of Empress Ci Xi. Your guide can arrange the lunch in advance. After lunch you can have a leisurely boat ride starting from the dock at the Marble Boat back to the entrance of the Summer Palace. Empress Ci Xi used the navy funds to build this 36-meter-long decorative stone boat.

Imperial Guard of Honor, Ming tombs.

Ming tombs.

82

The Tombs of Ming Emperors   The emperors of China always carefully planned and built gigantic tombs. Hong Wu, the first Ming emperor, was splendidly buried at Zhongsan near Nanjing. Yongle, the third Ming ruler, officially moved the capital to Beijing. He then personally selected the imperial burial site, about forty-eight kilometers west of Beijing, known as Shisan Ling, or the Thirteen Ming Tombs. Thirteen of the sixteen Ming emperors were buried on this site. En route to the Ming tombs you will pass a tall white marble gateway, which was sculpted in A.D. 1540. Next you come across the Great Red Gate (Dahung Men), a vast structure over 36 meters high, and a gigantic white marble turtle (Pei Ting) erected in 1426 by Hongxi to the memory of Emperor Yongle. Then you approach the procession of the Imperial Guard of Honor, fine marble carvings of pairs of camels, lions, elephants, horses, mythological animals (Qiling), and officials, set on either side of the road.

Only two Ming emperors' tombs have been excavated. Dingling, Emperor Wanli's burial site, is open to visitors as the "Underground Palace." It is the only remaining imperial tomb in excellent condition. Just before you descend to the entrance of Dingling you can clearly see the underground opening in the middle of the burial mound. Passing a descending staircase and entering the underground palace, you will see a huge gate made of a single block of fine white marble. There are seven such marble gates in this underground palace. Dingling consists of three main halls in a row. The front hall and the middle hall are the same size—7 meters high, 6 meters wide, and 58 meters long—and floored with special ceramic bricks from Suzhou. The middle hall is also the ritual chamber containing three handsomely carved stone thrones made of Han nephrite stone, pairs of vases and candle holders, an incense burner, and three huge blue and white ceramic jars used for the "eternal lighting." There is a chamber on either side of the middle hall. The back hall, the necropolis, is the largest of the three main halls, containing the three coffins and twenty-six chests full of imperial treasures—over three thousand items. Among the buried treasures are large quantities of blue-white porcelain, jade vessels, and daily utensils in silver and gold with delicate carving and precious stone inlay. Four exquisitely jeweled crowns for Wanli and his two empresses were also discovered. The empress's strikingly beautiful peacock crown is decorated with pearls and precious stones. From the treasure chests there are hundreds of imperial gowns and countless gold-threaded silks and borcades. After three hundred years of underground storage, they still retain their fabulous color and beautiful design. The excavation of Wanli's tomb from 1956 to 1958 has provided new knowledge and understanding of the past.

Beijing Zoo   The zoo is the home of over four thousand animals, including rare birds, reptiles, and the famous giant pandas. Also of interest are the big tigers collected from different parts of China.

Bei Hai Park   This beautiful park is situated on the shores of the Bei Hai Lake near the center of Beijing. It was first populated by the Liao dynasty over a thousand years ago. Later Kublai Khan also lived on this site. On the small island, the White Dagoba (Bei Ta) was built in 1651 by Shunzhi to commemorate the first visit of the Dalai Lama of Tibet. The White Dagoba is a landmark of

Beijing. The park includes temples, pavilions, bridges, gardens, and paths leading to the Temple of Everlasting Peace (Yongan Si), also built in 1651, and the White Dagoba. On the northern side stands the Ten Thousand Buddha Pavilion. To the west is the famous Nine Dragon Screen (Jiulong Bi), which is a wall of glazed ceramic tiles, colorfully depicting the playful nine dragons.

Coal Hill Park (Jing Shan)   Coal Hill (Mei Shan) is located north of the Palace Museum and east of the White Dagoba in Bei Hai Park. The park entrance is directly opposite the Gate of Divine Pride (Shen Wu Men) of the Palace Museum. A path takes you to the Pavilion of Ten Thousand Springs (Wanchun Ding) on the top of Coal Hill, where the last Ming emperor, Chongzhen, hanged himself in 1644 following his defeat by rebels. From the hilltop you can enjoy a panoramic view of Beijing.

Temple of Heaven (Tian Tan)   One of the most famous sites in Beijing, this group of well-planned ceremonial sites is located in a walled park in southeast Beijing. This complex was first built by Emperor Yongle in the fifteenth century and was restored by Emperor Qianlong in 1749 and again under the present regime. Covering 276 hectares, this complex consists of a processional avenue 723 meters long with three major temple sites on a north-south axis. Entering the South Gate you will see first the Altar of Heaven, or Circular Mound Altar (Huanqin Tan), then the Imperial Vault of Heaven (Huangqiong Yu), and finally the Hall of Prayer for Good Harvests (Qinian Dian).

The Altar of Heaven is a triple-tiered round marble terrace. The tiers represent, in ascending order, man, earth, and heaven. Each tier is surrounded by a beautifully carved white marble balustrade supported by 360 pillars. At this sacred altar emperors would make a sacrifice to heaven accompanied by ritualistic music and priests' chanting.

The Hall of Prayer for Good Harvests is the most important site on the park grounds. Surrounded by a three-tiered circular marble terrace, it has purple eaves and a cone-shaped roof covered with cobalt blue tiles. No steel, cement, or beams were used in the construction of this hall, which is 38 meters high and is supported by 28 massive wooden pillars. The four center columns, called the dragon-well pillars, represent the four seasons. Made of timber from the distant Yuan Province, they are 19 meters high with a circumference of two-and-a-half persons at arm's length. The ceiling of the hall is exquisitely painted in red and blue, with an elaborate gilt overlay. The emperor would spend the night here once a year, fasting and praying for a good harvest.

The Imperial Vault of Heaven is a smaller octagonal wooden building with a cone-shaped roof of cobalt blue glazed tiles and a golden top. This hall used to house the tablets of the Manchu imperial ancestors and the tablets to heaven, which were used during ceremonies. The Vault of Heaven is surrounded by a circular wall of polished bricks that has an opening to the south. This wall is known as Echo Wall, since whispers at one end of the wall can be heard at the opposite end.

Lu Xun's Residence Museum   The former residence of Lu Xun (1881-1936), the famous thinker and revolutionary writer, is located on Xi'an Tiao

Street in the vicinity of the Western Market. Displays of Lu Xun's pictures, manuscripts, calligraphies, and other personal articles can be seen here.

National Library of Beijing This well-known library was established in 1912. It houses the imperial collections of the Southern Song dynasty (A.D. 1127-1280), the Ming dynasty (A.D. 1368-1644), and the Qing dynasty (A.D. 1644-1911). Other collections include rare manuscripts dating back to the fifth century and wood-block prints from the ninth century. The library has over four million volumes.

Beijing University Established in 1898, this is one of the most famous universities in China. Well known for its academic leadership and excellent standing in the arts and sciences, the university is attended by many foreign students. The campus, which includes scenic lakes and gardens, is located in the Haidian District, a northern suburb of Beijing.

Beijing Dance School Established in September 1954, this is one of the leading schools in China for training professional dancers. Young students selected from various parts of China, including Xizang (Tibet), usually devote six or seven years to learning folk dancing or classical ballet. During their training, they also participate in stage performances. The school is made up of the teaching staff, the school orchestra, and the ballet troupe.

Beijing Art Gallery The gallery is located near the city center within easy walking distance of the Beijing Hotel. This massive building of Chinese architectural design presents selected works of art from different provinces in China. The exhibition may include modern oil and water-color paintings, sculptures, and graphics selected by the provinces. Occasionally the gallery also displays Western art.

Fragrant Hills Park (Xiang Shan) This delightful park is located in northwestern Beijing beyond the Summer Palace. You will be fascinated by the elegant designs of the temples, pavilions, and landscaped gardens. In the eighteenth century the emperor used the area for hunting and games. Today a modern hotel designed by the famous Chinese-American I.M. Pei is located here.

Sun Yat-sen Park (Zhongshan Gong Yuan) In this spacious park near the Tianan Men and the Palace Museum, you will see beautiful old cypress trees, pavilions, interesting garden paths, and greenhouses. In addition, the park contains the Altar of the Earth and Harvests, where the emperor made sacrifices to the gods for good harvests twice a year.

People's Cultural Park (Renmin Wenhua Gong) The People's Park stands on the eastern side of the Tianan Men Gate. Inside the park are three imperial halls that were originally used for religious ceremonies and a courtyard surrounded by old cypress trees. Today, an open-air theater presents folk plays and dramas in the summer.

The Great Wall (Wanli Chang Cheng) The literal translation of the Chinese name for the Great Wall is "the Long Wall of Ten Thousand Li." (*Li* is the Chinese measure for distance; 1 *li* = 0.5 kilometers.) The wall was built in the fifth century B.C. to protect China from the aggressive northern Tartars. Later, in 221 B.C, the sections of the wall were joined together by the Emperor

Qin Shi Huang Di. This monumental task involved over 300,000 laborers and took ten years to complete. The Great Wall was unused from the sixth to the fourteenth century and was restored in the Ming dynasty (A.D. 1368-1644). It was later abandoned. Today a few passes of the wall have been restored for tourists.

The Great Wall is the only manmade structure visible from earth orbit. Winding six thousand kilometers through northern China from Shanhai Guan on the east coast to Gansu Province in north-central China, the Great Wall stands 6½ meters high. Towers 11 to 12 meters high were built into the wall every 180 to 270 meters. Its sides are made of earth, brick, and stone, and the top of the wall is paved with bricks set in line to form a path for soldiers and horses.

Nankow Pass and Bada Ling Pass are about 65 kilometers from Beijing and can be reached by car or train in two or three hours. Comfortable shoes should be worn for the short but steep climb to the Great Wall. From the towers you can enjoy a breathtaking panoramic view and trace the distant, endlessly snaking wall through the magnificent northern mountains.

Your guide can arrange for your group to be served a box lunch in a reception room at the foot of the wall after your energetic walk. Following your lunch break you may still have time to visit the Ming tombs in the afternoon.

Temple of Heaven.

Long Corridor, Summer Palace.

ACCOMMODATION

Beijing Hotel   Changan Boulevard. Phone: 552231, 556531, 558331.

This is one of the most prestigious and comfortable hotels in China. The rooms of the sixteen-story hotel are spacious and have views of the city or of Changan Boulevard and Tianan Men Square. The hotel is located near the center of Beijing, the Palace Museum, Tianan Men Square, and the Beijing shopping district. The rate is Y50 ($33.50 U.S., $37.50 Canadian) for a room with twin beds and Y150 ($100.00 U.S., $112.50 Canadian) for a suite.

In this hotel you will find restaurants, a bank, post and telegraph offices, a hair salon, a barbershop, arts and crafts stores, and a bar and billiards room. The hotel dining room is in the lobby and provides both Chinese and Western dishes. Private banquet rooms and a Japanese restaurant are located on the second floor.

Friendship Hotel   Haidian Road. Phone: 890621.

This six-story hotel is located in the northwestern side of Beijing and is about twenty minutes by car from the city center. The hotel includes dining room, post office, bank exchange, hairdressers, billiards room, and craft shop. The rate is Y24 ($16.00 U.S., $18.00 Canadian) per day for a double room.

Minzu (Nationalities) Hotel   West Changan Avenue. Phone: 668541.

Located west of the Palace Museum and next to the Minorities Cultural Palace, this hotel is a short distance from the Tianan Men Square. The rates are Y14 ($9.40 U.S., $10.50 Canadian) for a double room and Y40 ($27.00 U.S., $30.00 Canadian) for a suite. The hotel has two restaurants, which provide Chinese and Western menus separately, a post office, a bank, a gift shop, hairdressers, and a bookstore.

Chienmen Hotel   Yunan Street. Phone: 338731.

This nine-story hotel is south of Liuli Chang Street and near Hoping Men. It has a dining room, a post office, hairdressers, and a crafts shop. The rate is Y20 ($13.40 U.S., $15.00 Canadian) per day.

Xin Qiao Hotel   Dongiaomin Lane. Phone: 557731.

The hotel is in a gray-brick six-story building. It is located near the city center and in the old legation quarter. The hotel has a Chinese restaurant on the lobby floor and a Western restaurant on the top floor. There are bars, a pool room, and a roof garden available for the hotel guests. The rate is Y40 ($26.80 U.S., $30.00 Canadian) per day for a double room.

Huachiao Ta Shia (Overseas Chinese) Hotel   Wang Fujing Main Street. Phone: 558851.

Specially built for the overseas Chinese guest, this hotel has a central location near the Wang Fujing shopping district, the Beijing Art Gallery, Tianan Men Square, and the Palace Museum. The hotel has an air-conditioned Chinese restaurant, a crafts and fruit store, and a post office. The hotel desk provides bank exchange, makes travel arrangements, and procures train or airline tickets as well as tickets to the theater and sports events. The hotel also arranges group excursion tours. The dining room offers an excellent Chinese menu for hotel guests and their friends. The rates are about Y15 ($10.00 U.S., $12.00 Canadian) for a double room, and Y25 ($17.00 U.S., $19.00 Canadian) for a suite.

RESTAURANTS

Beijing offers a fine selection of Chinese restaurants specializing in the regional cuisine of Shanghai, Beijing, Sichuan, and Shantung, among others. The local restaurants are known for their northern or Pekinese style of cooking, which emphasizes duck, lamb, and wheat dumplings, buns, and noodles. Many hotels have excellent facilities for both casual dinners and elaborate banquets. It is convenient to entertain your Chinese hosts or friends in your hotel dining room, and, since they rarely have the opportunity to go into a hotel for foreign visitors, they will probably appreciate the chance to dine in a hotel restaurant. However, you must try some of the interesting restaurants in the city.

NORTHERN CHINESE RESTAURANTS

Beijing Roast Duck Restaurants   Their special features are roast duck wrapped in Chinese pancakes and served with green onion and sweet plum sauce. Dishes made of duck liver and meat with vegetables are also served.
— Hong Bin Lou (Important Guests' Restaurant), 82 West Changan Dajie. Phone: 330967.
— Qianmen Roast Duck Restaurant, 32 Qianmen Dajie. Phone: 751379.
— Beijing Big Duck Restaurant, 13 Wang Fujing. Phone: 553310.
Dinner reservations are usually required. Your guide can help you with this.

Fang Sang Restaurant   (Fang Sang: the Kitchen of the Empress Ci Xi at Bei Hai Park)

This is one of the best Northern restaurants in Beijing. Beautifully situated in the scenic Bei Hai Park, this famous restaurant is worth a visit for its views and the special cuisine favored by Empress Dowager Ci Xi. Its specialties are many, including shark fin with pigeon eggs, the assorted cold plate or *Pin Pan*, minced pork stuffed in sesame seed buns, and the empress's favorite pastry of tiny cornmeal cubes and chilled pea cakes. There are private dining rooms for banquets. It is necessary to make a lunch or dinner reservation in advance.

Summer Palace Restaurant   Ting Li Guan. Phone: 281926.

Located on the north bank of the Kunming Lake in the Summer Palace, this restaurant is noted for its lovely settings and its seafood dishes. Their specialties are Chinese hors d'oeuvres, skewered meats, various fish, and special desserts.

Hong Bin Lou (the Pavilion of Noted Guests)   82 West Changan Dajie. Phone: 330967.

This Northern Chinese restaurant, which faces the Central Post Office on West Changan Avenue, specializes in Moslem food. The menu offers a fine selection of Peking-Mongolian dishes except pork. You must try the fried mutton ravioli, Mongolian hotpot, and the tasty mutton shashlik here. You may reserve a private room for group banquets in advance.

Pienyi Fang   7 Hsien Yu Kou on Qianmen Dajie. Phone: 750505.

This is an old Manchu restaurant that has been in service for centuries. The house specialties are duck marinated in wine, pigs' kidneys, and sweet-and-sour fish. If you are interested, you may request a quick visit to the kitchens.

SHANTUNG RESTAURANTS

Feng Ze Yuan (the Horn of Plenty)   183 Zhushikou Street West. Phone: 332828.

This is considered the best restaurant in Beijing. Shangtung cuisine uses the special flavors and riches of the sea in a wide variety of dishes. The restaurant's specialties are braised shark fin, cuttlefish-roe soup, duck's liver, raw abalone with mushrooms, and roast duck. For dessert you must try the toffee apples, which are the best in Beijing.

Shoudu Restaurant (Capital Restaurant)   60 Wang Fujing. Phone: 554581 or 552594.

This restaurant provides excellent Shantung food. The dinner menu offers a fine selection of meats, seafood, duck, and chicken. For banquets you may preorder the dinner simply by stating the amount of money to be spent per person (usually Y20 to Y25). Then the chefs will arrange a detailed menu for your group. Shoudu is located near the Wang Fujing business district, a short walk from the Beijing Hotel.

Tung He Ju (Peace and Harmony Restaurant)   3 Xi Si Nan-Dajie. Phone: 660925.

This is a good Shantung restaurant. It offers many Northern Chinese dishes, including meats, seafood, and wheat buns.

Sichuan Restaurant   51 West Rong Xian Lane. Phone: 336356.

This restaurant specializes in the hot and spicy food of Sichuan Province. The hot-sour soup, tea-smoked duck, and hot-pepper chicken are especially good.

Mount Omei Restaurant   Hsi Tan Street. Phone: 660085.

Foreign visitors may use the small dining room on the first floor, where you can order hot, spicy Sichuan dishes, including chicken, minced pork, and beancakes and noodles with red-hot sauces.

Wu Fong Chai (the Pavilion of the Five Perfumes)   In the Eastern Market.

This restaurant offers such fine Shanghai cuisine as braised fish, pork-liver sausages, soft turtles and crabs, and fried eels.

Zhen Jiang Restaurant   Hsun Nei Dajie. Phone: 662115, 662289.

This popular restaurant provides an excellent selection of Shanghai cuisine in seafood, meats, chicken, and duck, plus Shanghai pastries.

International Club Restaurant   Qienguo Men Wai. Phone: 522144.

If you want a steak one night, try the International Club Restaurant, which serves both Chinese and Western food. Your Chinese hosts and friends might enjoy going to this restaurant also.

Jin Yang Restaurant (Sunny Shanxi Restaurant)   241 Zhu Shi Kou Street West. Phone: 334361, 331669, 332120.

This restaurant serves the Northern Chinese cooking of Shanxi Province. Its specialties are fragrant crisp duck, deep-fried prawns, and chicken sautéed with hot pepper.

Huai Yang Fan Zhuang (Huai Yang Restaurant)   212 Xidan Bei Dajie. Phone: 660521.

Yangzhou food is the specialty here, including eel with sesame oil and garlic, crisp chicken, smoked yellow pike fish, sautéed prawns, and the Three Whites (chicken, fish, and bamboo shoots sautéed in wine sauce).

SHOPPING

Department Stores Beijing has two department stores, the Beijing Department Store (*Beijing Baihuo Dalou*, which means "Beijing Hundred Products Big Store") and the Dong Feng (East Wind) Department Store. In both you can find local arts and crafts, silks, jewelry, Chinese wine and spirits, cotton shirts, toys, handmade silk blouses, shoes, candies, radios, and Mao hats, as well as many other items. These stores are a good place to pick up attractive and inexpensive gifts. Both are open from 9:00 a.m. to 8:00 p.m. daily.

The Handicraft Store Located at 200 Wang Fujing, this store has a fine selection of Chinese crafts, including pottery, paintings, calligraphy, papercuts, ivory and stone carvings, cloisonné and lacquerwares, batik, linens, and bamboo and cane articles. All are quite reasonably priced.

Friendship Store Reserved for foreign residents and visitors in Beijing, this modern store is located near the International Club on Changan Jie. Here you will find a wide variety of high-quality goods, ranging from fur coats to wine, as well as a tailor shop, dry-cleaning service, and watch repair shop. The selection of jewelry and jade carvings (modern or antique items) is excellent. The price is quite fair, with a plentiful selection. If you are not sure about the jade and semiprecious stones, consult one of the older Chinese clerks. Although you might need the aid of an interpreter, you will find their knowledge and help invaluable. Silk, cashmere sweaters, and hand-embroidered silk blouses are the best buys here. You also can find good art supplies and Chinese brushes.

The Markets of Beijing When you are in China, you must visit a market. In Beijing, the Dong Feng (East Wind) Market and the People's (Renmin) Market are worth a visit. Both of them are close to the Beijing Hotel. At the markets you will find fruit stalls, restaurants, and shops selling special food and snacks. The market clerks are usually helpful and polite to foreign visitors—as long as they know what you want! The seals counter in the Dong Feng Market has an excellent selection of both antique and modern seal stones, red seal ink, inkstones, inksticks, water-color brushes, stationery, and rice papers.

Arts and Crafts Trust Company (the Beijing Theater Shop) Located at 12 Chongwenmen Dajie Street near the Beijing Hotel, this interesting antique and secondhand store carries old opera costumes, gowns and robes once worn by the gentry, antique jewelry, silver and crystal, old clocks, brass wares, and used fur garments and hats. If you like antiques, you must make a quick visit here.

Liuli Chang If you are interested in Chinese antiques, you must visit Luili Chang, a small district of antique shops and art specialty stores in old Beijing. You can start at Rong Bao Zhai (Studio of Glorious Treasure) in Hufang Lu. It was originally a place where art scholars, artists, and rich collectors could buy old paintings and art supplies and have mountings done for scroll paintings.

Today it has expanded to carry modern paintings and wood-block prints of famous paintings. If you are lucky, the friendly clerk might show you some of the original antique painting and calligraphy collections, which command a fabulous price. If you make arrangements in advance, you may observe the special workshop of Chinese wood-block printing in the back quarters of Rong Bao Zhai. It is an invaluable educational experience for art students, teachers, and collectors, and will enhance your appreciation of the ancient art form of Chinese wood-block printing,

Just across from Rong Bai Zhai is a small store specializing in old seals, antique inkstones, and books that are several hundred years old and have unique wooden covers. If you walk eastward, you will see a Xin Hua bookstore, where you can buy Chinese books in the arts, literature, history, and political science as well as novels and modern posters. At 70 and 80 Liuli Chang are the best antique stores, which sell a variety of antiques: carvings of jade, ceramics, ivory, wood, and semiprecious stones; snuff bottles; cloisonné and lacquerwares; metalwork. These items are generally from the Qing dynasty to the early 1900s, not exceeding 120 years old. The painting shop at 63 Liuli Chang sells original modern water-color paintings, old Chinese paintings, and calligraphy. The clerks are usually delighted to chat with foreign art connoisseurs. It is here that you can buy work by such masters as Xu Beihong and Chi Baishi if you have $10,000 to $20,000 U.S. or $12,000 to $24,000 Canadian to spare! You can buy the paintings of Chi Baishi's two sons here for much less. At 92 Liuli Chang you will find additional choices of modern paintings, which are the work of budding artists or the artisans of the arts and craft centers in Beijing.

Books   There are many Xinhua bookstores, which are the main stores carrying the major Chinese books, in Beijing. At 235 Wang Fujing the Foreign Language Book Store carries many new and old books (printed before the Cultural Revolution), postcards, and art books. In the Dong Feng (East Wind) Market near the Beijing Hotel, there is a book section where you can buy old or used books in both English and Chinese. If you are a book lover, you must make a quick visit to this market. I found a few rare old art books here.

Seals   In China, on documents or checks, a personal seal or chop bearing your full name is more important than a personal signature. These seals make unusual and interesting gifts. In Beijing there are three well-known seal shops: 261 Wang Fujing, 20 Liuli Chang, and the seal counter of the Dong Feng Market. The seal may be made of copper, stones, or jade. Beijing is noted for its little copper seals with a carved lion on the top. However, many different types of colored marble stones are used for seals. Depending on your personal preference, you can select a single stone or a pair of stones ranging from a few *yuans* to thousands of *yuans*. (Chicken blood stones or yellow-earth stones are for the art collectors!)

After you select the seal, you may choose the style of Chinese characters you wish. If you prefer the antique seals, the store can erase the old names and carve yours on it. The seal counter of the Dong Feng Market does excellent seal carving and is not pressed with large volumes of rush work from foreign visitors.

Furs In China you will find a good selection of furs, including sable, mink, and rabbit. Available as ready-made hats, jackets, and coats, they are inexpensive by Western standards. However, the style might not be as fashionable as the styles shown in New York or Paris. Furs may be found at 192 Wang Fujing and on the second floor of the Friendship Store. The fur section at the Trade Fair in Guangzhou (Canton) has a good selection of fur garments and fur rugs.

Carpets Chinese carpets, which are world renowned, are available in Beijing at the Friendship Store and at 208 Qian Men. Both stores carry a variety of carpets, rugs, and mats in the traditional designs of Tiajin, Xinjiang, Inner Mongolia, and Xizang (Tibet). In China, good carpets are expensive.

Major Antique Stores	Address	Phone
Baoguzhai Shop of Paintings and Calligraphy	63 E. Liuli Chang	330146
Cuizhenzhai Shop of Modern Pottery and Porcelain	17 W. Liuli Chang	
Guanfuzhai Shop of Seals and Inkstones	34A W. Liuli Chang	331209
Moyuange Shop of Contemporary Paintings and Calligraphy	58 E. Liuli Chang	330146
Palace Museum, Foreign Guest Service Department	Palace Museum	555031
Qingyuntang Shop of Stone Rubbings	20 W. Liuli Chang	331209
Yunguzhai Shop of Ancient Pottery and Porcelain	80 E. Liuli Chang	336682
Yunyuzhai Shop for Green Jades	108 E. Liuli Chang	
Zhenahuan Shop of Metals and Stones	70 E. Liuli Chang	331951

Major Arts and Crafts Department Stores in Beijing	Address	Phone
Beijing Arts and Crafts Department Store	200 Wang Fujing	556816
Beijing Museum of Chinese Arts	Palace Museum	443119
Beijing Painting Shop	289 Wang Fujing	553409
Kong Bao Zhai	W. Liuli Chang	333352

Bookshops and Department Stores	Address	Phone
Beijing Department Store	Wang Fujing Street	
Dong Feng Market	Wang Fujing Street East	

Foreign Language Press	235 Wang Fujing Street	
Friendship Store	Jiangguo Menwai Street	593531
Xidan Shopping Center	120 Beidajie, Xidan	
Xinhua Bookstore	214 Wang Fujing Street—in Dong Feng Market—Wang Fujing Xidan Shopping Center	
Zhongguo Bookstore	115 E. Liuli Chang	

ENTERTAINMENT

Beijing Opera   The Beijing opera, or *Jing Ju*, which means the "Opera of the Capital," is one of China's major dramatic art forms. Developed over many centuries, the opera combines literature, traditional music, dancing, pantomime, acrobatic feats, and stylized singing and acting. An orchestra of string and percussion instruments is used, the drummer acting as the conductor. The actors wear dramatic facial makeup and elegant costumes. It is a fantastic experience to see this famous opera company, which, in recent years, has performed in Europe, the United States, and Canada.

Ballet   In Beijing the New China Ballet Troupe regularly presents well-known revolutionary ballets, which are basically Western ballets using stylized acting to depict the class struggle in China. Since the summer of 1978 Western ballets such as *Swan Lake* have reappeared on the Beijing stage. The most popular and newly created ballet on the Beijing stage is *The Little Match-Girl*, which was adopted from Hans Christian Anderson's story and is performed by the Beijing Dance School. The Beijing Dance School also created a modern ballet drama that is a moving remembrance of Premier Zhou Enlai. Although ballet tickets are hard to come by for visitors and local residents, you may be able to get some with the help of your guide.

Concerts   Since the Cultural Revolution, Western classical composers and their work have been sharply criticized and banned. After the fall of the Gang of Four in 1976, the forbidden Western music began to be played again in China's major cites. The Central Orchestra of Beijing regularly presents classical symphonies. Sometimes a visiting Western symphony orchestra or noted artists might present joint concerts with their host-musicians.

Acrobatic Show   This is one of the most popular and enjoyable forms of entertainment in China for all ages. It combines an amazing mixture of excellent acrobats, jugglers, conjurors, and dancers. The performance usually lasts for two to three hours. After a busy day of sightseeing, it is relaxing to see this show.

Beijing opera.

Acrobatic show.

Beijing Puppet Show Beijing is noted for its puppet theater, in which classical operas or modern heroic stories are acted out by puppets. The three-feet-high puppets are manipulated on sticks by young actors, who perform the dialogue and sing below the stage. The imaginative stage settings, modern sound, and interesting visual effects help create a memorable and enjoyable show.

Drama In Beijing there are many theaters presenting classical dramas or modern plays in Chinese. If you have command of the Chinese language, you will enjoy such performances as "Yang Kai-hui," a new play depicting Chairman Mao and his wife Yang's heroic life. You need not know Chinese, however, to appreciate the singing, music, superb acting, and spectacular stage designs in "Juo Wenjin," a music-drama based on the life of the third-century poetess and writer Juo Wenjin. It is a truly magnificent production.

Sports Sports and games are extremely popular among Chinese families. The huge, modern Beijing Capital Colosseum (Beijing Ti Yu Guan), an indoor sports stadium with a seating capacity of twenty thousand, is well worth seeing. For a current program of athletic events consult your tour guide.

BEIJING TELEPHONE GUIDE

Taxis	337431, 557461
Bank of China	330452
Post Office	555414
International Club	522144
Capital Hospital	553731
China International Travel	557558, 557496, 551379
China Travel Service (at Overseas Chinese Hotel)	551129, 553509

Travel Service and Airlines

China International Travel
  Service (*Luxingshe*)
  East Changan Street, Beijing   557558, 557496, 551379
  Cable "LUXINGSHE."

Civil Aviation Administration of China (CAAC)

Information, Beijing Airport	552515
City Office, Zhu Shi Da Jie	555531
Domestic Ticket Office, Zhu Shi Da Jie	554415
International Ticket Office, Zhu Shi Da Jie	557878
Cargo Office, Zhu Shi Da Jie	552945
Customs, Zhu Shi Da Jie	550054
Ethiopian Air, Jianguomenwai 2-2-12	523285
Air France, Jianguomenwai 2-2-12	523894
Air Romania, Jianguomenwai 2-2-12	523552
Iran Air, Jianguomenwai 2-2-51	523249
Japan Airlines, Jianguomenwai 2-2-12	523457
Pakistan Airlines, Jianguomenwai 2-2-61	523542, 523989
Swiss Air, Beijing Hotel, Room 5015	522231, Ext. 5015

Changchun Geological College.

Changchun No. 1 Auto Plant.

CHANGCHUN (Changchun)

Jilin Province

The capital of Jilin Province, Changchun, is located on the Yitong River in the central Northeast Plain. With a population of 1.5 million, the city is characterized by its broad, tree-lined streets and many administrative buildings. Much of this thousand-year-old city was built during the Japanese occupation of 1933-45, when the city was known as the capital of "Manchukuo." At the end of World War II, China regained control of Changchun.

In 1953, China's first automobile plant was opened in Changchun. Today it is the largest center of the industry, manufacturing trucks, tractors, and automobiles, including the official "Red Flag" limousines. The city's light industries produce optical instruments, pharmaceutical products, machine tools, railway cars, textiles, clocks and watches, and food.

Jilin University, Changchun Geological College, and Jilin Provincial Library are interesting places to visit. Nanhu Park, the Xinli Cheng Reservoir, and the Workers' Park are also popular sightseeing spots. Sports-minded visitors might like to see the Changchun Gymnasium, which is the home of many Northern Chinese athletes. Changchun is also the home of one of China's largest film studios, the Changchun Studio.

The spacious and comfortable Changchun Guesthouse accommodates foreign visitors.

CHANGSHA (Changsha)

Hunan Province

Changsha, the capital of Hunan Province, is located on the Xiangjiang River about 525 kilometers northwest of Guangzhou, and about 1,350 kilometers south of Beijing. It is on the express train line from the north of China to the south. Although traditionally the major trading center for the rich agricultural Hunan Province, which produces 15 percent of the rice of China, Changsha has more recently diversified its economic base. Today it is a city devoted primarily to light industry and operates many rice mills, chemical plants, electronics, machinery, and metal works. It has a population of approximately one million.

Changsha is perhaps most important for its association with Chairman Mao Zedong, for it was here that he lived and studied from 1913 to 1918. Mao's experiences and observations in Changsha had a profound influence on him and provided the basis for his political thinking and revolutionary activities.

In addition to being a significant political and commercial center, Changsha also serves as the provincial center for culture and education. Its educational facilities include Hunan University, a teacher training school, the Institute of Metallurgy, and the Institute of Chinese Traditional Medicine. Culturally, Changsha has its own local opera company and is renowned for its marionette and shadow-puppet shows.

HISTORY

Changsha is one of China's ancient cities, dating back about three thousand years. In January 1972, during an excavation of the Western Han tombs (206 B.C.-A.D. 24) at Mawangdui, an eastern suburb of Changsha, archaeologists unearthed a collection of particularly fine and well-preserved artifacts. These indicate that a highly civilized culture existed here during the Han period. During the Song dynasty (A.D. 960-1280) Changsha was established as an educational center with the founding of a college on Mount Yuilu. The well-known philosopher Zhu Xi taught there. During the Ming dynasty the Emperor Hong Wu had a large wall with nine gates built around the city of Changsha. In 1644, with the change in administrative regions under the Qing dynasty, the city became the provincial capital of Hunan.

When Changsha was opened to international trade in 1904, many Europeans and Americans moved into the city and began to assert their cultural and religious influence. Gradually these foreigners established merchant businesses, export factories, churches, and schools. Yale University set up a medical college here. Shortly thereafter, with the building of the railway, Changsha became an important agricultural port, exporting tea, tobacco, rice, and cotton, and a center for light industry.

From 1913 to 1918 Chairman Mao received his teacher training at the First Normal School. After the founding of the Chinese Communist Party in 1921, he returned to Changsha to establish the local Party Committee and directed its early activities here.

PLACES TO SEE

Hunan First Normal School Although the original buildings of the First Normal School were destroyed during the civil war, the school has been faithfully reconstructed to appear just as it was when Mao attended. Some of the rooms have been set aside and converted into a small museum. These have been set up like the original classrooms where he taught and held meetings for the young students and illiterate peasant workers of Changsha and Qingshuitang. The museum displays samples of Mao's schoolwork as well as photographs and records associated with his early career and revolutionary activities. Today the school is still used as a teacher training facility, which has a staff of ninety and an annual enrollment of about one hundred students in the three-year program. In addition, an elementary school for practical training is also administered by this normal school. Requests to visit the school must be made in advance.

Hunan Provincial Museum Located in Martyrs Park, this museum contains not only a special collection of revolutionary documents but also the famous relics from local Han tombs excavated in 1965 and 1972. A new thermo-controlled museum section was specially constructed to house the archaeological finds from the two groups of Western Han (206 B.C.-A.D. 24) tombs at Mawangdui 1 and 3. For more details, please refer to the section entitled "Major Museums of China."

Hunan Provincial Embroidery Factory Hunan is renowned for its lovely embroidery, and located here in Changsha is one of the four best embroidery factories in China. The factory has a staff of over two hundred, thirty of whom are devoted to artistic design and finding new techniques of embroidering. So far, they have perfected over seventy different stitches. Subjects include figures, landscapes, flowers, birds, animals, and political leaders and themes. This embroidery is used mainly for public exhibitions and for decoration in public buildings, as well as for gifts of international exchange.

Hunan Pottery Exhibition Hall　Several cities in Hunan produce colorful ceramic wares and fine porcelain. Established in 1974, the exhibition hall has on display over three thousand representative types of pottery, including Changsha and Lilin wares. There are two exhibits annually. A small gift shop is open to visitors.

The Former Office of the Hunan Communist Party Committee　The Qingshuitang (Clear Water Pond), which is located southwest of Martyrs Park, was formerly the site of the first office of the Hunan Communist Party Committee. Today the small house, where Mao Zedong lived in 1921 and in which committee meetings were held, has been turned into a museum. Displayed here are revolutionary documents and records associated with the early activities of the Hunan Communist movement.

Aiwan (Loving Dusk) Pavilion　A popular retreat of Mao Zedong, this pavilion is situated on Yue Lu Hill on the west bank of the Xiangjiang River. Built in 1792, it was named after a poem written by the Tang poet Tu Mu. The pavilion overlooks Hunan University and commands an excellent view of the city.

ACCOMMODATION

Hunan Guesthouse　This hotel is located in Martyrs Park and is the city's finest accommodation for foreign visitors. Built in 1959, this nine-story building has more than 250 rooms and can accommodate 600 people. The hotel facilities include three dining rooms, a gift shop, and a local crafts shop. In addition, the hotel has a barbershop, post office, bank, laundry, and taxi services. Hotel rates are Y14 - Y18 (about $11.00 U.S., $12.00 Canadian) for a room with twin beds. A suite is Y60 ($40.00 U.S., $45.00 Canadian).

CUISINE

Hunan food is noted for its spicy dishes flavored with hot pepper. However, the hotel menu usually offers more bland and less spicy meals for visitors. If you are adventurous, you might request real Hunan food through your guide or the dining room staff. Beancakes and chicken and vegetables, especially the winter-melon prepared in Hunan hot sauces, can also be a special treat.

SHOPPING

The Hunan embroidery is lovely but expensive. However, in addition to embroidery, Hunan is also known for its traditional regional handicrafts, which include ceramics, shellwork, bamboo carving, and embroidered watercolor paintings. The small ceramic figurines and miniature shell ornaments are particularly recommended. A good selection of these crafts can be found in either the local department store or the hotel shops.

Marketplace, Changzhou.

CHANGZHOU (Changchow)

Jiangsu Province

Changzhou is located halfway between Zhenjiang and Suzhou in Jiangsu Province on the old imperial Grand Canal. Founded under the Sui dynasty (A.D. 589-618), the city became an active port on the canal during the period when tribute rice, grown on the surrounding Yangtze plain, was collected and shipped north to the imperial capital Beijing. Changzhou's traditional local handicrafts include wood carving, papercuttings, and inlaid woodwork. Today Changzhou is a center for the textile and food industries.

Visitors will enjoy the Tianning Temple, a historical building known for its architecture and design. The Red Plum Pavilion (Hongmei Tang) is another interesting site because of its scenic beauty and history. The Changzhou Museum, located in the Qu Qiubai's house, displays a collection of local historical and cultural relics of Changzhou.

Chengde Palace.

CHENGDE (Chengteh or Jehol)

Hebei Province

Chengde, meaning "Inherited Virtue," was the summer resort of the imperial family of the Qing dynasty (1644-1911). Located 250 kilometers northeast of Beijing in Hebei Province, it can be reached in four hours from Beijing and makes an excellent day trip. At an elevation of 350 meters, the resort occupies a basin that remains pleasantly cool during the hot summers. Thus, it is also often referred to as the "Mountain Village for Escaping the Heat."

The construction of Chengde was begun by Emperor Kangxi in 1703 and completed by Emperor Qianlong in 1790. The whole resort extends over an area of about 560 hectares, which is surrounded by mountains, thick forests, and small lakes. Thus, Chengde is even bigger than the Beijing Palace Museum and Summer Palace together.

The principal part of the summer residence consists of the palace complex, the Bishushanzhuang, and grounds, which are entirely encompassed by a long red wall. Outside the walls, several other temples and pavilions are set among the hills and trees to the east and north. Unlike the main palace, which is built in the traditional Chinese style, these pavilions and temples are modeled on the simpler Tibetan style. Throughout the palaces and pavilions, however, the architectural elements are of a simplistic design and neutral color, harmoniously in keeping with the natural surroundings.

The main entrance to the Chengde resort has three traditional gateways. Inscribed on a plaque over the center gate is the name of the gate in Chinese, Mongolian, Tibetan, Arabic, and Manchu. The major residence complex, situated in the southeast corner of the walled area, consists of four palaces: (1) The Main Palace (Zheng Gong) is the largest and contains the throne hall (Nanmu Hall), which was built from the fine-grained aromatic hardwood called *Nanmu*. Here the Qing emperors received foreign envoys and the nobility of China. Behind the hall are the library and private apartments.   (2) the Hazel Grouse Studio (Songhao Zhai), east of the Main Palace, was used by empresses and the imperial families.   (3) The young emperor Qianlong attended school in the Wind in the Pines, or Ten Thousand Streams (Wanhe Sonfeng), a smaller palace north of the Hazel Grouse Studio.   (4) The East Palace (Dong Gong) was used by the emperors for official functions.

Beyond the palace, to the northeast, the series of interconnecting lakes surrounded by gardens, pathways, and pavilions frequently offered a pleasant retreat for the imperial household during the heat of the summer. In 1793, Emperor Qianlong received Lord Macartney, England's first envoy to China, in a pavilion on the north shore of the lake. Beyond the lake-center pavilions, on a small islet, stands a tower called the House of Mists and Rains, where the Qing emperors used to study and watch the misty clouds and rain over the distant hills.

Northwest of the palace complex is the famous Wenjin Pavilion, which was built in 1774 to house the imperial library collection of the Emperor Qianlong. Among the books this library contains are the 79,000 volumes of the "Complete Works of the Four Treasures" (classics, history, philosophy, and literature), or *Siku Quanshu*, and the "Collections of Ancient and Modern Books," both of which were compiled during the eighteenth century.

If visitors decide to stay in Chengde for more than one day the Chengde Hotel, situated south of the palace in town, offers comfortable accommodation.

Blue and white vase of the Qianlong period.

Hanging white jade jar.

Baoguangsi Monastery, Chengdu.

CHENGDU (Chengtu) Sichuan Province

Chengdu, the provincial capital of Sichuan Province, was a political, economic, and cultural center as early as 400 B.C. Situated on a broad plain at an elevation of 153 meters, it is surrounded by intensively cultivated land, which produces wheat, rice, tea, tobacco and a variety of plants and herbs used for medicinal purposes. In addition to being an agricultural center, Chengdu has also developed into an important industrial city, with a total population of over three million. For centuries it has also served as a provincial center for culture and education. Today Chengdu has twelve colleges and thirty-two technical institutes as well as the Opera Art Institute. The latter preserves a tradition of local Sichuan opera that dates back some two thousand years.

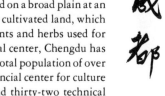

HISTORY

Chengdu is an ancient city with a history that is two thousand years old. In the Three Kingdoms period (220-265), it became the capital of the kingdom of Shu Han under Lui Bei. For a short period during the Tang dynasty (618-907), it was occupied by the Emperor Xuan Zong and his court after the emperor had fled his rebellious subjects, who were led by An Lushan. Shortly after, Chengdu was almost destroyed by the Mongols. During the tenth century, under the Five Dynasties (907-960), the king of Later Shu had hibiscus flowers planted along the walls of the city, giving rise to the name *Furong*, or "City of Hibiscus." With the fall of the Ming dynasty in 1644, Chengdu was taken by a group of rebels who maintained the city as an independent domain for three years. It was finally established as a permanent garrison under the Qing dynasty. Du Fu, the great Tang dynasty poet (712-770), also lived in Chengdu, after escaping the An Lushan revolt in Xi'an. During his three years in Chengdu, Du Fu wrote several hundred poems, many of which relate the suffering caused by the civil rebellion.

PLACES TO SEE

Du Fu Cao Tang   Although the original thatched cottage in which the poet Du Fu lived no longer exists, an eighth-century shrine marks the site of his garden. In addition, the surrounding buildings have been restored over the centuries and contain displays associated with the poet and his life, including several editions of his works. Many Chinese scholars and political leaders, including Chairman Mao Zedong, have visited this shrine. It is a tradition to visit the Du Fu Cao Tang on the seventh day of the first lunar month (mid February).

Wu Hou Shrine   Situated southwest of the city, this Tang dynasty shrine was built to commemorate the life and achievements of the famous third-century scholar and military strategist Wu Hou 181-234), also known as Zhuge Liang. Over the centuries the shrine has been reconstructed several times. In 1952 further restoration was undertaken, and it was designated as an official historical site.

Sichuan University   This well-known institute of higher education was established in 1927. Today it has many colleges, including colleges of the arts, the sciences, medicine, and engineering.

Wan Jiang Park   This park, which is located in the southern suburbs of the city overlooking the Jinjiang (Brocade River), was designed during the Qing dynasty and is noted for its cedar wood pavilions. Its forest contains over a hundred different varieties of bamboo.

River View Pavilion   Situated near the East Nine-Arch Bridge, this three-story wooden structure stands above the water on the bank of the Jinjiang. An interesting teahouse is now located in the pavilion.

Baoguangsi Monastery   This Buddhist monastery is situated about thirty kilometers northeast of the city. Although the monastery dates back before the seventh century A.D., many of the carvings, statues of Buddha, and pagodas were made during the Tang dynasty (618-907). The complex, which at one time held a community of some three thousand monks, consists of several halls, courtyards, and other buildings. Lohan Hall is of particular interest for the five hundred Lohans (disciples of Buddha), which are represented in a variety of poses and expressions.

Tujianyan Dam and Green City Peak   Located forty kilometers northwest of Chengdu, this two-thousand-year-old dam was built to channel water from the Min River into a vast irrigation system in the valley below the Green City Peak. A monument to early Chinese technology, the dam is still in use today. Since 1949, it has been expanded and improved to provide irrigation for over six million hectares of crop land.

Teahouses   Teahouses are an integral part of Sichuan life, serving as centers for conducting business and for social gatherings. For example, the teahouse on Dongfang Street in Chengdu is a popular battleground for chess enthusiasts. Other teahouses provide such entertainments as storytelling and musical performances. For the Chinese, a teahouse is a popular and inexpensive place to spend leisure time.

ACCOMMODATION

Jinjiang (Brocade River) Guesthouse Built in 1956, this is a fairly comfortable hotel located on the west side of Renmin Road in the old town. It has a gift shop, post office, barbershop, and twenty-four-hour laundry service. The dining room serves excellent food.

Chengdu Hotel This new hotel, built in 1979, is also located on Renmin Road South. It has five hundred rooms and offers comfortable accommodation, modern facilities, a relaxed atmosphere, and good food.

CUISINE

Sichuan food is considered a specialty among the many Chinese regional cuisines. Visitors can sample the hot, peppery dishes at the Chengdu Restaurant on Sheng Li Road East, or at the Furong Restaurant on Renmin Road. If you like hot food you must try the famous carrying-pole noodles (*dandanmian*), which were originally sold by a vendor who carried the cooked food on two poles. Other local favorites are Grandma Chen's beancurd (*Chenmapo doufu*), and strange-taste chicken (*Guaiweiji*). The use of medicinal herbs and flower petals is another unique aspect of Sichuan cooking. You might want to try fried lotus flowers, chicken strips with orchid petals, or duck cooked with medicinal herbs. Chengdu offers two hundred varieties of snacks, such as sweet, glutinous rice dumplings and boiled meat dumplings.

SHOPPING

The local Sichuan crafts, which include lacquerware, pottery, brocade, bamboo, and plaited straw-wares, are available in almost all the local shops. In particular, embroidery and Shu brocades are well known for their fine quality and make excellent gifts. Silver filigree is another Chengdu specialty. Delicately designed human figures, animals, flowers, bamboo, and pine are used for wall decorations and jewelry pieces.

In Sichuan Province there are special marketing days called *Ganzhang*, which means "rushing to market." Periodically, the farmers and merchants bring their merchandise to a designated marketplace for open selling and buying. Visiting the market can be a fascinating experience.

Sichuan panda.

Food stalls, Chongqing.

CHONGQING (Chungking)

Sichuan Province

The city of Chongqing, in Sichuan Province, was the war capital of China from 1939 to 1945. The old city was built on a rocky promontory at the confluence of the Jialing and Yangtze Rivers. Today, with a population of six million, it is China's largest municipality, encompassing the surrounding agricultural and industrial area to the west of the city. Because of its location, Chongqing developed as a major transportation junction, linked by land routes to the north and by the Yangtze and Shanghai to the east. It has also become an important industrial center, manufacturing steel, machinery, chemicals, and textiles. Educational institutions in Chongqing include several universities and technical colleges, the Sichuan Academy of Fine Arts, and the Chongqing Working People's Palace of Culture.

During the Second World War, Chongqing was the capital of the Nationalist government. However, at the same time, members of the Communist Party were also active, with their base located in Red Crag Village in the western suburbs of the city. When the Japanese invaded China, the two parties negotiated and agreed to unite their efforts against the common enemy.

Today visitors are usually taken to Chongqing to embark on a two-day river cruise through the Yangtze Gorges, which are located between Chongqing and Wuhan.

PLACES TO SEE

Red Crag Village (Hongyan Cun) During the Second World War, the Communist Party representatives, Zhou Enlai and others, established the

Eighth Route Army office and the Southern Bureau of the Central Committee here in Chongqing. Located in the western suburbs, it is now a museum dedicated to the Revolution.

Cassia Garden   This was the place in which Mao Zedong stayed during his visit to Chongqing in August 1945 to negotiate the ill-fated truce with the Nationalist leader Chiang Kaishek.

Loquat Hill   This is the highest point in the city and commands a view of Chongqing and the river.

Southern Mountain Park (Nanshan Gongyuan)   Nanshan Park, which is located on the south bank, can be reached by ferry. It overlooks a magnificent landscape of terraced rice fields, the city, and the river.

Southern Hot Springs (Nanwen Quan)   A trip to these hot springs, which are located twenty kilometers south of the city, makes a pleasant excursion. The sulfurous springs are surrounded by beautiful lakes, gardens, and pavilions.

ACCOMMODATION

The People's Hall Hotel   Located on Renmin Road, in the center of the city, this wing of the People's Hall is often used for conferences. Built in 1954 in the style of Beijing's Temple of Heaven, it offers comfortable, spacious rooms.

Yuzhou Hotel   Although providing more comfortable accommodation, this hotel, which is situated in a park in the southeastern suburbs, is some distance from the city center.

CUISINE

Chongqing offers typical hot, spicy Sichuan food, which is famed for its pickled vegetables, chicken and duck dishes, and red hot noodles. You can sample some of these dishes in the hotel dining room or venture to the local food stalls and restaurants.

SHOPPING

At the Friendship Store or the local department stores, visitors will find a variety of local products and crafts such as silk, brocade, pottery, lacquerwares, silver crafts, and bamboo products. If circumstances permit, visitors should take the opportunity to go to the local market, where farmers, craftsmen, and shopkeepers sell their special products and goods.

ENTERTAINMENT

Teahouses   In Sichuan Province the local teahouses have become important social and cultural centers. Occasionally, local musicians perform at the teahouses, providing pleasant afternoon or evening entertainment.

Sichuan Puppet Show   One of the popular forms of entertainment in Chongqing is the puppet theater. Performances are usually based on Chinese folktales or well-known historical stories.

Starry Park Beach, Dalian.

DALIAN (Talien) Liaoning Province

Dalian, also known as Darien or Luda, is located in the northwestern province of Liaoning on the southern tip of the Liaoning Peninsula. In 1905 both Dalian and Port Arthur (Lushun) immediately to the south were leased to Japan, and for the next forty years the Japanese enlarged and improved the harbor area, which is completely ice-free throughout the year. The Soviet Union later took control of Dalian as a result of the 1945 Yalta Agreement. Since the early 1950s, when the city was once again restored to China, the Chinese have further developed the harbor facilities.

Today Dalian is China's third largest foreign trade port city, receiving ships from more than one hundred nations. Its modern harbor facilities are capable of handling the great volume of shipping, and more recently it has become China's largest deep water oil port. In addition to trade activities, Dalian has become an industrial city involved in ship and locomotive building, food processing and refining, and the manufacture of chemicals and textiles. It also operates several smaller craft factories, which produce shell pictures and glass items. Foreign visitors may take a tour of the harbor and see some of the local factories, with their day-care and medical facilities. A visit to one of the workers' residential neighborhoods will complete the picture of daily life in Dalian.

After Shenyang, Dalian is an important cultural center of the province. It is also an attractive seaside resort, surrounded by hills and offering excellent recreational areas and beaches. Dongshan, Tiger Bay, and Xinghai are the three major beaches and are located just south of town. Within the city, much of the past influence of the Russians can be seen in the architecture, open squares, and bilingual signs.

Visitors are usually accommodated at the Dalian Guesthouse. This old-fashioned Victorian-style hotel, built in 1907, offers reasonably comfortable rooms and services. The dining room is recommended for its fresh seafood dishes.

Factory workers, Daqing.

DAQING (Taching) Heilongjiang Province

Located in a formerly barren area in southwestern Heilongjiang Province just north of Harbin, Daqing is a busy industrial and agricultural center. During the 1930s, geological surveys undertaken by the Japanese revealed the existence of large oil reserves. Initial drilling and exploration began in the 1950s, and oil was struck in 1959, despite the fact that the Soviet Union withdrew its technical assistance in the project. Since then, Daqing has become China's model industrial development; hence Chairman Mao's famous dictum, "In industry, learn from Daqing." By 1975 Daqing was supplying 80 percent of the country's oil. Although production has declined over the past few years as a result of the decreasing oil reserves, Daqing still supplies China with a high proportion of its oil.

Today, in addition to oil-related activities, Daqing has expanded to include industrial and agricultural production. Some fifty small village units scattered over the 1,000-square-kilometer oil field make up this community complex, which is serviced by day-care, medical, and educational facilities.

Visitors who wish to stay overnight here in Daqing can be accommodated in one of the guesthouses, which are all very simple.

Seated Buddha, Yungang Grottoes.

DATONG (Tatung) Shanxi Province

Datong is the largest city in north Shanxi Province and is situated on a plateau bounded by the Great Wall to the north and to the south. It can be reached easily by train from Beijing, which is about 250 kilometers to the east. Established during the Spring and Autumn Period (770-476 B.C.), it became a capital of the Wei empire during the fifth century A.D. and of the Liao empire during the tenth century. Today, with a population of 150,000, it is one of China's major producers of coal and it is also a center for light industry, manufacturing, and the production of pottery, carpets, shoes, and crafts. Apart from a few temples within the city walls, Datong is best known for the Yungang Grottoes, which are located sixteen kilometers west of town.

PLACES TO SEE

Nine Dragon Screen (Jiu Long Bi) This early Ming screen is located in the center of Datong near the Drum Tower. The screen, which is about forty-six meters long, two meters thick, and six meters high, is covered with colorful glazed ceramic tiles, and depicts nine dragons fighting for the sun.

Huayan Monastery (Huayan Si) Located in the southwest corner of the old city, this Buddhist temple dates back to the Liao dynasty of the tenth century A.D. and takes its name from the Buddhist sect, Huayan, which was founded during the Tang dynasty. Further construction took place during the eleventh and twelfth centuries. During the Ming dynasty (1368-1644), the monastery was divided into an upper and lower temple. The Upper Huayan is a well-preserved structure containing religious statues and paintings dating from the early Ming and Qing periods. The main hall of the Lower Huayan was built in 1048 and houses the library of the Buddhist sutras as well as several Liao statues. The museum of Datong is located in the buildings in front of the lower temple.

Yungang Grottoes   This world-renowned repository of early Buddhist art is located at the southern base of the Wuzhou Hills, sixteen kilometers west of Datong. Although it took about 145 years to complete this spectacular project, most of the carving was done between 460 and 494 during the Northern Wei dynasty. Hewn from the cliffside, the caves extend from east to west along the sandstone hills for about one kilometer. A total of fifty-three stone caves contain over fifty-one thousand finely carved stone statues of Buddha, Bodhisattva, and flying hapsarahs as well as countless birds, animals, pagodas, and ornamental motifs. The largest statue of Buddha stands seventeen meters, while the smallest is just a couple of centimeters high. The statues in this vast collection were executed in a variety of styles, and their graceful, lifelike forms assume many different poses and expressions. Although all of these carved images convey religious meaning and stories, they are also invaluable works of art that provide artists and historians with a better understanding of the culture of ancient China.

Ceramic Factory of the Meikuo Guo District   Established in 1971, this factory was originally built to meet the needs of the local market. Since then, the factory has expanded considerably, and today a staff of 260 produces ceramic wares for the local market as well as for export to Japan, Africa, and France. The artistic designs and innovative styles and techniques are of particular interest.

Carpet Factory   This factory was established in 1970 by eight housewives who made small cooking tools out of surplus steel wires. In late 1972 they decided to attempt carpet making, and by 1973 they were producing their own self-designed carpets. Today this factory produces three styles of carpets: the Beijing type, the Shanxi type, and the artistic style. The staff take great pride in the elegant carpets they produce, which are all hand woven on looms.

ACCOMMODATION

Datong Guesthouse   Located in the southern quarter of the town, outside the lower fortifications, this hotel provides only very simple and basic accommodation for foreign visitors.

Yungang Grottoes.

111

Terraced fields, Dazhai.

DAZHAI (Tachai) Shanxi Province

Dazhai is a small village in the Taihang Mountains of Shanxi Province. Before the 1950s it was a poor rural area marked by barren hills, dry and rocky soils, and a susceptibility to flooding. Nevertheless, it was seen to have potential, and in 1953 fifty families set up China's first agricultural cooperative here. Through repeated hard work and determination, the original Dazhai Production Brigade transformed the desolate fields into productive farmland, which in four years produced twice the previous annual yield. Although the brigade members initially encountered overwhelming difficulties caused by flooding, they achieved great success by constructing a series of terraces, embankments, and a long irrigation gully.

Today Dazhai serves as the exemplar for the rest of the country; hence the motto "In agriculture, learn from Dazhai," which is quoted throughout rural China. During conferences in 1975 and 1976, it was recommended that agricultural projects undertaken in Dazhai be implemented in other regions of China. Over the past few years the Dazhai commune has expanded considerably and is continually developing more sophisticated methods of increasing production. Chemical fertilizers have recently been introduced, and modern machinery and processing equipment have replaced the old manual tools that were originally used to cultivate the land.

Since its creation, the Dazhai commune has been popular with both foreign visitors and native Chinese. Model workers from rural areas all over China are often rewarded with a special visit to Dazhai, for it embodies the revolutionary spirit of accomplishment.

A visit to Dazhai necessitates an overnight stay. Visitors can be accommodated in the community guesthouse, which is simple and typical of the northern Chinese style of dwelling.

Mogao Caves, Dunhuang.

DUNHUANG (Dunhuang)

Gansu Province

Dunhuang, an oasis along the Danghe River in the Gobi Desert, is located at the foot of the snow-capped Qilian Mountains in western Gansu Province. As a result of its abundant water supply and dry climate, Dunhuang has long enjoyed great prosperity; it also offers spectacular scenery. It can easily be reached by train or plane from Lanzhou.

Dunhuang was established in 111 B.C. as a prefecture under the Emperor Wi Di of the Western Han Dynasty (206 B.C.-A.D. 24). As one of the major stops along the ancient Silk Road, it developed into an important cultural, religious, and economic center. From the rest of Asia, many ideas such as Buddhism were disseminated along the Silk Road and readily embraced in Dunhuang. Zhu Fafu, the Bodhisattva of Dunhuang, translated the Buddhist canons and sutras from Sanskrit and propagated them extremely successfully. Eventually numerous Buddhist monasteries, temples, shrines, and grottoes were established along the Silk Road, among them Dunhuang's Mogao Caves. From the fifth through the eleventh centuries Dunhuang flourished as a great Buddhist center, attracting not only devout pilgrims, but scholars and artists as well.

PLACES TO SEE

Mogao Caves These caves, which were only discovered in the past century, date back to the fourth century A.D. and represent one of the finest collections of early Buddhist art in China. According to some Tang tablets found on the site, work on the caves was begun in A.D. 366 under the Jin dynasty, and continued over some one thousand years until the late Yuan dynasty. Apparently the caves were finally abandoned and sealed when the monks took flight from foreign invaders. Thereafter the caves were plundered and suffered considerable damage over the centuries. Following their discovery, many of the treasures, including ancient manuscripts and scrolls, were removed by foreigners. Today, these can largely be found in various museums and private collections around the world. Since 1943, however, the Dunhuang Cultural Research

Institute, established by the state, has overseen the preservation of this historical site and in recent years has successfully restored many of the caves. In addition, the institute serves as a center for art history research and training. Hewn into the sandstone cliff face, the caves of Mogao extend over a distance of approximately sixteen hundred meters. Four hundred and ninety-two caves have survived and visitors can view these caves from modern platforms and walkways secured to the cliff. The caves, which are of various sizes and shapes, contain several thousand statues of Buddhas and Bodhisattvas, wall carvings, and frescoes ranging in style from the early Eastern Jin dynasty through to the Song and Yuan dynasties. In addition to their religious and artistic significance, these caves provide an invaluable chronological record of early Chinese culture. The historian can look at the murals and decorations and learn a great deal about the court life, costumes, architecture, customs, and habits of former dynasties.

According to the different styles and periods during which the caves were decorated, the caves at Dunhuang can be divided into three major groups. For example, in the earliest caves (A.D. 366-580) to the south, the predominant figure is the Sakyamuni Buddha, who is accompanied by smaller Lohans and Bodhisattvas. Simple bas-reliefs and tempera frescoes around the cave walls depict mythological figures, landscapes, scenes from the life of Sakyamuni, and tableaux of daily life.

Gradually the fresco painters and sculptors developed more innovative techniques, which are evident in the second group of caves dating from the Sui (589-618) and Tang (618-907) dynasties. Characteristic of this period are the giant statues of Buddha (the tallest of which is thirty-three meters) carved from the cave walls and modelled with clay. The statues were then painted to emphasize the fine detail and contours of the figure. Also, in the mural paintings of the Tang period artists achieved a far greater degree of realism, incorporating magnificent scenes from daily and court life into their depictions of religious stories. A fine example of this can be seen in the painting "The Pure Land."

By the tenth century, Buddhism in Dunhuang lost much of its impetus, and thereafter few additions and cave decorations were made. During this late period, portrait painting and large mural decoration were the principal artistic activities within the Mogao caves. Among the portraits that of the Five Dynasties (907-960) Emperor Li Shengtian is perhaps the finest. The most interesting Yuan murals include the map-like view of the Wutai Mountains and surrounding landscape, which can be seen in cave 61, and the large painting in cave 465, which is a colorful tableau of fourteenth century activities such as pottery making, weaving, milling, and herding.

Although Buddhist caves within the Dunhuang group include the Yulinsi Cave and the Thousand Buddha Cave, the Mogao caves are considered to be the most important and impressive.

Visitors can be accommodated in a very small and simple guesthouse on the caves site; however, as accommodation is extremely limited it is best to make arrangements in advance through your travel guide.

EMEISHAN (Mount Omei)

Sichuan Province

Emeishan is one of the four famous Buddhist mountain sanctuaries in China. Located forty kilometers west of Leshan in Sichuan Province, the site can be reached by road. The mountain rises to an altitude of over three thousand meters and from the summit, providing it is a clear day, one can see the distant peaks of the Tibetan mountains to the southwest. Although the sanctuary, which contains some seventy temples, evidently dates back to the Eastern Han dynasty of the second century A.D., most of the building was undertaken during the sixth century. Later, in the sixteenth century, when the Buddhists made Emeishan one of their sacred mountains, many of the temples were renovated and enlarged.

Access to the temples is along rugged footpaths carved out of the rock. The distance from the base to the summit is about sixty kilometers, and since the climbing can be quite arduous and dangerous all visitors are accompanied by a local guide who is familiar with the mountain.

The temples that are usually visited include: (1) the Temple for Protecting the Country (Baoguosi) located at the base, which contains the Library of the Sutras; (2) the Temple of the Crouching Tiger (Fuhusi); (3) the Temple of the Sound of Thunder (Leiyingsi); (4) the Temple of Ten Thousand Years (Wanniansi), which honors the Bodhisattva Puxian, Emeishan's patron saint; (5) the Hongchun Temple; (6) the Temple of the Magic Peak (Xianfengsi); and finally (7) the Temple of the Golden Summit (Jingdinsi), from which the phenomenon of the spectacular Precious Light of Buddha can be seen.

The Temple of Ten Thousand Years, which dates from the fourth century, was in remarkably good condition until this century. However, in 1946, during the period when the Guomindang, led by Chiang Kaishek, occupied Emeishan, this temple was almost destroyed by fire. Fortunately the hall containing the magnificent gilt statue of the Bodhisattva Puxian astride a life-size bronze elephant survived.

Emeishan is also a sanctuary for wildlife, with the dense forest of cedars and azaleas providing a home for a great variety of rare animals, including pandas, monkeys, antelopes, birds, and insects, frogs, and exotic butterflies.

Visitors are usually provided with meals and accommodation in simple guesthouses within the temples. Arrangements for overnight stays must be made in advance at the registration facilities at the foot of the mountain.

Shiwan pottery bear.

FOSHAN (Foshan)

Guangdong Province

Foshan is located sixteen kilometers southwest of Guangzhou in Guangdong Province. Originally a religious center, it was for centuries renowned for the three statues of Buddha carved into the hillside during the Tang dynasty 618-907); hence its name, which is translated as Buddha Hill. By about the fourteenth century, Foshan developed as a major center for the pottery industry. This tradition of pottery-making, however, dates back further than the Ming dynasty, for in recent excavations in the surrounding area, many ancient Shiwan pottery kiln sites were unearthed, which indicates that pottery was being produced here during the Song dynasty (960-1280). Although Foshan's importance diminished with the growth of Guangzhou, the pottery industry still flourishes today. In addition to pottery, Foshan also produces a variety of other traditional arts and crafts such as papercuts and lanterns.

PLACES TO SEE

Zumiao (Ancestral Temple)   This Taoist temple, which was built in the Ming dynasty (1368 - 1644), and later restored during the Qing dynasty, has now been converted into a museum. The displays include a 2,500 kilo bronze Buddhist statue, ancient pottery, and Han tomb figurines as well as several other artifacts discovered in this area. Within the huge courtyard of this temple is a stage surrounded by traditional verandas and balconies that was used during the nineteenth century for performances of local plays.

Arts and Crafts Center   Located in the former Ren Shou Si Temple, this center provides an opportunity to see local craftsmen at work designing papercuts, fabric flowers, and lanterns. The finished products are on display in the showroom and are also available for purchase in the center's shop.

Shiwan Pottery Factory   Visitors are usually taken to the Shiwan Pottery Factory, the most renowned of the several factories in Foshan. Ceramic tiles and bricks used in building, domestic pottery, and a variety of traditional decorative wares and ornaments are the major products manufactured here. Examples of Shiwan pottery are available in several local shops as well as in the factory shop. The miniature figurines and flower vases are particularly worthy of note.

ACCOMMODATION

A visit to Foshan is usually regarded as a day-excursion from Guangzhou. However, if visitors wish to stay overnight they can be accommodated in the Old Foshan Guesthouse, which also provides lunches for day-visitors.

The West Lake, Fuzhou.

FUZHOU (Foochow)   Fujian Province

Fuzhou, the capital of Fujian Province, is located in southeastern China on the north bank of the Minjiang. A suburb to the south on Nantai Island is linked to the mainland by two bridges.

Fuzhou was founded in the sixth century as a river settlement and port. Its present name appears around the eighth century. During the Five Dynasties (907-960), Fuzhou became the capital of the autonomous state of Minyue; later it became an international trade port. At the beginning of the Ming dynasty, the city walls were built. In 1842, the Treaty of Nanjing made Fuzhou an open port, and Europeans settled on the south bank of the river. In the nineteenth century, the city was known for its tea, timber, lichee nuts, silks, lacquerwares, wood engravings, umbrellas, and horn combs. Since 1949 the city has developed light industries in machinery, chemicals, and arts and crafts.

PLACES TO SEE

Hua Lin Temple   Situated on the southern slope of Blibing Mountain, this temple was first built during the Tang dynasty (618-907) and was restored under the Song, Ming, and Qing dynasties.

The Gushing Spring Temple (Yong Quan Si)   This eighth century shrine, located on the western slope of the Gushan (Drum Hill) just east of Fuzhou, is famous for possessing one of Buddha's teeth. In addition, there are two magnificent octagonal ceramic pagodas, which date from the Song dynasty (960-1280), situated within the temple grounds. Each pagoda has nine tiers and is adorned with hundreds of sculpted relief figures of Buddha. The Gushan rises to a height of about nine hundred meters and is renowned for its beauty and historical sites as well as its spa.

福
州

White Pagoda Monastery In the western foothills of Mount Yu is the magnificent White Pagoda Monastery, where the famous patriot and scholar Yan Fu pursued his studies over a hundred years ago. Yan spent many years translating such works as Darwin's *Evolution of the Species* from English into Chinese. Today the monastery houses the Yushan Library.

Qi Jiguang Memorial Temple This temple was built in honor of the famous Ming general Qi Jiguang, who led his army from Zhejiang to Fuzhou and defeated the Japanese pirates. The temple contains a bust of this heroic man. Surrounding the temple are the decorative Drunken Stone Pavilion, Pingyuan Terrace, and Penglai Pavilion, as well as rock gardens, bamboo groves, and evergreens.

Ding Guang Pagoda and Ebony Pagoda At the foot of Mount Yu, the two pagodas stand opposite each other, forming one of the scenic sights of Fuzhou. The Ding Guang is a seven-tiered octagonal white pagoda, about forty-one meters in height. Visitors can enjoy a full view of the islands and the sea from the top of this pagoda. The Ebony Pagoda, constructed in A.D. 789 of dark stones, is also a seven-tiered octagonal structure, but it is slightly smaller than the Ding Guang. The bottom tier, which is in the shape of an overturned lotus, is elegantly carved with dragons and phoenixes.

The West Lake This manmade lake is located in an enchanting park northwest of the city. Created some seventeen hundred years ago, it is surrounded by lovely gardens, pavilions and bridges. Next to the Cloud-Treading Bridge is the Cassia Studio, which was once used as a study by Lin Zexu, an eminent statesman of the mid-nineteenth century. The Fujian Provincial Museum, situated beside the Jade Belt Bridge, houses historical relics dating from the third century.

ACCOMMODATION

Foreign visitors may stay at either the Fuzhou Guesthouse or the Fuzhou Hotel. In both cases, the accommodation is very simple yet comfortable.

SHOPPING

The local handicrafts of Fujian Province include ivory, wood, and stone carvings, lacquerware, and bamboo basketry. These products are available at the local Friendship Store and Fuzhou Department Store.

Ivory carving.

Mausoleum of the Seventy-two Martyrs of Huanghuakang.

GUANGZHOU (Kwangchow or Canton)

Guangdong Province

Guangzhou, the capital of Guangdong Province, is situated on the northern Zhujiang (Pearl River) Delta and on the South China Sea. For centuries it has been an important international trade port, located only 145 kilometers northwest of Hong Kong. Today Guangzhou is the most important center in southern China, supporting a population of over three million. As a major industrial city, Guangzhou has shipbuilding facilities, refining and food processing plants, and factories producing chemicals, textiles, automobiles, machinery, steel, and rubber products. Agriculture, light industry, and traditional handcrafting are also major commercial activities of the city. As a cultural and educational center, Guangzhou has several excellent museums and many institutes of higher learning, including Zhong Shan University, a medical college, teacher training colleges, and eleven technical and research institutes. In addition to its political, economic, and cultural importance, Guangzhou is also the host city for the biannual (spring and autumn) Chinese Export Commodities Fair and a principal point of entry for visitors to China. It is a pleasant, tropical city, attractively landscaped with many parks and open areas.

HISTORY

Guangzhou, which until recently was familiarly known as Canton, has been associated with China's foreign trade and commerce for well over two thousand years. By the Qin dynasty (221-206 B.C.), it was already a foreign trade port maintaining regular contact with foreign countries. During the Han period (206 B.C.-A.D. 220) Roman merchants visited Guangzhou to exchange their cargoes of glass, wool, and linens for Chinese silks, pottery, and other handicrafts. A Moslem colony appeared during the seventh century, signaling the beginning of foreign immigration into the city, which was eventually to have a dramatic influence on Guangzhou's development. Later, in A.D. 714, under the Tang dynasty, special trade officials were appointed to set up an office in Guangzhou and oversee the city's foreign trade activities. Thus, Guangzhou became China's first official export trade port. Through the tenth century the city established contacts with Persian, Hindu, and Arab traders.

By the middle of the sixteenth century, the Portuguese, Spanish, Dutch, and British were seeking to establish trade concessions in Guangzhou. In 1699, the British East India Company opened its first concession outside the city walls. With the settlement of foreigners, a Chinese administrative official, the Viceroy, was appointed to control trade. However, despite prohibition and strong opposition from the Chinese authorities, the British began to import opium into China. This eventually led to the Opium Wars (1840-1842 and 1856-1860) and subsequently to the Treaty of Nanjing. Finally, an island in the Zhujiang south of Guangzhou, now known as Hong Kong, was released by the Chinese as a foreign concession.

During the past century, Guangzhou has had a significant role in China's revolutionary development. In April 1911, the Chinese Revolutionary League, led by Dr. Sun Yat-sen, launched an armed insurrection in Guangzhou to oppose the reactionary Qing regime. Although his army succeeded in overthrowing the ancient imperial system, it was not until 1923 that Sun Yat-sen founded the Nationalist Party (Guomindang) in Guangzhou. In 1926, Mao Zedong established the National Peasant Movement in Guangzhou and trained many Communist cadres here. In 1927 the Communists confronted the Nationalists in the famous Canton Uprising.

During the Sino-Japanese war, from 1938 to 1945, the city was again under foreign control. Since 1949, Guangzhou has greatly developed its industry, agriculture, science, crafts, and commerce, and retains much of its independence and individuality.

PLACES TO SEE

Chinese Export Commodities Fair   Also known as the Canton Trade Fair, this event is held twice annually from April 15 to May 15 and from October 15 to November 15. It is open daily from 8:30 to 11:30 a.m. and from 2:00 to 5:00 p.m. For more information on the Trade Fair see the section entitled "Conducting Business and Foreign Trade in China."

Yuexiu Park   This is the largest and one of the most popular parks in the city, located within walking distance of the Trade Fair and the Dong Fang Hotel. A fourteenth century five-story building known as the Zhenhai Lou (Tower for Overlooking the Sea) is situated on the hilltop in the park. Once a guarded post overlooking the river, today it houses the Guangzhou (Canton) Museum. The exhibits include historical relics, art treasures, and a collection of ceramics from the Neolithic period through to the present. A teahouse is situated at the top of the tower. In addition, this park has a number of sports facilities, pavilions, and gardens. Visitors can also hire boats to see the lake within the park.

Guangzhou Zoo   Situated in the northeast quarter of Guangzhou, the zoo occupies an area of over one and a half hectares. Considered one of the best in China, it is perhaps only surpassed by the Beijing Zoo. Visitors will see over two hundred species of animals here, but the pandas are really the top attraction. The zoo is open from 7:30 a.m. to 5:30 p.m. and facilities on the grounds include a shop and restaurant

Peasant Movement Institute   In 1924, this institute was founded by the Third Congress of the Chinese Congress Party for the purpose of training young people of the peasant class to further the cause of the Communist Party. Mao Zedong was in charge of the Institute from March 1926 to 1927, and many of the supporters of the movement such as Zhou Enlai taught here. The Institute, however, lasted only a short while for in 1927, as a result of the Canton uprising, it was closed. Today, the Institute, which is situated on the site of a former sixteenth century Confucian temple, has been restored. Visitors will see Mao's bedroom and office, dormitories, dining room, and lecture room.

Exhibition Hall of the Revolution   Situated next to the Peasant Movement Institute, this modern building contains a collection of Communist leaders' texts and historical photographs.

Guangzhou Cultural Park   This park is Guangzhou's largest cultural and recreational center. It is situated on south Renmin Road, a short distance from the river, and covers about eight hectares. Within this carnival-like setting there are numerous facilities for sports and entertainment including a concert hall, theater, opera house, cinema, aquarium, teahouses, and several exhibition pavilions. In addition, one will find the Chinese playing chess and basketball, and roller-skating. Visitors can see a wide variety of exhibits and open stage performances here during the day; however, for evening concerts and events, arrangements for tickets must be made in advance through your guide.

Dr. Sun Yat-sen Memorial Hall   Situated on Dongfeng Road, this splendid octagonal pavilion, with its colorfully tiled roof, was built in 1925 to commemorate Dr. Sun Yat-sen. It is used for concerts and stage performances and can seat five thousand people.

Zhong Shan University   Occupying what was formerly Lingnam University, the Zhong Shan is the oldest and largest university in Guangzhou, and offers excellent arts, science, and medical programs. Visitors who are interested in visiting the university may make special arrangements with the tour guide.

Hall of the Chinese Export Commodities Fair, Guangzhou.

Temple of the Six Banyan Trees (Liurongsi)   Built in A.D. 479, this temple owes its unusual name to the eleventh century poet, Su Dongpo, who while visiting there was inspired by the presence of six banyan trees growing outside the temple. Since then it has been restored several times and today is occupied by the Guangzhou Buddhist Association. Special permission is required to visit the temple. The pagoda dates from the sixth century. It rises about fifty-five meters from an octagonal base and is of architectural interest for within the nine-story structure there are seventeen internal stories.

The Huisheng Mosque   This mosque dates from the seventh century A.D. and is considered to be the oldest in China. It is believed that it was founded by an uncle of Mohammed. Although still used by the local Moslem community, visitors are permitted to see the main temple pavilion, courtyard, and prayer hall. The minaret, a modern twenty-eight-meter-high structure, towers above the mosque. A balcony at the top of the minaret commands an excellent view of the city of Guangzhou.

The Mausoleum of the Seventy-two Martyrs of Huanghuakang   This monument is dedicated to the memory of the seventy-two martyrs who lost their lives in the revolutionary uprising of March 29, 1911, which was but one of the many attempts to overthrow the Qing dynasty. Situated in a park in the northeast corner of the city, the mausoleum was built in 1918 with the support of overseas Chinese.

The Seven-Star Crag   Situated about 113 kilometers west of Guangzhou, near Zhaoqing, this area is popular for its beautiful mountainous landscape, lakes, and caves. One particular group of caves resembles the seven stars of the Big Dipper constellation. Within some of the caves, such as the Kuan Yin Cave, there are many stalactites, which take on unusual shapes and forms.

ACCOMMODATION

Dong Fang Hotel   Renmin Road North. Phone: 69900.

The Dong Fang, which is mainly for Western, English-speaking visitors, is a huge complex containing 1,100 rooms and a lovely garden courtyard. Located across the street from the exhibition hall of the Chinese Export Commodities Fair and within walking distance of the railway station, it is ideal for businessmen. However, it is far from the city center and the Pearl River bridge, where the local activities are centered.

A new wing was added to the old section of the hotel in the early 1970s. The rooms are plain, clean, and air-conditioned; some have a television and a small refrigerator. Although the Dong Fang is one of the best hotels in Guangzhou, the rooms in the old section tend to be drab.

The hotel has three restaurants, a bar and a café, four retail stores, a post office, a bank, and telecommunications facilities. Each floor has its own service desk. Rates are Y40 ($27.00 U.S., $30.00 Canadian) for a double room and Y150 ($100.50 U.S., $112.00 Canadian) for a deluxe suite.

Liu Hau Hotel   Renmin Road North. Phone: 68800.

Although this hotel caters to the overseas Chinese, on rare occasions Western guests may be accommodated there. Adjacent to the Commodities

Trade Fair grounds and the railway station, and near the main office of the Postal and Telegraph Services, the hotel has a restaurant, hair salon, retail store, bank, bookstore, and postal and telegraph services. Rates are Y20 ($13.40 U.S., $15.00 Canadian) for a single or double room and Y40 ($27.00 U.S., $30.00 Canadian) for a suite.

Bai Yun Hotel   Huan Shi Road East. Phone: 67700.

Located in the northeastern part of the city, across the street from the Friendship Store, the Bai Yun (White Cloud) opened in 1977. This pleasant, thirty-three-story hotel has air-conditioned rooms, which are attractive and comfortable, and a lovely inner courtyard with a rock garden and waterfall. The hotel's Chinese restaurant is open all year round; a Western dining room is open during the Guangzhou Fair and during the tourist season. Other services include a bank, hair salon, postal and telegraph office, and gift shop. A bus takes visitors from the hotel to the exhibition hall during the Fair. Rates are Y25 ($16.75 U.S., $18.75 Canadian) for a single or double room and Y40 ($27.00 U.S., $30.00 Canadian) for a suite.

RESTAURANTS

One of the biggest delights of Guangzhou is the selection of Cantonese restaurants. Distinguished by its appeal to the eye and subtlety of flavors, Cantonese cuisine is also known for its variety and use of fresh ingredients. In contrast to the austerity of restaurants in Beijing, restaurants in Guangzhou often have beautiful settings.

Ban Xi   Liwan Road East. Phone: 85655.

Located in Liwan Lake Park in western Guangzhou, this restaurant overlooks a lake and is surrounded by beautiful landscaped gardens, tropical foliage, and bamboo trees. The food is outstanding and includes a wide range of pastries. A number of lovely private dining rooms are available for special banquets. Your guide can help you make reservations and arrange the dinner menu. The cost per person will be about Y20-Y30 ($13.00-$20.00 U.S., $16.00-$24.00 Canadian).

Bei Yuan   318 Dengfen Road North. Phone: 32471.

The Bei Yuan (North Garden) is a famous old restaurant in a beautiful setting of ornamental pools, winding paths, and refined gardens. The food is excellently matched to the attractive site. The specialty of Bei Yuan is Shao Xing chicken, which is cooked whole and has a delicate flavor. Sharkfin, seafood dishes, and Dim Sum are outstanding in this restaurant. Dinner banquets may be prearranged.

Nan Yuan   120 Qianjin Road. Phone: 50532.

The Nan Yuan (South Garden Restaurant) is another beautifully land-scaped garden restaurant. Small dining pavilions with delicate stained-glass windows are available for private dinners. The food is excellent and includes a wide selection of meats, poultry, seafoods, and pastries.

Kwangchow (or Guangzhou) Restaurant   2 Wenchang Lukou. Phone: 87136, 87840, 23493.

This restaurant is housed in an old teahouse with many terraces and stairs. Its delicious food and informal atmosphere make it a local favorite. An excellent banquet, including goose, seafood, frog's legs, quail, and sweet pastries, may be preordered for groups of ten to twelve at a cost of Y20-Y30 per person.

Datong Restaurant 63 Yuan Jiang Road. Phone: 88697, 86983, 20318.

Located on the top floor of a modern building, the Datong Restaurant offers a fantastic view of the Pearl River. The food is excellent; specialties are peacock chicken, straw mushrooms with crabmeat, and Dim Sum.

Yu Yuan Restaurant 90 Liwang Road South. Phone: 88552, 88689.

This restaurant is in a modern building with a rock garden and fish pond in the central courtyard. The menu offers a wide choice of dishes, including sautéed squab, Peking Duck, freshwater fish, and local vegetables, which are its specialties.

Snake Restaurant 43 Jianglanlu Road. Phone: 21811, 24679.

This is a unique restaurant in China, specializing in snakes and monkeys. It is mainly for the daring, who will have the chance to see the preparation of a live snake for cooking. Fresh snake bile sac, chicken soup with snakes, and "Dragon and Tiger Stew" (snake and cat meat stew) are the specialties of the house. The dinner menu also offers a variety of meats, poultry, seafoods, and local greens if you have a weak stomach.

Vegetarian Fragrance Restaurant 167 Zhongshan Road. Phone: 86836.

This restaurant is a special delight for vegetarians and an interesting and enjoyable experience for nonvegetarians. All dishes are prepared from vegetables, but they may look or taste like seafood or meat.

Wild Fragrance Restaurant Beijing Road. Phone: 30337, 30997.

This specialty restaurant offers exotic game and seafood, including quail, lark, dog stew, and turtle. The menu also provides good duck, chicken, Yunan ham, and vegetable dishes.

Renmin Restaurant Zhongshan Road Four. Phone: 32493.

The Renmin restaurant serves Hakka cooking. Its specialty is salt-baked chicken.

Muslim Restaurant Beijing Road. Phone: 30475.

This restaurant is famous for its mutton hotpot, beef meatballs, and many other Muslim dishes.

Economical Restaurant Shamian Island. Phone: 20763.

One of the less expensive restaurants, the Economical Restaurant serves large portions of both Western and Chinese food.

Northern Beauty Restaurant Liberation Road. Phone: 30941.

A five-minute walk from the Dong Fang Hotel, this restaurant serves a good selection of poultry, meat, and seafood dishes. Dim Sum offers a variety of choices at a reasonable price.

SHOPPING

The Friendship Store Yuan Kiang Road. Guangzhou's four-year-old Friendship Store is adjacent to the Bai Yun Hotel. It offers a wide range of mass-produced goods, including canned food, beverages, bicycles, appliances, luggage, silks and cotton, clothing, and handicrafts. The store is open from 9:00 a.m. to 9:00 p.m.

Nan Fang Department Store   1 Yuan Kiang Road.

The largest retail store in Guangzhou, the Nan Fang is a good place to watch the Chinese shopping. Here you will find clothing, textiles, sporting goods, bicycles, spare parts, television sets, and linens.

Jiang Nan Native Products Store   399 Zhong Shan Road.

This store specializes in basketry and bamboo articles.

Guangzhou Antique Shop   146 Wen Teh Road.

This store has a wide selection of antiques but emphasizes ceramics, paintings, and small carvings.

Guangzhou Antique Warehouse   Huang Shu Road.   Here there are four rooms filled with antiques, but purchases must be of Y5,000 or more. Payment is by letter of credit, and goods must be shipped from the store.

First Cultural and Antique Supplies Store   322 Beijing Road.

This shop sells art supplies, brushes, ink, and stone chops.

TELECOMMUNICATION AND POST

Guangzhou Cable Bureau	Zhong Shan Road III	Ph: 71617
Guangzhou Telecommunications Bureau	Liu Hua Square	
Guangzhou Post Office	Yuan Kiang Road I	Ph: 87649
Guangzhou Parcel Delivery Station	Lia Hua Square	

TRANSPORTATION AND TRAVEL SERVICES

Guangzhou may be reached from Hong Kong and Kowloon by plane, hovercraft, or express train. The China International Travel Services in Hong Kong and Kowloon can assist you with travel reservations.

Guangzhou-China International Travel Service	865 Chieh Fang Road	Ph: 33454 Cable: 1954 Guangzhou
Guangzhou China Travel Service	Hai Zhu Square, next to the Hua Chiao (Overseas Chinese) Hotel	
CAAC (China Administration of Civil Aviation of China)	Booking Office: 980 Chieh Fang Road North	Ph: 33684
	International Passenger Service	Ph: 31769
	Domestic Passenger Service	Ph: 33590
	Cargo Service	Ph: 31600

125

Rail Services:	Guangzhou Railway	
	Station	Ph: 33333
	South Station	Ph: 85981

ENTERTAINMENT

Numerous cultural activities and sports events take place in Guangzhou throughout the year. Visitors and businessmen may enjoy the acrobatic shows, the Chinese opera, sports, and the dance troupes from different regions of China. There are also many local movie theaters for the interested visitor.

The world champions, Chinese women's volleyball team.

Along the Li River.

GUILIN (Kweilin)

Guangxi Zhuangzu Autonomous Region

Guilin, the former capital of Guangxi Zhuangzu Autonomous Region, is world renowned for its scenic beauty, which over the centuries has been immortalized by Chinese poets and painters. Surrounded by solitary pinnacles of limestone and steep hills, which rise out of the plain of rivers, lakes, and paddy fields, this city boasts one of the most breathtaking natural landscapes in China.

Guilin was founded by Emperor Qin Shi Huang Di in 214 B.C. as a small settlement on the west bank of the Li River. At the same time the emperor built a canal linking tributaries of the Yangtze and Pearl Rivers. Thus, the settlement developed into an important junction on the transportation route between central and southern China. Guilin was then designated as the provincial capital under the Ming dynasty (1368-1644). In 1914, the capital was moved to Nanning to the southwest.

Since 1949, a variety of industries have been established in Guilin, producing such commodities as machinery, fertilizers, silk and cotton textiles, and medicines. Local arts and crafts are also still produced. In addition, it has developed its agricultural base producing crops of bamboo, rice, and grain. Throughout the city cassia (*osmanthus*) trees grow in great abundance, hence the city's name, which in English means "Sweet Osmanthus Wood." Various by-products of the cassia tree include wine, herbal medicines and teas, and fragrant oils and perfumes.

Visitors will enjoy not only the natural setting of Guilin, but also many of the local attractions such as the pavilions, temples, pagodas, and caves on the surrounding hills.

PLACES TO SEE

Former Palace of the King of Wang Zheng   The first Ming emperor, Hong Wu, made one of his sons king of Jing Jiang in 1369. The king then built his palace on the Peak of Solitary Beauty in the center of Guilin. Under the Qing dynasty, the imperial residence became an examination hall and today is the site of the Guangxi Provincial Teachers' Training College.

Fu Bo Shan   From the pavilions situated at the summit of this hill one can get a superb view of the city and the hills to the east. Legend has it that a mythological giant man appeared on this hill and after destroying the wild demons and monsters there he pierced a hole in the mountain, which exists to this day.

Returned Pearl Cave   Situated on the south slope of the Fu Bo Shan is the Returned Pearl Cave (Huan Zhu Dong). According to an old legend, a dragon once lived in a pool in this cave. When it got dark, the dragon would take out his precious pearl, which was so brilliant that it illuminated the cave. An old fisherman observed this and stole the precious pearl. Later he was so overcome with guilt that he returned the pearl to the cave; hence the name "Returned Pearl Cave." The cave contains natural pillars of granite, as well as numerous Buddhist carvings and calligraphic tablets.

Thousand Buddha Cliff   Located to the left of the Returned Pearl Cave this cliff is known for the carvings of over three hundred Buddha statues, some of which date from the Tang dynasty (A.D. 618-907).

The Elephant's Trunk Hill (Xiang Bi Shan)   This unusual rock formation on the west bank of the Li River resembles a huge elephant dipping his trunk into the river. The pagoda on its summit, called the Pu Xian Ta, contains the carved statue of the Buddha of Universal Virtue.

Seven Star Hill   Rising to the east of the city, this hill can be identified by its seven peaks, which resemble the formation of the seven stars of the Big Dipper constellation. Within the hill are six large caverns formed long ago by underground rivers. These caves are associated with many famous legends and, according to inscriptions around the walls and entrances, were renowned as early as the seventh century A.D.

Boat Excursion along the Li River   A boat trip down the Li River from Guilin to Yangshuo must certainly be a highlight of any visit to Guilin. The eighty-five-kilometer trip usually takes about six or seven hours, beginning near Guilin in the morning. During the river cruise you can relax and enjoy the magnificent landscape along the river shore, take photographs, and observe such intriguing river activities as the cormorants diving for fish from the fishermens' boats. Visitors are also usually served a light lunch on the boat. The boat trip ends at the lovely rural town of Yangshuo and from there you will be driven back to Guilin, arriving back at your hotel around 4:00 p.m.

The Reed Flute Cave   Located about eight kilometers northeast of the city, this five-hundred-meter-long cave is perhaps the most spectacular in this area. Its stalactites and stalagmites resemble the shapes of humans and animals of Chinese legends, and are illuminated by colorful spotlights. Visitors will also see lovely scenes such as the Flowing Waterfall, the Great Headless Carp, and the Fruit and Flower Mountain here. The cave took its name from the reeds growing in front of the entrance, which made fine flutes as well as a natural cover to disguise the cave.

ACCOMMODATION

The Lijiang Hotel Located in the center of the city on the shore of Banyan Lake, this fourteen-story hotel commands a spectacular view of the surrounding mountains and city. It is a new hotel, opened in 1976, which was built to accommodate an ever-increasing number of visitors. The rooms are pleasant and comfortable and during the winter are heated. The services and facilities provided by the hotel are good and include a restaurant serving both Western and Chinese food, a bank, post office, telegraph office, gift store, and food store.

The Banyan Lake Hotel This hotel is reserved for official dignitaries and delegations visiting Guilin, and offers relatively luxurious accommodation. Several interesting local specialty dishes are served in the hotel dining room.

SHOPPING

Guilin is known for its stone carving, bamboo products, embroidered linens, and the local cassia wine and tea. Visitors can find a fair selection of local crafts and products at the Friendship Store or local shops.

The Elephant's Trunk Hill.

Fu Bo Shan, Guilin.

Minority nationalities in Guiyang.

GUIYANG (Kweyang)   Guizhou Province

Guiyang, the capital of Guizhou Province, is situated on a tributary of the Nanming River and on the railway line leading to Guangxi Province in the west and to Sichuan Province in the south. The population of Guizhou Province consists of Miao, Bu yi, Yi, and Dong minorities, and the Han.

Guiyang was founded during the Han dynasty (206 B.C.-A.D. 220). A protective wall was built around the city during the Ming dynasty (1368-1644), and Guiyang became the provincial capital during the Qing dynasty (1644-1911). Today the city manufactures machinery and arts and crafts. At an altitude of three thousand feet, Guiyang is surrounded by lovely hills and scenery.

PLACES TO SEE

Guizhou Provincial Museum   This museum houses recently excavated art treasures from the province as well as other art collections and mineralogical, historical, and cultural exhibits.

ACCOMMODATION

Visitors may stay in the Guiyang Guesthouse, a rather plain and simple hotel.

130

HAINAN ISLAND   Guangdong Province

Hainan, the second largest island in China, is located off the southwest coast of Guangdong Province. Many overseas Chinese came from Hainan to southeast Asia and North America.

Haikou, the capital of Hainan Island Administrative Area, is the political, economic, and cultural center of the island. Situated on the north coast of the island, it faces the Leizhou Peninsula across the Qiongzhou Strait. Historical sites within the city include the Temple of Five Celebrities, the Temple of Su Dongpo, the Dongpo Academy of Classical Learning, and the Tomb of Hai Rui. Today Haikou has become an important industrial city producing several commodities for the export market. Its industries include shipbuilding, canning, and the manufacture of rubber and textiles.

Sanya on the southern coast of Hainan is a beautiful city full of flamboyant tropical flowers and trees, which line the streets. Situated on the west shore of Sanya Bay is Tian-Ya-Hai-Jiao; the poem "Tian Ya," which is inscribed on a rock beside the sea, was written by the famous poet Su Dongpo of the Northern Song (A.D. 960-1127) when he was relegated to the island of Hainan. Today Sanya is a seaside resort for both Chinese and Western visitors.

海南島

Three Pools Mirroring the Moon, Xi Hu, Hangzhou.

HANGZHOU (Hangchow)
Zhejiang Province

Hangzhou, the capital of Zhejiang Province, is situated on the northern bank of the Qiantang River near the Bay of Hangzhou on the southeast coast of China. For centuries it has been renowned for its scenic beauty, the major attraction being West Lake (Xi Hu) with its causeways, which are charmingly decorated with flowers and trees, and its bridges, islands, and pavilions. As a popular resort it has attracted visitors from all over the world, including many foreign dignitaries, since the time of Marco Polo. Located 1,145 kilometers from Beijing and only 161 kilometers from Shanghai, Hangzhou can easily be reached either by air (two and a half hours from Beijing and twenty minutes from Shanghai) or by train.

HISTORY

Hangzhou, which dates back over two thousand years, was for several centuries merely a small fishing village. However, in the sixth century A.D., it rapidly grew into a large commercial center as a result of the building of the Grand Canal between Beijing and the fertile Yangtze River Delta. In the twelfth century when the Jin forced the imperial court south from Beijing, a son of Emperor Hui Zong escaped and established his palatial residence in Hangzhou. Thus, the city became the imperial capital throughout the Southern Song dynasty (1127-1280) and developed as one of China's most important centers of culture and trade. Although the capital was moved to Beijing under the Yuan dynasty (1280-1368), Hangzhou continued to flourish as a major commercial, political, and cultural center until the middle of the nineteenth century. The city was then almost entirely devastated in the Taiping Rebellion. At the end of the nineteenth century Hangzhou was opened as a foreign trade port.

Since 1949, the city has been rebuilt on reclaimed land to the east of the lake, and many industries have been established here. Today it has a population of 980,000 and an industrial output of machine tools, iron, steel, chemical fertilizers, and petroleum products. Agriculturally, Hangzhou is renowned for its Longjing tea. It also maintains its reputation as a major producer of silk, cotton, brocades, and sandalwood products.

The city of Hangzhou is not very large. The center of the city is occupied by relatively modern office buildings, residential complexes, schools, and a shopping district. Its most notable streets are Lakeside Avenue, Zhongshan Lu, and Huping Lu. Visitors may enjoy a leisurely walk around the lake and city center. In addition, there are public buses, which run along Lakeside Avenue. Scattered on the surrounding hills are several temples and pavilions, which are really the only surviving remnants of the twelfth-century city.

PLACES TO SEE

The West Lake (Xi Hu) Xi Hu is a small lake divided into three parts by two very ancient and picturesque tree-lined dikes. Originally part of the Qiantang estuary, the lake was gradually formed by silt deposits and the construction of the dikes and causeways. The Bai Juyi Causeway (Baiti) is to the north and the Su Dongpo Causeway (Suti) is to the west. The Bai Causeway, built in the ninth century, extends from the Hangzhou Hotel, along the southern shores and back up to the shoreline to the northeast. It is named after the poet Bai Juyi, who was also a governor of Hangzhou. The Su Causeway is connected by six bridges and dates from the eleventh century. It too is named after a poet, the famous Su Dongpo, who was prefect of Hangzhou. The purpose of the two causeways is primarily to control the tidal waters, yet they also provide scenic pathways for viewing the lake. There are three islands in West Lake: The Gushan, the Three Pools Mirroring the Moon, and the Island of Mid-Lake Pavilion. Visitors can walk along the Bai Causeway to Gushan, the largest of the islands, or a leisure boat can take you to the other two islands.

Three Pools Mirroring the Moon Situated in the southern part of West Lake, this island contains four small lakes or ponds, which are in fact one lake divided by islets and linked by bridges. Several beautiful pavilions built around the edges can be reached by winding pathways and bridges. The island is a lovely spot attractively landscaped with willows and colorful lotus plants, which blossom in the summer. Three seventeenth-century stone stupas are located in the water off the south shore of the island. Each stupa is about one and a half meters high with five recessed windows, which once held lighted candles. The reflection of candle- and moon-light in the lake created beautiful shadow images of the San Tan (Three Stupas); hence the name of this island.

Mid-Lake Pavilion On this small artificial island, situated between the San Tan and the Gushan, there is a beautiful pavilion surrounded by attractive flower gardens. Visitors may get off the boat and take the short walk around the island, although most of it can be seen from the boat.

Xiling Seal Engravers' Society   Situated on the western side of Gushan, these buildings were once occupied by a group of Chinese scholars, intellectuals, and seal engravers who founded their society here at the beginning of this century. Visitors may view the small collection of prints of various old seal styles housed in the pavilion. Original seals and seal-stones, modern as well as old, can be purchased at a nearby shop.

Zhejiang Provincial Museum   Also located on Gushan, this museum is housed in the old Wenlan Ge Building, which was the library of Emperor Qianlong during the eighteenth century. The museum collection consists of historical relics and archaeological finds from the province, which are arranged in chronological order. The most notable pieces include Han (206 B.C.-A.D. 220) pottery and bronzes, iron tools of the Song and Yuan dynasties (the tenth through the fourteenth century), and fine ceramics and historical paintings of the Ming and Qing dynasties (fourteenth to twentieth century).

Lin Yin Temple   This Buddhist temple, which is situated at the foot of the hills to the west of the lake, dates back to the fourth century A.D. Although it was destroyed numerous times through the centuries it was carefully restored in 1956 after having been neglected for almost a century. Within the front hall of the temple, also known as the Hall of the Celestial Kings, is a large laughing Buddha of carved and gilded camphorwood. A smaller gilt figure stands behind the Buddha. In addition, there are the four finely carved guardian statues standing along the sides.

The rear hall of the temple, which dates from the eighteenth century, contains a giant carved Buddha, twenty meters high. In the temple grounds, the four Buddhist columns, which are decorated with carvings, and the two stone stupas date from about the tenth century.

Dragon Well   In the hills southwest of the lake, tea plantations owned and cultivated by the Growing Brigade of West Lake Commune at Mei Chia Wu produce the famous "Longjing" (Dragon Well), the treasured Chinese green tea. If you make your request in advance, a quick tour of the "Dragon Well" can be arranged.

Tiger Spring   Many natural mineral springs can be found in the surrounding hills of Hangzhou. The spring water of the Tiger Spring to the south is renowned for its fine tea-brewing qualities, for its natural sweet taste, and for its unusual mineral content. The old temple Hubaosi has been converted into a tearoom where you can enjoy the view and sample the famous Longjing green tea brewed with Tiger Spring water.

Yue Fei Temple and Tomb   Yue Fei (1103-1141) was a famous national hero of the Song dynasty. His tomb, which is situated in the hills behind the Hangzhou Hotel, was built in 1221, and features magnificent halls surrounded by ancient trees.

Hangzhou Silk and Brocade Mill   This silk mill in the middle of the city has grown tremendously since the 1950s, and produces beautiful brocade, quilt covers, and silk pictures and fabrics. The 1,700 workers and 300 looms turn out about three million meters of silk, much of which is designed for export.

ACCOMMODATION

Hangzhou Hotel   Situated on Lakeside Avenue on the northeast shore of West Lake, this is the principal hotel for foreign guests. The accommodation is quite luxurious compared to most other Chinese hotels, with large and comfortable rooms and pleasant landscaped surroundings. The hotel also has a good dining room overlooking the lake, which serves some of Hangzhou's local specialty dishes.

Overseas Chinese Hotel   This hotel, which is also located on the lake front, is reserved specially for overseas Chinese visitors.

RESTAURANTS

Hangzhou offers some of China's finer cuisine. In addition to the hotel dining rooms, the city has several other good restaurants where visitors might venture to sample some of the excellent local specialty dishes. It is, however, advisable to consult with your guide beforehand.

Lou Wailou Restaurant   Situated in the southeast corner of Zhongshan Park, this restaurant is highly recommended for such local specialties as the sweet and sour carp, freshwater shrimp, stewed duck tongue, honeyed ham, cassia soup, and fresh vegetable dishes.

The Tian Waitian Restaurant   Located near the Linyin Temple to the west, this restaurant is also very good. As at the Lou Wailou, all the ingredients are very fresh and succulent, and the dishes are well prepared.

SHOPPING

Visitors will find a variety of handicrafts, including brocade, silk, fans, tea, basketware, chinaware, chopsticks, embroidery, and parasols in Hangzhou. A good selection of antiques, including old jade, paintings, and ceramics, is available at Wen-wu Store on Lakeside Avenue.

Tiger Spring, Hangzhou.

Ice sculpture, Harbin.

HARBIN (Harbin)   Heilongjiang Province

哈
尔
宾

Harbin, the capital of Heilongjiang Province, is located about 1,120 kilometers north of Beijing. As a modern industrial and rail transportation center, it has a population of over two million. Today Harbin is one of China's major manufacturing centers, producing steam turbines, electric motors, and machine tools. The city is quite European in appearance with its Western-style buildings and broad, tree-lined promenades.

HISTORY

This area was inhabited in the eleventh century by the Nuzhen, ancestors of Manchu. The name *Harbin* derives from the Manchurian *Alejin*, meaning "ground for sunning fishing nets." In 1896, Tsarist Russia and the Qing court signed a secret treaty to build a railroad from the Chinese city of Manzhouli on the Sino-Russian border through Harbin to Vladivostok, Russia. Harbin became the administrative headquarters of the project and henceforth a major transportation center for both the Chinese and the Russians. During the first half of this century, many foreign consulates were also established here; at one time there were one hundred thousand foreign residents from thirty-six countries living in Harbin. In 1946, at the end of World War II, the Chinese once again took control of Harbin.

PLACES TO SEE

Riverside Park   Harbin is also known as the "City of Parks" because of the many parks situated along the Songhua River. Riverside Park, on the south bank, is an attractively landscaped area covering ten hectares and filled with colorful flowers.

Children's Park   This is the only park in China with a children's railroad. Built in 1956, the two-kilometer miniature railroad runs between models of Beijing Station and Harbin Station. The small train is drawn by diesel-locomotive and pulls seven colorful coaches that can hold two hundred passengers. The special feature of this miniature railway is that the station managers, engineers, conductors, guards, crew, and ticket sellers are all school children under the age of thirteen. So they work and play at the same time.

Spring Festival In China it is a tradition to hang decorative paper lanterns in celebration of the Lunar New Year. In addition, lanterns are sculpted out of enormous blocks of ice taken from the Songhua River. Shaped into flowers, animals, or human figures, they are lighted in the public squares and parks at nightfall. It is a fantastic sight.

ACCOMMODATION

The *Harbin Guesthouse* and *China International Travel Service Hotel* are the two hotels in which most visitors stay while in Harbin. The rooms are comfortable, and the services are adequate.

Spring Festival activities on the Songhua River.

Xiaoyaojing Park, Hefei.

HEFEI (Hofei) Anhui Province

Hefei is situated in the middle of Anhui Province, north of Chao Lake. It was founded as a trading town in the Han dynasty (206 B.C.-220 A.D.). In 1949, it became the provincial capital and was linked by rail to Beijing and Shanghai. Today it has developed into an industrial center with iron and steel mills, a power station, and chemical and textile factories.

PLACES TO SEE

Bao Gong Temple Dedicated to the honest and fearless judge Lord Bao of the Song dynasty, this temple is located at the south gate of Hefei.

Anhui Provincial Museum This museum houses a fine collection of cultural relics discovered in the province. The display includes a reproduction of a jade burial suit found in Anhui.

Ming Jiao Si Temple This temple dates from the eighth century A.D. It was specially built to house an iron statue of the Buddha, which is over five meters in height. Its Terrace for Appointing Generals was constructed in the twelfth century.

Anhui University and *East Is Red Commune* may also be of special interest to visitors.

ACCOMMODATION

The *Hefei Guesthouse* is a small, plain hotel for visitors. The dining room provides good food.

Children at play, Inner Mongolia.

HOHHOT (Huhehot)

Inner Mongolia Autonomous Region

Inner Mongolia, the largest of China's five autonomous regions, is located in China's north, bordering the Soviet Union. A population of 8.6 million inhabits this area, which covers 450,000 square kilometers. Today only 20 percent of the population is Mongolian; most of the inhabitants are Hans, who originally settled in the area after 1949 to modernize it. Other minority nationalities residing in this region include Hanchu, Manchu, Hui, Koreans, Tahur, and Owenk.

On May 1, 1947, Inner Mongolia was established as the first autonomous region in China. Administratively, it has four regions, which are further divided into three municipalities and forty-three counties, also called Banners (*Qi*).

The economy of Inner Mongolia is based on animal husbandry; there are over seven million acres of fertile grasslands here. With the modernization of China, the traditional herdsmen were forced to relinquish their nomadic way of life and to adjust to organized communal living. Irrigation systems were built, trees were planted, and pastures were enclosed. Since these measures were taken, grain output has increased. The rich mineral deposits of coal, chromium, copper, aluminum, iron, gold, silver, asbestos, and sulfur make this region a natural site for industry. Baotou, the largest city in Inner Mongolia, has a highly developed mining industry.

呼和浩特

Hohhot was founded in 1581 by the last Mongol emperor, the Altan Khan, and has been the capital of the Autonomous Region of Inner Mongolia since 1952. Located at the edge of the grasslands, it is about 425 kilometers northwest of Beijing. Hohhot can be reached from Beijing by a one-hour plane trip or by a very interesting ten-hour train trip.

Summers are pleasant, with average temperatures around 20° C. Winters are extremely cold and dry; for five to six months the temperatures drop to between -20° C and -40° C. Agriculture is well developed on the Hohhot plain, where the population is mainly Chinese. There are some food processing and mechanical industries here.

PLACES TO SEE

Wu Dang Zhao Monastery   This monastery was founded in the eighteenth century. Built in the Tibetan style, it has seven different halls which contain the sutras and statues of Buddha.

The Drum Tower (Gulou)   As part of the Great Wall, this huge, two-story pavilion with balconies and decorative roofs is supported by a massive foundation.

Wanbuhua Yanjing Pagoda   Built in the tenth century by Liao emperor Shengzong, this pagoda is located in the eastern suburbs of Hohhot. Many historical inscriptions can be seen on the interior walls of the pagoda, which is an eight-story octagonal brick building. Each side is about six meters wide.

Wutazhao Pagoda   This pagoda is located in the Pinkkang district of the old town in Hohhot. Also known as the Gadeng Si or the Jingang Baozuo Ta, this splendid pagoda has seven stories with green glazed tile roofs and white stone parapets. It stands on a white brick base on a large terrace surrounded by sturdy ramparts. Five smaller pagodas, which were built in 1740 and are covered with beautiful carvings and figures, occupy the terrace.

Ulanmuchi Dance Troupe,
Inner Mongolia.

Xilitu Zhao (Yanshou Si)   This monastery, built in the Sino-Tibetan style during the Ming dynasty, is also known as the Great Hall of the Sutras. A large wooden Ming gate covered with Mongolian inscriptions leads into this massive two-story building, which has a sharply upturned roof decorated with elaborate bells, animals, dragons, and clouds at the corners. A wide veranda is supported by pillars. Another well-known monastery in Hohhot is Dazhao, which is built in the same style as the Xilitu Zhao.

Shuanger Ta (Two Ears Pagoda)   This magnificent white pagoda, built in the classical style, acquired its name from the two carved lobes that protrude from the pointed ridge of the roof. The base consists of four tiers resting on a stone plinth. The interior walls are gracefully decorated with patterns of clouds and symbols of longevity.

Visits to the Grasslands   Tours have been organized to take visitors on an overnight trip to the grasslands. Visitors will have the chance to see a *yurt* (a Mongolian tent made from animal hides), and meet the local residents.

ACCOMMODATION

The Friendship Hotel offers visitors comfortable accommodation and pleasant hospitality. The hotel dining room provides an excellent menu of both Mongolian and Chinese food.

CUISINE

Mongolian food consists mainly of roasted or boiled mutton served in large chunks. The traditional tea is a warm broth supplemented with goat's milk, butter, and grains.

SHOPPING

Visitors will find a Friendship Store counter in the local department store, where a good selection of local jewelry, leather goods, and colorful Mongolian gowns and boots is available.

Teacher and students, Hohhot.

Thousand Buddha Mountain, Jinan.

JINAN (Tsinan)   Shandong Province

Jinan, the capital and political center of Shandong Province, is situated in a valley between the Huang He River and the Taishan Mountains. Archaeological remains indicate that part of Jinan was originally one of the sites of the Longshan culture of the Neolithic period. During the Song dynasty it was designated as a provincial capital and for centuries has flourished as a traditional center for the production of silk. With the development of the railway, it became a major junction on the Beijing-Shanghai and Qingdao lines, stimulating further expansion of the city. Today the population of Jinan is approximately 1.7 million, and its industries include metallurgy, and the production of machinery, chemicals, textiles, and agricultural items. It is also a major regional center for higher education. Shandong University, Shandong Medical School, and a teacher's training college and polytechnic institute are all established here.

PLACES TO SEE

The Fountain and Black Tiger Springs   Jinan is also known as the "City of Springs" because more than a hundred natural hot springs appear all over the city. The streams eventually flow into Daming Lake to the north of the city, which has become a popular recreational area. Attractively landscaped parks have been built around four of the springs. The Fountain Spring (Bau Tu Quan) is located to the southwest of the city in a park landscaped with gardens, ponds, bridges, and pavilions. The Black Tiger Spring (Hei Hu Quan) in another park to the southwest is perhaps the most interesting. Here the water flows through three tiger heads sculptured in black stone.

Li Qing Zhao Museum   This small museum is located in a house in the same park as the Fountain Spring. It contains portraits and the works of China's famous poetess Li Qing Zhao, who, it is said, lived here during the eleventh and twelfth centuries. She had a sad and lonely life, which is tenderly expressed in her poems.

Thousand Buddha Mountain (Qianfo Shan)   Near the summit of this mountain, which is south of town, are hundreds of carved Buddhas, some of which date from the seventh century. The monastery at the top is closed to the public; however, from the nearby path visitors may get a splendid view of Jinan and the Huang He River.

Shandong Provincial Museum   This museum, which is located on West Wenhua Road in the old city, contains a fine collection of Neolithic black pottery from the Longshan culture, dating back to about 2,500 B.C. This type of pottery is characterized by a smooth and glossy black surface and a delicately thin and well-balanced form.

ACCOMMODATION

Jinan Hotel   This hotel, on Jinger Road west of the old city, is situated in a pleasant garden setting. The rooms are clean and spacious. The dining room, however, offers a very limited menu.

Nanjiao Hotel   This seven-hundred-room hotel, located to the south of the city, is Jinan's finest accommodation. It has an indoor swimming pool, air conditioning, and a good restaurant.

Thousand Buddha Mountain Monastery.

Celadon vases, Jingdezhen.

JINGDEZHEN (Chingtechen)

Jiangxi Province

Jingdezhen is located in northeastern Jiangxi Province, east of Poyang Lake and on the south bank of the Changjiang, a tributary of the Yangtze River. Before the Tang dynasty (618-907), the town was called Hsin-ping-chen. Later the name was changed to Chang-nan-chen, indicating that it was situated on the south bank of the Changjiang. Since 1949, Jingdezhen has been a municipality under the Jiangxi provincial government. The city covers a large area, and has a population of 450,000.

For centuries Jingdezhen has been China's most important center for the production of ceramics. It is particularly renowned for its fine porcelain. Pottery was first produced here during the second century B.C., and gradually more sophisticated firing techniques were discovered and perfected.

From the second to the sixth century Jingdezhen produced pottery objects according to imperial court orders, as for example the animal statues that were made during the Sui dynasty (589-618). In the Tang dynasty the volume of ceramics produced increased as a result of the popularity of tea drinking and the demands of the export markets. During the reign of Jingde (1004-1007), Northern Song pottery was marked "made during the Jingde period" and was intended for export abroad as well as for domestic use. As the source of fine porcelain, Jingdezhen thus became well known as the capital of Chinese ceramics.

The kilns were built in the southeast part of the town, as it was there that the special raw material kaolin (a unique combination of local minerals and fine white clay extracted from Mount Kao Ling) was found. During the Qing dynasty, imperial officers were appointed to control the quality and quantity of the ceramics production. Ceramics destined for the foreign market were transported from the nearby Poyang Lake to the Yangtze River and from there overseas.

Today, modern technology and skills are used in the making of ceramics, resulting in better quality and increased productivity. At the same time individual creativity has been encouraged in the design of modern pottery. Since 1955 the variety of ceramics has increased significantly; over five hundred different wares with some three thousand designs are now available. In addition, new ceramics factories and plants have been established to manufacture ceramics chemicals, machinery, and tools. Thus, there is still great vitality in the ceramics industry in Jingdezhen. The ceramics produced for the export market are displayed at the Spring and Fall Trade Fairs in Guangzhou.

PLACES TO SEE

Jingdezhen Ceramics Institute   Established in 1954, this institute maintains a staff of thirty, including an art historian, archaeologists, ceramic specialists, and researchers. The institute is divided into the departments of Art Exhibition, Ceramics History, Archaeological Studies, Administration, and Planning. For ceramics scholars and collectors the institute's exhibition not only is a pleasing visual experience but also offers a good historical survey of Chinese ceramics from the Han dynasty (B.C. 206-A.D. 220) to the Qing dynasty (A.D. 1644-1911).

Jingdezhen Ceramics Research Institute   The main purpose of this institute, which was established in 1954, is to improve ceramics technology and artistic designs in order to enhance the quality and quantity of local ceramics production. The institute also sets the standard for ceramics in national and international exhibitions. There are two hundred staff members employed in the institute.

Riguo Porcelain Plant and *Fine Art Porcelain Plant*   These plants are Jingdezhen's two major producers of porcelain. They both make a wide range of quality products. Riguo's porcelains come in seventy different glazes and are noted for their high quality. The Fine Art Plant has earned an international reputation for classical paintings on porcelains. Visitors may arrange a tour to see one of the plants with the help of a tour guide.

Hudian Ancient Kiln Site   There are over thirty ancient kiln sites in the area around Jingdezhen. At the Hudian kiln site, which is located on the outer edge of the city, fine porcelains of the blue-white and Qingbai (shadowy-blue) type were produced throughout the Southern Song, Yuan, and Ming dynasties (from the twelfth century to the seventeenth century). The finished wares were then exported to the Middle East and Central Asia by way of the Silk Road.

Research and excavation have been carried out on the site in recent years. A small museum has recently been built on the kiln site.

ACCOMMODATION

Jingdezhen Guesthouse This pleasant hotel, built for visitors and Chinese delegations, is situated on a treed hillside away from the town and factories. The rooms, although simple, are spacious and comfortable. The staff are most pleasant and helpful. A small dining room provides good Chinese food. Visitors should sample the mushrooms, which are a local speciality.

SHOPPING

While here, visitors should take advantage of the reasonable price of the local pottery and porcelains. There is a large ceramics store that carries all the different types of ceramics from the local plants, including dinner sets, small tea sets, decorative plates, vases, and fine figurines. The eggshell thin porcelain bowls and vases, which are decorated with hand-painted landscapes, are rarely seen in the West.

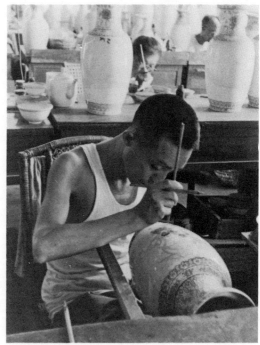

Ceramic artist at work, Jingdezhen.

Figurines, Jiangxi.

JIUJIANG (Jiukiang) Jiangxi Province

Jiujiang is a busy port city on the Yangtze River in north Jiangxi Province. Founded in the Han dynasty over two thousand years ago, it has been a traditional export center for Chinese tea, wine, bamboo, and porcelain for centuries. In 1862, Jiujiang was opened for foreign trade. At the same time the British established a concession west of town but were eventually forced out in 1927. Visitors usually only stop in Jiujiang briefly on their way to see the scenic resort of Lushan, which is located on Poyang Lake a few kilometers northwest of the city.

PLACES TO SEE

Gantang Lake and *Nanmen Lake* Jiujiang is situated on the shores of Lakes Gantang and Nanmen, which are separated by a causeway built in 821. The lovely Yanshui Pavilion on the island of Lake Gantang features a series of halls, pavilions, and landscaped gardens. A bridge now links it to the shore. In 1972 the pavilion was converted into an exhibition hall for displaying historical relics discovered in Jiangxi Province.

ACCOMMODATION

Jiujiang Guesthouse If visitors have occasion to stay in Jiujiang, this small hotel is really the only accommodation available.

147

Xiangguo Si Temple, Kaifeng.

KAIFENG (Kaifeng) Henan Province

The old city of Kaifeng, formerly the capital of Henan Province, has had a turbulent history. Situated on the North China Plain east of Zhengzhou and south of the Huang He River, it has suffered hundreds of floods caused by the constantly changing course of the river. Over the centuries, Kaifeng has been designated capital of various provinces, kingdoms, and empires. It first became a capital during the Three Kingdoms Period (220-265). Although it lost prominence through the Tang dynasty, Kaifeng was restored as the northern capital of the empire that existed during the Five Dynasties era (907-960). Thereafter it was rebuilt as the imperial capital of the Song dynasty, but this position was short-lived. Its final demise occurred in 1126, when the barbarian Jins overran and destroyed the city. Today the city has a population of half a million, and although it has not been greatly developed as an industrial city it does manufacture such light industrial products as chemicals, machinery, and tools. Kaifeng is also renowned for its handicrafts, the most famous of which is the local Bian embroidery.

PLACES TO SEE

Dragon Pavilion (Longting) Located to the northwest within the old city walls, this building is all that remains of the imperial palace of the Northern Song dynasty. It was rebuilt under the Qing emperor Kangxi (1662-1723) as the Palace of the Life of Ten Thousand Years (Wan Shou Gong). The area surrounding the pavilion, which borders on Yang and Pans Lakes, has been made into a park.

Iron Pagoda (Tie Ta) This tall, slender pagoda, so named because of its brown glazed tiles, stands at the northeast side of Kaifeng. Originally a wooden structure, it was destroyed by fire in 1044 and was rebuilt in 1049 as a thirteen-story octagonal brick pagoda fifty-four meters high.

Yuwang Tai (Chui Tai) This pavilion is located in the southeastern part of the town in a lovely park. Historically, it was built for the famous musician Shi Kuang during the Spring and Autumn Period (770-476 B.C.). During the Tang dynasty the great poets such as Li Bai and Du Fu also visited there.

Xiangguo Si Temple This Buddhist temple, which is located at the south end of the old city, dates back to the sixth century A.D. Over the centuries, the original temple was expanded and restored several times. During the Song dynasty it was the largest Buddhist monastery in China. The present building dates from the Qing dynasty, about 1766. Today the main halls are used for exhibitions, while some other areas of the temple have been converted to a library, a children's palace, and a department store.

Pota Pagoda In 1841 the Tianqingsi monastery in south Kaifeng was destroyed, and all that remained was this brick pagoda. When originally built during the tenth century, the pagoda had nine stories. However, during the fourteenth century three of the stories collapsed and were subsequently replaced by three miniature stories. Each of the hexagonal bricks covering the pagoda is decorated with a small Buddha, but at present these cannot be examined closely since the area surrounding this monument is not open to the public.

ACCOMMODATION

Kaifeng Hotel Located on Ziyou Road in the old town, this hotel occupies a number of buildings and offers spacious and comfortable accommodation.

SHOPPING

The local *Friendship Store* is located to the east of the Xiangguo Temple. Here you can find the famous Bian embroidery, which is made of fine, delicate stitches of silk thread. Local hand-crafted papercuts, pottery, and paintings are also available.

Pota Pagoda, Kaifeng.

Dianchi Lake, Kunming.

KUNMING (Kunming)

Yunnan Province

Kunming is the capital city of Yunnan Province, a region in the south of China bordering on Vietnam, Burma, and Laos. Situated on the Yunnan Plateau at an elevation of about 1,894 meters, Kunming is bounded by Dianchi Lake to the south and mountains to the north, east, and west. Because it is near the Tropic of Cancer, the weather is warm and mild all year. Thus, it is often called the "City of Eternal Spring."

Kunming is one of southwest China's relatively new industrial cities. For centuries it served as a provincial market center. With the building of the French-Indochina railway in 1910, Kunming was finally linked with larger centers to the north and east and consequently outgrew its old provincial character. Since the 1930s it has rapidly developed into a major regional manufacturing center supporting a population of about 1.5 million, including several minority groups. Today its industrial output includes textiles, chemicals, mining equipment, building materials, and various metal products.

In addition to its importance as a regional center for industry and transportation, Kunming also serves as the provincial center for culture and education. Its educational institutions include Yunnan University, the Institute for Nationalities, and the Kunming Normal School. Kunming is also an important regional military base.

HISTORY

Kunming was founded in about 100 B.C. under the Han dynasty (206 B.C.-A.D. 220) and for centuries flourished as a regional market and export center. In the eighth century it was chosen as a subsidiary capital of the kingdom of Nanzhao, and in 1280 it was again designated a regional capital by the princes of Yunnan. During this latter period, Kunming was visited by Marco Polo, who was impressed by the local wealth of the city created by the export of timber, precious metals, salt, and local crafts. Kunming then became a walled city in 1382, under the Ming dynasty (1368-1644), and until the end of the nineteenth century it remained a relatively isolated center.

Although Kunming has since been transformed into a modern commercial city, some of the cobbled back streets of the old town still exist.

PLACES TO SEE

Yunnan Provincial Museum   Located in the public park, the Yuantong Shan, on the north side of the city, this museum contains several special collections, including recent local archaeological finds, some Han bronzes, and artifacts made by the province's minority nationalities.

Daguan Park   This park is situated southwest of the city, on the edge of Dianchi Lake. Located within the park is the City Zoo, which contains many of China's rare native animals.

The Temples of the Western Hills   Clinging to the sheer rock cliffs near the summit of the Western Hills, some seven kilometers from Kunming, is a group of ancient buildings and temples, the earliest of which dates from the thirteenth century. After traveling by road, visitors must take the winding footpath the rest of the way, passing through tunnels and corridors hewn out of the rock.

The first structure encountered along the way is the fourteenth-century temple that was once the villa of the Nanzhao ruler during the Song dynasty. Slightly beyond this is another temple, added later, which contains some beautiful Buddhist carvings dating from the Ming dynasty.

Eventually you will reach a stone arch, the Dragon Gate, and a group of caves carved out of the rock. Most of this work was done between 1781 and 1853 by the Taoist monk Wu Laiqing and a few local stonemasons. Their beautiful carvings include figures of the Kuixing muse, animals, and fanciful images of flowers, fruit, and birds, which decorate the ceilings. The terrace near the Dragon Gate commands an impressive view of Dianchi Lake below and Kunming in the distance.

Finally, there is a Taoist temple beyond the Dragon Gate. It dates from the thirteenth century and was used as a villa during the Yuan dynasty (1280-1368).

The Stone Forest   Located about one hundred kilometers southeast of Kunming is one of China's most spectacular natural formations, the Stone Forest. Fantastic monolithic limestone pillars, ranging from five to thirty meters in height, are clustered together like trees in a great forest. While some of the stones bear inscriptions carved over the centuries by poets and artists, others are outstanding for their extraordinary shapes. Visitors are usually taken along a trail, which meanders through the forest, and eventually reach a pool out of which rises a swordlike pinnacle of rock. From the pool, you can climb to the highest point in the forest, Lotus Peak.

Wuhua Shan (Five Flowers Hill)   Located in the center of the city, this hill offers a bird's eye view of the city and its surroundings. There are many temples and houses to be seen on this hill as well.

Cuihu Lake (Green Lake)   This is a lovely willow-lined lake in northeastern Kunming surrounded by gardens, temples, and pathways.

Golden Hall   This temple, which is situated a few kilometers northeast of the city, is part of a Ming dynasty palace. The temple, however, was not built until 1671, during the Qing dynasty. Set on a marble base, this structure is of particular interest because the gates, pillars, arches, and beams, as well as numerous statues, are all of gilded bronze.

ACCOMMODATION

Kunming Hotel   Located in the city center, this hotel has clean and spacious rooms and adequate services. The dining room serves good local food, including Yunnan ham, which is famous throughout China, much as Virginia ham is prized in the United States. Steamed chicken and stuffed pancakes are also local specialties.

SHOPPING

Local handicrafts, many of which are made by the minorities, include silver, ceramics, lacquerwares, Miao embroidery, swords, jewelry, and clothing, boots, and hats. They can be found in several of the local shops such as the Arts and Crafts Store, the hotel shop, the Friendship Store, the Minorities Store, and the department store.

Cuihu Lake, Kunming.

LANZHOU (Lanchow) Gansu Province

Lanzhou is the provincial capital of Gansu Province, which is situated in northwestern China. Its central location in northern China together with its position on the upper Huang He River makes Lanzhou a natural crossroad for transportation and communication. From this city railway lines and roads extend north, south, and west, linking eastern China with the remote autonomous regions of Xingjiang, Inner Mongolia, and Xizang. In addition, regular flights connect Lanzhou with Beijing, Chengdu, Urumqi, and Hohhot. Although evidence of a Neolithic culture has been found in the area surrounding Lanzhou, until recently the city has not had any historical or political significance. Since the building of the railway in 1952, Lanzhou has become a major distribution and industrial center manufacturing petrochemicals, fertilizers, and machinery.

PLACES TO SEE

Five Spring Hill (Wu Quan) Lovely pavilions, gardens, and the Chong Qing Temple (built in A.D. 1374) are situated in this scenic park in Lanzhou. The local zoo is also here.

The Binglingsi Forty kilometers west of Lanzhou, near Yongjing, are the ancient cave temples, the Binglingsi, which were discovered in 1952. Historical inscriptions indicate that these caves date back to A.D. 513. Construction and wall decoration were carried out over a period of about a thousand years (from the sixth to the seventeenth century). Some caves contain carvings and frescoes that were executed as early as the Wei dynasty (sixth century), while others contain mural paintings, sculptures, religious shrines, and pagodas of a later date, the most recent from the Ming dynasty. Within the upper temple is an enormous carved statue of Buddha from the Tang dynasty. The lower Bingling is of particular interest for its fine Song and Ming frescoes.

ACCOMMODATION

The Lanzhou Guesthouse This is a simple and comfortable hotel located in the main part of the city.

SHOPPING

Gansu Province is well known for its beautiful hand-loomed carpets, with their colorful geometrical designs. They are available in the local shops of Lanzhou, where visitors will also find local handcrafted pottery, papercuts, and woven items.

Path of Nine Turnings on Lingyun Hill, Leshan.

LESHAN (Loshan) Sichuan Province

The city of Leshan is located about two hundred kilometers south of Chengdu in Sichuan Province. A naturally fortified city, Leshan sits atop a rocky headland at the junction of the Min, Tatu, and Chingyi rivers. From Chengdu, Leshan can be reached either by road or by river ferry. The two main attractions near Leshan are located on the hills across the river from the city. Motorboat service to and from these sites is provided for visitors.

PLACES TO SEE

Lingyun Temple Directly across from Leshan, on the opposite bank of the river, is the Lingyun Hill. Here a gigantic seated Buddha, seventy meters in height, was carved into the sandstone cliff face during the eighth century. Work on this monumental figure started in A.D. 713 and took nine years to complete. In addition to being well proportioned, it is cleverly constructed, with a hidden channel cut through the body to prevent weathering at the surface. Although the best view of the Lingyun Buddha is from the Leshan side of the river, visitors can appreciate the size of the figure by climbing the steps to the head. From this vantage point one can also get a good view of the Leshan and the surrounding area.

Wulong Temple A short distance downriver from Lingyun Hill, southeast of Leshan, is the Wulong Hill. The Wulong Temple, which was built here during the Tang dynasty, has now been converted into a small museum and displays calligraphy, paintings, Buddhist canonical books, and inscriptions of Su Dongpo, a noted scholar and poet of the Song dynasty.

ACCOMMODATION

Leshan Guesthouse Visitors staying in Leshan will be accommodated in this small but comfortable hotel.

Sheep grazing, Northern Xizang.

LHASA (Lhasa)

Xizang Autonomous Region (Tibet)

Lhasa, "City of the Sun," is situated on the Lhasa River, a tributary of the Yarlung Zamba, in Xizang Autonomous Region. The city is 3,800 meters above sea level and is completely surrounded by mountains. Because of Lhasa's high altitude, visitors may experience dizziness and shortness of breath upon arrival. Founded in the seventh century by King Songtsan Gambo (617-650) and his Chinese princess, Wen Cheng, Lhasa is today the cultural, religious, economic, and political capital of Xizang.

PLACES TO SEE

Suglakang Temple   The oldest monument in Lhasa is the Suglakang Temple, which was built in A.D. 652 to house the Buddha statue that Han Princess Wen Cheng brought with her from China when she married King Songtsan Gambo in 641. Originally built by Chinese architects and Tibetan workers, the temple has been rebuilt over the centuries, most recently in 1660.

The Suglakang Temple is three stories high and has a flat roof ornamented with gilded copper canopies to protect the shrines and sanctuaries inside. A carmine gate inscribed in gold leads into a courtyard and galleries. Frescoes on the gallery walls depict infernos, heavens, deities, monsters, and the arrival of Princess Wen Cheng. A well in the courtyard reminds visitors of the legend of the holy spring that miraculously appeared when the princess arrived 1,300 years ago. The Buddha she brought with her is housed in the inner chapel. Seated on a gilded throne and wearing a thick gold crown, the statue has a gilded face with blue-lidded eyes. The Buddha is dressed in rich brocade embroidered with gold thread and wears gold necklaces studded with precious pearls, turquoise, and coral. There are many other chapels with Buddhist statues, as well as a shrine containing life-size statues of King Songtsan Gambo and his two wives, Princess Wen Cheng and his Nepalese wife. A collection of Ming musical instruments, tablewares, and Songtsan Gambo's helmet are stored in the treasure chamber of this temple.

Potala Palace   Located in the heart of Lhasa, the Potala Palace, originally known as the Red Palace, was built by King Songtsan Gambo for Princess Wen Cheng in the seventh century. The name *Potala* means "Buddha's Mountain." Standing atop a cliff over 3,700 meters above sea level, the palace has a thirteen-story tower that can be seen from almost anywhere in the city.

The Potala Palace was destroyed and rebuilt many times. A chapel and statues of the king and his wives are all that remain of the original palace. The present palace was reconstructed in the mid-seventeenth century by the fifth Dalai Lama (1617-1682) and has 1,000 rooms, 10,000 chapels, and about 200,000 statues of all sizes, as well as six large gates. It took fifty years, many thousands of serfs, and 2.13 million taels of silver to build this present Potala.

Stone stairs lead to the palace's eastern gate and a wide platform where celebrations took place on holidays or religious occasions. West of the platform are chanting halls and living quarters for the palace's 154 lamas. Above the platform, passing through a winding corridor, is the important East Main Hall, where the Dalai Lamas conducted official ceremonies. The West Main Hall, or the Hall of Sacrifice, houses dome-shaped stupas containing the embalmed remains of the deceased Dalai Lamas. The fifth and the thirteenth Dalais have the most impressive tombs, which are about eighteen meters high, covered with gold leaf, and studded with precious stones. In front of the stupas are incense burners and butter lamps.

At the top of the White Palace, which the thirteenth Dalai Lama added in the twentieth century, are the Dalai's living chambers, including prayer halls, sitting rooms, storage halls for the sutra, and bedrooms. They are all luxuriously decorated with silk, jewels, and handmade carpets. At one time only high-ranking officials were allowed to enter these chambers; today they are open to the public.

The Potala's stone foundation is set deep in the hill. The outer wall is several meters thick, with copper support to give additional strength. The upper structure of the palace is made of wood, and the rooms of the main buildings are in traditional Han style with upturned decorative eaves and tinkling bells at the corners.

The palace murals, which are treasured as works of great artistic merit, depict religious themes, Tibetan life, historical events, and the special meetings between the fifth and thirteenth Dalai Lamas and the Qing emperors.

In 1961 the Potala was designated a national cultural site to be given protection. Today the palace and other religious sites are under the care of the Tibet Committee for Management of Cultural Relics.

Marketplace on Barkor Street   A great variety of local farm produce, food, and handicrafts are bought and sold in this busy marketplace of Lhasa. A new trade policy was made to encourage the open market of Tibetan handicrafts. Thus, visitors will find an excellent selection of Tibetan crafts, including lovely inlaid silver bowls and jewelry, Tibetan knives, colorful fabrics (such as the woolen *pulu* used for clothing), traditional carpets, mats, and paintings, at the Barkor Market.

ACCOMMODATION

Lhasa Guesthouse This is the only official guesthouse in Lhasa for foreign visitors. Situated on the main street, it is relatively small, with only sixty rooms. Accommodation is clean and reasonably comfortable, although hot water is not always available. The guesthouse also has a dining room.

Suglakang Temple, Lhasa.

Potala Palace, Lhasa.

Young potter at the Luoyang Ceramic Workshop.

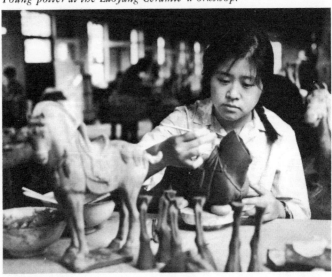

LUOYANG (Loyang) Henan Province

Luoyang, in Western Henan Province, is located at the base of the Mangshan hills and north of the Luo River. South of the river are the Longmen Grottoes, which are some of the most famous caves of ancient Buddhist sculptural art in China. Luoyang covers an area of 1,100 square kilometers and has a population of just over one million. It is about 120 kilometers east of Xi'an.

Luoyang and the surrounding area were inhabited as early as the Neolithic era (about 5,000 B.C.) by the Yangshao and the Longshan cultures. Although several sites in the surrounding district had been established as capitals in the Xia (2205-1766 B.C.) and the Shang (1766-1122 B.C.) dynasties, it was not until 770 B.C. that Luoyang was chosen as imperial capital of the Eastern Zhou dynasty (770-256 B.C.) Subsequently, it periodically was the imperial capital of the dynasties of Eastern Han, Wei, Jin, Northern Wei, Sai, Tang, and Liang over a period of more than one thousand years. Thus, Luoyang is often called the "Ancient Capital of Nine Dynasties." Luoyang was also an important historical and cultural center over the centuries. Buddhism was first introduced here in the first century A.D., and by the fifth century carving on the Longmen Caves had commenced. Later, under the Tang dynasty, it attracted many renowned artists and scholars.

Since 1949, Luoyang has developed as an industrial center manufacturing tractors, machinery, ball bearings, mining equipment, and glass. The tractor plant was the first to be built in China. Luoyang is also a major agricultural producer of corn, wheat, cotton, tobacco, peanuts, and livestock.

Archaeological teams have recently excavated several ancient city sites, palaces, and tombs in Luoyang. The earliest site, found in the eastern section of the city, is that of a capital of the Xia dynasty, which dates back to about 2000 B.C. The other sites discovered in the area date from the Zhou, Han-Wei, and Sui-Tang periods. The two Han tombs have been removed from where they were originally found and are now situated in Wang Cheng Park, which also was the site of the Zhou palace. Many of the treasures that were unearthed during these excavations are presently displayed in the local museum of Luoyang.

Luoyang has long been renowned for its arts and crafts. The gray and white pottery and colorful glazed Tang pottery were originally made here. Luoyang also produced the famous lanterns and silk flowers for the imperial palaces of the Ming and Qing dynasties. Today the craftsmen continue to produce fine handicrafts that are exported to Europe, America, and Southeast Asia.

PLACES TO SEE

Longmen Grottoes These spectacular caves are located on the north bank of the Yishui River, about twelve kilometers south of Luoyang. At this point in the river the cliffs rise like towers on either side of the river—hence its name, which means "Dragon's Gate." Stretching about one kilometer across the north cliff there are 1,352 grottoes, 750 niches, and 40 pagodas containing approximately one hundred thousand statues of Buddha. Work was begun on these caves in A.D. 494 under the Northern Wei dynasty (A.D. 386-534) and continued over a period of four hundred years, spanning seven dynasties. The largest Buddha in China, carved during the Tang dynasty (A.D. 618-907), is over seventeen meters high and is housed in Longmen's biggest cave. In contrast, the smallest statue of Buddha is a mere two centimeters in height and is but one of the more than fifteen thousand statues in the Cave of the Ten Thousand Buddhas, which dates from the seventh century.

In addition to statues of Buddha, the caves are filled with thousands of statues of Bodhisattvas and guardians as well as carvings of lotus flowers and animals. There are also many calligraphic inscriptions to be found on the cave walls, such as the several hundred medicinal recipes inscribed in the Cave of Prescriptions.

All of these statues, carvings, and inscriptions at Longmen are invaluable records for the archaeologist and art historian, for they represent some of the finest artistry and religious history of China.

Luoyang Museum This municipal museum contains a representative collection of artifacts dating from the Neolithic Yangshao and Longshan cultures through to the Song dynasty. Of particular interest are the shells, which were used as money several thousand years ago; the three-thousand-year-old "pottery bean" drinking cup; the Shang and Zhou bronzes; the stone chimes, which date from the Spring and Autumn period; and the many fine examples of pottery from the Neolithic red and black forms to the Song porcelains. In addition there are displays of the treasures unearthed in the recent archaeological excavations.

White Horse Temple This Buddhist temple, which is situated fifteen kilometers east of Luoyang, was one of the first to be established in China. Founded by two monks in A.D. 68 under the Western Han dynasty, it was built to house the Buddhist sutras they had brought from India. It is said that the monks arrived on two white horses—hence the name of this temple and the presence of the two stone statues guarding the entrance gates.

Guan Di Temple Guan Di (or Guan Yu) was a hero of the Three Kingdoms period (A.D. 220-265). A general under the emperor Liu Bei, he was highly respected for his loyalty and patriotism. In the sixteenth century, during the Wanli era of the Ming dynasty, a memorial temple was constructed over his burial site.

The Imperial Tombs of the Song Dynasty Seven of the nine emperors of the Song dynasty, as well as the father of the first emperor, were buried in Gongxian. The tomb of the third emperor, Yongding, who died in 998, is the most interesting, as it is the best preserved of the tombs. Although the building around his tomb no longer exists, the procession of the magnificent stone sculptures of animals, foreign envoys, and officials still stands guarding the imperial burial site. The four gates, which once stood in the square wall around the tomb, were also guarded by a pair of crouching lions. In addition to these imperial tombs it is believed that over one hundred other members of the imperial family are buried in the surrounding area.

The Gongxian Caves This group of Buddhist caves is situated on the north bank of the Yiluo River just a few kilometers northeast of Gongxian. Built in the late Northern Wei dynasty, they are smaller than but similar in style to the Yungang Caves at Datong. The Gongxian Caves consist of five grottoes carved out of the soft sandstone of the Dali Hill, and contain several statues of Buddha that are characteristic of the Northern Wei style. Unfortunately, the caves have suffered the effects of weathering and time. There is a small guesthouse in Gongxian, but the accommodation and facilities are rather limited.

Shaolinsi, Dengfeng Also known as the Little Forest Temple, Shaolinsi is situated northwest of the town of Dengfeng, which is about eighty kilometers southeast of Luoyang. Founded in A.D. 496, during the Northern Wei dynasty (386-534), this monastery became a major center of Chinese Buddhism. For centuries it has also been internationally renowned for its traditional training of martial arts, which were originally developed as routine exercises to be done between long periods of meditation. *Shaolin Quan*, a wrestling form developed by the monks of this temple, is still used in China and Japan. The brick floor in the main Hall of the Thousand Buddhas bears the old marks made by the monks who practiced their martial arts here. It is believed that the Chan Buddhist sect, which emphasizes meditation and introspection, was introduced to Shaolinsi in the early sixth century by the Indian monk Boddhidarma (known as Damo by the Chinese).

The Forest of Stupas (Talin), Shaolinsi On the hillside southwest of the Shaolinsi are 220 small stone towers, which, over the centuries, were erected to mark the graves of the senior members of the temple monastery.

Songshan Temple Situated in Dengfeng County, this temple was originally built in A.D. 508 as a leisure palace by Emperor Xuanwu of the

Northern Wei dynasty. In 520, he constructed fifteen pagodas and palaces here. One of the pagodas, a tall twelve-sided brick stucture, is reputed to be the oldest pagoda still standing in China.

Zhongyuemiao (Temple of the Central Peak)   This Taoist temple, at the foot of the Central Peak of the Song Mountains, dates from the eighth century of the Tang dynasty. It was subsequently enlarged in the Song dynasty for the Song emperors, who used this temple for making their sacrificial offerings, and again under the Ming and Qing dynasties. Near the temple are two stone monuments that were erected to mark the visit of Emperor Wu of the Han dynasty, who came to the Song Mountains in 110 B.C.

ACCOMMODATION

Friendship Hotel   Luoyang's Friendship Hotel is located on Tangyuan Road in the Cantonese community, known as the Canton Market, to the west of town. As one of the more modern hotels in China, it offers very comfortable and hospitable accommodation. The dining room serves both Western and Chinese food, although the menu is somewhat limited.

Longmen Grottoes, Luoyang.

NANCHANG (Nanchang)

Jiangxi Province

Nanchang is the capital city of Jiangxi Province and is situated on the east bank of the Ganjiang River, which flows into Poyang Lake to the northeast. Nanchang is an old city dating back to the Han dynasty (206 B.C.-A.D. 220). When ceramics became one of China's popular export commodities it developed into the major trading and distribution center for porcelains and ceramics, most of which were produced in Jingdezhen to the east. More recently, Nanchang was an important center of activity during the revolution. It was here that Chiang Kaishek, leader of the Nationalist Party, the Guomindang, set up headquarters in 1927. In an attempt to openly oppose the Guomindang, the Communists rallied their forces together to form the Red Army and led their supporters into the famous August Uprising of 1927. Defeated in Nanchang and driven underground by the Guomindang, the Communists then retreated to the mountains on the Jiangxi-Henan border.

Today Nanchang is an important railway junction on the lines that link Shanghai with Guangzhou and the provinces to the south. With a population of about 700,000, it has also developed as a major regional center for industry, manufacturing aircraft, electronics, textiles, and machinery.

PLACES TO SEE

Jiangxi Provincial Museum   A fine art collection of paintings, ceramics, and recent archaeological finds from this province are housed in this museum.

Museum of the Revolutionary History of Jiangxi   This museum contains a display of records and photographs, which document the revolutionary uprising of August 1, 1927, as well as subsequent events and activities of the Guomindang and the Communists. Another revolutionary museum is located in the Jinggang Mountains to the southwest, where the Communists established their headquarters until 1931.

ACCOMMODATION

Jiangxi Hotel   This large hotel complex, which is situated in the center of town, offers comfortable accommodation and good service. During the summer, some of the rooms are air conditioned. The hotel facilities include a barbershop and post office and a dining room, which serves a fairly good selection of Chinese dishes.

Water-color painting of Yangtze River Bridge, Nanjing.

NANJING (Nanking)   Jiangsu Province

Nanjing, the capital of Jiangsu Province, is one of China's oldest cities. It is also one of the most naturally scenic cities in the country, situated in a valley with the Yangtze River to the north and the Purple (Zijin) Mountains to the east and south. Nanjing has long been an important national center—hence its name, which means "Southern Capital." This also refers to its long history, for over the centuries Nanjing was chosen as a national and state capital several times.

Nanjing was already an important manufacturing center in the Ming dynasty (1368-1644), producing timber, ceramics, and metal products. Since 1949 its industrial base has been greatly expanded, and today it supports a population of about two and a half million. Its factories produce a variety of goods and materials, including textiles, machinery, motor vehicles, tools, scientific instruments, iron, steel, and cement. The rich agricultural land surrounding Nanjing yields crops of grain, fruit, vegetables, and tea.

In addition to its importance as an industrial city and river port, Nanjing has also been renowned for centuries as a cultural and educational center. During the Ming dynasty, the Imperial College attracted scholars and intellectuals from all over the country. Today its university is considered to be one of the finest in China. There are also many technical institutes, colleges, and research centers established here.

The city itself is very attractive, with its wide tree-lined boulevards and traditionally styled buildings. Also, many of the gates and sections of the old wall, which were erected during the Ming dynasty, still surround the inner city. The most spectacular feature of Nanjing, however, is the famous double-tiered Yangtze River Bridge, a monument to the achievements of twentieth century engineering in China. Completed in 1968, it spans over fifteen hundred meters and links the Yangtze River Basin with the north.

HISTORY

Archaeological discoveries have provided evidence that Nanjing was inhabited as long ago as the Paleolithic period, about 4000 B.C. However, it was not until the eighth century B.C. that the city really began to develop. Following the unification of China in the third century B.C., Nanjing became a strategically important center. Subsequently it was chosen as the state capital of six consecutive dynasties from A.D. 220 to A.D. 589. With the exception of the Tang dynasty (A.D. 618-907) the city was not of such significance again until the fourteenth century, when the Ming emperor selected Nanjing for his imperial capital. During this period Nanjing was greatly expanded and fortified; most of the city is still contained within the original walls. Although the capital was later moved to Beijing, Nanjing continued to flourish as a great commercial and cultural center through the nineteenth century. During the Taiping Rebellion in the 1850s the city was, for a short period of ten years, the seat of the Taiping. Thereafter, it was chosen as the national capital of the Republicans during a three-month period in 1912 before the government moved to Beijing, and, during the civil conflict between the Guomindang and the Communists, Nanjing was taken by Chiang Kaishek as the capital of the Nationalist government.

PLACES TO SEE

The Mausoleum of Sun Yat-sen (Zhongshan Ling)   The tomb of Dr. Sun Yat-sen, the great Chinese patriot and founder of the first Republic of China in 1911, is situated on the southern slope of Zijin Shan (Purple Mountains) to the east of the city. This magnificent monument is set within beautifully landscaped grounds, which cover eight hectares, and was completed in 1929, four years after the death of Dr. Sun. Visitors enter through the first three-arched gate, which bears the Chinese character inscription *Boai*, meaning "universal love." After passing along an avenue bordered by pines and cypresses you reach the main gate, over which is engraved *Tian xia wei gong*, meaning "the world belongs to everyone." These calligraphic inscriptions are two of the famous maxims quoted by Dr. Sun Yat-sen.

From the main gate there are 392 marble steps leading up to the memorial pavilion, a white granite structure with a two-tiered roof covered with blue glazed tiles. The white and blue are the symbolic colors of the Nationalist Party. Within the mausoleum, quotations from Dr. Sun's works as well as extracts from the 1912 Constitution and National Charter are inscribed on the surrounding walls. In the middle of the hall is a white marble seated statue of

Dr. Sun, mounted on a carved pedestal, which bears the signature of the French sculptor Landowski and is dated Paris, 1930. Behind the statue is a door opening into a circular domed vault where the actual coffin is placed. A lovely view of the surrounding hills can be seen from the terrace of the mausoleum. Above the tomb is another recumbent marble statue of Dr. Sun Yat-sen.

Yuhua Tai (Rain of Flowers Terrace)   Small and colorful pebbles, which resemble flower petals, can be found in this park south of Nanjing. According to the legend, a Buddhist monk of the sixth century, Yuan Guang, preached here and so moved Buddha that a "rain of flowers" fell from heaven. Many ancient temples and tombs have been built here, although none have survived. Within the park today there is a small museum and a modern stele, which was erected in memory of the Communist patriots who were executed by the Guomindang (the Nationalist Party) between 1927 and 1949.

Xuanwu Lake   This lake is situated in a park outside the north walls of the old city. Surrounded by hills, it is a popular leisure spot for both residents and visitors. In the center of the lake there are five islets named after the five continents, which are connected by dykes and bridges. The whole park is beautifully landscaped with old pines, cypresses, and rock gardens, and in summer the lake is covered with floating lotus flowers. Since the park was opened to the public in 1911, an open-air theater, concert hall, zoo, skating rink, and children's park have been built here. In addition, parts of the lake have been converted into swimming areas. While water buffalo freely graze along the edges of the lake, the pandas and lions are housed in the zoo on Luozengge islet.

Jiangsu Provincial Museum   Situated in a modern Chinese-style building on the eastern side of the city, this museum contains a collection of artifacts and treasures ranging from the prehistoric era through to the Qing dynasty of the early twentieth century. The exhibits are divided between several rooms and are presented chronologically. Ancient stone tools, Shang bronzes, Han pottery, jewelry, ivory, jade, and Qing scrolls are but a few of the fine examples on display here. The museum collection also includes recently unearthed art relics from the Nanjing area.

Taiping Museum   This museum, which is housed in the former palace of the Taiping "Celestial Emperor," Hong Xiu Quan, is located in the southern section of the city. The exhibits include the historical records, texts, maps, seals, and cannons of the revolutionary group, the Taiping Heavenly Kingdom (1851-1864).

The Ming Tomb of the Emperor Tai Zu   Emperor Tai Zu (1327-1398), also known as Hong Wu, was the founder of the Ming dynasty, and seventeen years before his death he had his tomb built here in the Purple Mountains to the east of Nanjing. Unfortunately, this site was damaged during the Taiping Rebellion. However, much of it has been restored in recent years. To reach the tomb you must pass through the Great Gate and follow the traditional path, the Sacred Way, a distance of one and a half kilometers. Upon entering through the Great Gate you will see a tall stele mounted on a stone tortoise. From here the Sacred Way passes over a small bridge and then opens on to the long processional path, guarded on either side by statues of animals, warriors, and court officials. You then enter a gate and proceed through a series of courtyards, terraces, and pavilions and cross another bridge, at the end of which you will have reached the building containing the tomb of the Emperor. The Empress of Tai Zu is also buried here.

Nanjing University   This well-known university, which was established in 1902, has an excellent reputation and attracts many foreign students.

Zijin Shan (Purple Mountain) Observatory   This observatory, which is located on the summit of the Purple Mountains to the northeast of Nanjing, is one of the largest in China. In addition to the observatory, which was founded in 1934, there is a large research center and museum of astronomy. The museum collection includes several ancient bronze astronomical instruments as well as a number of reproductions. Besides the Ming bronze replica of an ancient sundial, the most notable reproductions are of two armillary spheres. One of these celestial globes was originally cast over two thousand years ago under the Han dynasty; the one shown here was reproduced in the seventeenth century. The other armillary sphere is a replica made by the French of a more sophisticated instrument, showing the position of the stars and planets, which dates from the Yuan dynasty.

ACCOMMODATION

Nanjing Hotel   Located on the Zhongshan Road North (phone: 34121), the Nanjing Hotel has a lovely garden setting and peaceful atmosphere. The rooms are simple and comfortable. Hotel facilities include a beauty salon, retail store, and postal and telegraph office. The dining room serves good local specialties, such as Nanjing flat duck, dried beancurds, and pickled vegetables.

CUISINE

Nanjing is noted for its flat duck, also called Nanjing duck, and its delicious cherries and watermelon. In autumn you can sample the plump lake crabs.

SHOPPING

You will find a good selection of silk fabrics, porcelains, and antiques in Nanjing. One of the best places to find these items as well as local arts and crafts is at the People's Market on Zhongshan Road South. The local crafts include fine antique reproductions. However, should you wish to find some authentic Chinese antiques, ask your guide to take you to a Wen-wu store.

Nanjing ducks.

Young volunteers at the commune, Nanning.

NANNING (Nanning)

Guangxi Zhuangzu Autonomous Region

Nanning, the capital of Guangxi Zhuangzu Autonomous Region, in southern China, is located on a plain south of the Daming Hills and near the confluence of the Zuojiang and Yongjiang rivers. The southernmost of China's major cities, it is situated on the railway line to Vietnam. In addition, it is linked by air to Changsha, Guangzhou, Beijing, and Hanoi. Since 1977 Nanning has been included in short sightseeing tours from Hong Kong that also cover Guangzhou and Guilin.

Established during the Yuan dynasty in the thirteenth century, it developed as a trading center linked to Vietnam and Southeast Asia. In the twentieth century Nanning became an industrial center and today has sugar refineries, food processing plants, chemical fertilizer factories, flour mills, and a tractor plant. The Nanning area produces rice and sugarcane and is China's major producer of tung oil. With a population of 500,000, Nanning is the cultural center of Guangxi.

EVENTS AND PLACES TO SEE

Dragon Boat Festival In 295 B.C. the poet and statesman Qu Yuan drowned himself in Miluo River north of Changsha after having been falsely accused by a nobleman. The Dragon Boat Festival, which was banned during the Cultural Revolution and revived in 1978, commemorates the vast search party of boats that went looking for his body. During the festival, which is held on the fifth day of the fifth moon (usually in early to mid June), lavishly decorated dragon boats compete in regattas.

Yiling Stalactite Cave About twenty kilometers outside of Nanning is a large natural cave containing interesting formations that are entitled "fruit bowl," "city skyline," and so on. Other formations suggest human or animal shapes.

ACCOMMODATION

The Friendship Hotel This older hotel is located within walking distance of the town center. The rooms and the services are basic.

Ming Yuan Hotel Also located a short distance from the town center, this three-story hotel offers plain and comfortable accommodation.

QINGDAO (Tsingtao) Shangdong Province

Qingdao, the "Green Island," is situated in Jiaozhou Bay on the southeast coast of the Shandong peninsula. It is about twelve hours from Beijing by train and is linked by air to the major cities in China. The second largest city in Shandong Province, Qingdao has a population of 1.5 million.

In 1898 the Chinese ceded the small fishing village of Qingdao to the Germans, who extended the railway line from Jinan to Qingdao and began producing Qingdao beer, which is still considered the best beer in China. As a result of these developments, Qingdao became a modern town and harbor. After the First World War, all German-held territories, including Qingdao, were ceded to Japan. In 1923 Qingdao was finally returned to China.

Today Qingdao is one of China's most important ports as well as a popular seaside resort, with a beautiful beach and large, European-style villas. It is also an industrial center, manufacturing textiles, tools, weaving looms, tobacco, and wine, and is one of China's four carpet centers.

PLACES TO SEE

Qianhai Pier While you are enjoying the beach, stop at this favorite spot at the end of the city's main thoroughfare, Zhongshan Road. First built in 1891, the pier has been extended and renovated several times and today reaches 440 meters out to sea. Situated at the south end of the pier is a traditional-style octagonal pavilion and a semicircular breakwater.

Zhongshan Park Covering eight hundred thousand square meters, this park is the largest in the city. There are over three hundred thousand trees, and the park is particularly noted for its peach trees, tea shrubs, and gardens of medicinal herbs. A festival of art exhibitions and live performances takes place from mid-April to early May, while the cherry trees are in full bloom.

Laoshan (Mount Lao) Famous for its spring water, which is the main element of the excellent Qingdao beer, beautiful Laoshan rises 1,200 meters over the coastal waters. The mountain figures in local legends and was once thought to be the home of immortals.

Zhanshan (Limpid Mountain) Zhanshan overlooks the southern villa-dotted area of Qingdao. If you feel like a climb, visit the temple at the top, the Zhanshansi.

Qingdao Museum Located in the city, this museum houses local historical records and art treasures.

Sea Museum This aquarium contains over three thousand species of marine plants and fish, including many rare species.

QUFU (Chufu) Shandong Province

Qufu is renowned as the birthplace and shrine of the great Chinese philosopher and political thinker Confucius (Kong Qiu). Situated east of the Grand Canal and south of Jinan, this spectacular sanctuary can be easily reached by rail by taking the Beijing-Shanghai train as far as Yanzhou. From here it is just a short bus ride to Qufu.

The town of Qufu dates from the eleventh century B.C., when it became a state capital under the Zhou dynasty (B.C. 1122-770). In the period that followed, the Spring and Autumn era (B.C. 770-476), great technological, political, and philosophical advances occurred in China. It was during this time of achievement and enlightenment that Confucius was born, in 551 B.C.

Confucianism, the code of ethics and philosophy of social conduct that emphasizes humanity and confidence in man's abilities and responsibilities, had a profound influence on Chinese society over the next two thousand years. During his lifetime, Confucius spent many years traveling around the country, disseminating his social and political ideas throughout the imperial courts of China. Having gathered together a group of disciples, he then returned to Qufu, where he taught his followers until his death in 479 B.C.

While Confucius lived in poverty all his life, his seventy-six direct descendants were given important official appointments, accommodated in relatively luxurious residences, and treated with the utmost respect. The Confucian residence in Qufu was occupied by a Kong descendant as late as the 1940s.

Ever since the death of this great sage, Qufu has been revered as a sacred shrine of Confucianism, attracting scholars and pilgrims from all over the world. During the Cultural Revolution, the Confucian philosophy was severely attacked and the town suffered a considerable amount of damage as a result. Recently, however, Qufu has been restored and today is one of the most magnificent attractions in China.

PLACES TO SEE

Temple of Confucius (Kong Miao)   Dominating the town of Qufu is the great Temple of Confucius, which dates from 478 B.C. Over the centuries the original temple has been enlarged and restored many times and today covers an area of twenty-two hectares. Within this vast complex there are numerous pavilions, halls, and shrines elaborately adorned with glazed-tile roofs, magnificent carved pillars and motifs, and stone engravings.

After passing through a series of courtyards and gateways at the southern end of the temple grounds, you reach the Great Pavilion of the Constellation of Scholars, the oldest of the halls. This grand wooden structure, which is surmounted by a triple-tiered roof, dates from the late twelfth century.

The largest and most imposing pavilion is the Great Hall, situated in the center of the temple complex. Rebuilt in 1724, its façade features several enormous columns carved with twisting dragons, which support the lower roof. The two-tiered structure stands on a marble terrace and contains a collection of steles and stone engravings.

Within the Pavilion of the Sage is a collection of stone tablets. The inscriptions on these tablets detail the life of Confucius. In addition to the principal shrines and pavilions dedicated to Confucius there are several smaller buildings to the north and east of the Great Hall, including the shrines honoring the wife and parents of Confucius, and the Silk and Metal Hall, where ancient musical instruments were once stored.

The courtyards within the temple grounds contain hundreds of steles and sacred trees. One tree in particular, near the Great Hall, is reputed to have been planted by Confucius himself.

Residence of the Kong Family   These buildings, which are situated just east of the temple, were the living quarters of the honored descendants of Confucius. The present residence, which dates from the sixteenth century of the Ming dynasty, consists of several hundred reception halls, offices, and private apartments as well as several courtyards and ornamental gardens. The great power and wealth enjoyed by the Kong family over the centuries is evident as one passes from the Great Hall through the public halls and residential apartments. Most of the original furnishings and family treasures have been

Lingxing Gate, Confucius Temple.

carefully preserved and are displayed as one might have seen them when the residence was still in use. The treasures on display, some of which date back to the Han dynasty (206 B.C.-A.D. 220), include beautiful ivory and jade pieces, gold and silver wares, ceramics, embroideries, and the splendid costumes worn by the descendants during official functions, receptions, and temple ceremonies.

Tomb of Confucius   Leaving Qufu by the North Gate, one will reach the Confucian Woods, the largest and oldest manmade forest in China. Within these woods are hundreds of steles and the tombs of Confucius and almost all of his descendants. An avenue flanked by ancient pines and cypresses as well as stone guardians, griffins, and panthers leads up to the small temple-shrine and tomb of Confucius.

ACCOMMODATION

Overnight visitors may be accommodated at either of the two modern hotels in Qufu or at the guesthouse, which is located in the western wing of the Confucius house.

SHOPPING

Qufu is renowned for two of its local wines, Qufu Wine and Shandong Fountain Wine, and for its traditional engraved woodcuts and stone rubbings, all of which can be found in the local shops.

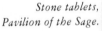

Stone tablets,
Pavilion of the Sage.

Shanghai harbor at night.

SHANGHAI   (Shanghai)

Shanghai, which means "Above the Sea," is the largest and most cosmopolitan city in China. Situated on the west bank of the Huang Po River, about twenty kilometers south of the Yangtze River estuary, this city is China's major international port and leading industrial center. It is also one of China's three municipalities (besides Beijing and Tianjin) directly under the control of the central government. Shanghai Municipality covers an area of over six thousand square kilometers and includes ten districts and ten suburban counties, supporting a total population of over ten million.

Shanghai is very much a modern metropolis, owing much of its appearance to Western influences, which predominated through the latter half of the nineteenth century. Grand European-style buildings line the Bund, the main boulevard along the west bank of the Huang Po River. Once the trade houses, banks, hotels, and clubs of foreign companies and entrepreneurs, these buildings now serve as local administrative offices, headquarters for the Chinese trade corporations, banks, and workers' clubs. This broad waterfront promenade affords a marvelous view of the busy harbor and city center. It is here on the Bund that local residences practice their *taiji* (shadow boxing) exercises and musical instruments in the early morning. Just west of the Bund is Shanghai's crowded shopping district, which centers around Nanjing Road.

Since 1949 Shanghai has developed into China's most important industrial and commercial center. Its major industries include electrical engineering, metallurgy, shipbuilding, processing and refining, and printing. In addition, a diversity of light industry has been established here with factories manufacturing machinery, electronic equipment, chemicals, textiles, pharmaceuticals, paper, and glass. Shanghai's harbor facilities have been greatly expanded over the past thirty years and today extend some sixty kilometers along the banks of the Huang Po River. As the largest port in China, it handles about half of the country's domestic and export trade. Although Shanghai is not a major agricultural center, the surrounding land is under intensive cultivation and yields enough produce and livestock to support the consumer needs of the municipality.

Shanghai is also considered one of China's most prominent centers of culture and education. It has eleven universities, of which Fudan University is the most renowned for its high standard of education, as well as many technical institutes and colleges. Culturally, Shanghai boasts several excellent performing arts companies and training schools. It also has a number of outstanding museums, parks, and children's palaces.

HISTORY

Although Shanghai was already an established fishing village during the Song dynasty (A.D. 960-1280), it was not until the seventeenth century, under the Qing dynasty, that the city achieved any historical or commercial significance. By this time it was a walled settlement and rapidly developed into a major production and trading center for cotton and silk. During the Kangxi era (1662-1723) of the Qing dynasty the harbor of Shanghai was built along the Huang Po River, and in 1842 it was one of the five ports opened up to foreign trade concessions as a result of the Nanjing Treaty.

The Europeans were soon settled in Shanghai with their trade houses, banks, clubs, and hotels established along the riverfront. Even though they were relatively unaffected by the Taiping Rebellion and subsequent uprisings through the period between 1853 and 1862, the foreigners did meet a great deal of resistance from members of the local Dagger Society, who persisted in raiding the European settlements until the society was suppressed in 1862. General discontent among the local Chinese continued, however, and by the end of the nineteenth century revolutionary groups opposed to the foreign concessions began to surface. The Chinese Communist Party was founded in Shanghai in 1921, Mao Zedong being one of the founding members. By 1925, the party was inciting rebellion among the intellectuals and workers in an attempt to bring about social reform. The final outcome of these revolutionary demonstrations was the Shanghai Massacre of 1927, the first in a series of purges undertaken by the Guomindang troops, who were led by Chiang Kaishek. As a result of all this social and political upheaval, many of the foreigners withdrew from Shanghai.

Shanghai was then occupied by the Japanese during the Sino-Japanese war (1937-1945). When the Communists finally defeated the Nationalists in 1949, the city was taken over by the state. The new government nationalized all existing businesses, and a major campaign was undertaken to abolish the conditions of depravity that had been generated by a century of foreign occupation, war, and civil turmoil.

PLACES TO SEE

The Shanghai Museum   In 1952, the former privately owned bank of Tu Yuehsheng was converted into the Shanghai Museum. The museum contains a representative collection of Chinese historical relics from the Paleolithic period to the modern era. It also houses the internationally renowned bronzes and some of China's finest paintings and ceramics. At the museum shop visitors can buy art books, postcards of the museum's collections, and reproductions of paintings. For further detail on the Shanghai Museum, please refer to the section covering the major museums of China.

Handicraft Research Institute   This institute, which is located on Nanjing Road, was established in 1956 to provide apprenticeship programs for those interested in acquiring the skills and craftsmanship of the traditional Chinese arts. Through lessons and study projects students learn the techniques of such arts as ivory and stone carving, silk and wool embroidery, papercutting, and silk flower and lantern making. Visitors may have a guided tour of the institute to observe the art masters and students at work.

The Children's Palace   The Shanghai Municipal Children's Palace is only one of the many children's educational centers or palaces in China. Located on Yanan Road in the former home of one of Shanghai's foreign entrepreneurs, this Children's Palace not only was the first to be established in Shanghai but is also the largest in China. The main purpose of these centers is to provide well-organized extracurricular activities in such areas as the arts, sciences, and sports to children between the ages of six and seventeen. In addition to the regular activities, free lessons are offered—for example, music, dancing, drama, electronics, and miniature airplane and ship building. Children may also join orchestras, theatrical groups, and sports teams organized by the center. If children show exceptional talents in any particular area, they then have the opportunity to receive special training and instruction from the highly qualified professionals. The success of the children's palaces throughout China is largely the result of the dedicated efforts of Sun Yat-sen's widow, Soong Ching-ling, who promoted the concept. Today eleven Children's Palaces exist in Shanghai.

The Shanghai Industrial Exhibition   This large exhibition hall is located west of the People's Park on Nanjing Road. Constructed during the 1950s by the Soviet Union, it was formerly known as the Sino-Soviet People's Friendship Building. A permanent exhibition displays samples of Shanghai's industrial and consumer products, as well as fine examples of Chinese arts and crafts. It can be of special interest to businessmen and visitors to learn some aspects of the Chinese economy from the exhibition.

Yu Yuan Garden   Also known as the Mandarin's Garden, this site once covered about five hectares in the old part of the city. It was commissioned by Pan Yuntuan, an important Sichuan official, in 1559 and completed in 1577. Landscaped in the traditional Ming style, the garden is divided into three sections by walls crowned with tiles that resemble dragon scales. The garden features several attractive ponds, hillocks, bridges, and rockeries as well as thirty pavilions, some of which have been converted into small teahouses. The Yu Garden also has some historical significance. In 1853 the Dagger Society established its headquarters in the Hall for Heralding Spring here. Later, in 1862, it was used by the imperial troops and foreigners in their attack on the Taiping. Although almost ruined and subsequently neglected over the next hundred years, the garden was completely restored to its former magnificence in 1956.

Sun Yat-sen Museum   Situated in the former French concession adjacent to Fuxing Park, this house is where Dr. Sun, founder of the Chinese Republic, resided when he came to Shanghai in 1911. Today this two-story building has been converted into a historical museum dedicated to Sun's life and revolutionary activities.

Shanghai Stadium.

Lu Xun Museum   This museum, which is located south of Hongkou Park, was formerly the home of the famous Chinese revolutionary, thinker, and writer Lu Xun (1881-1936). His writing and leadership in literary circles had a tremendous impact upon the revolutionary movements of China in the 1920s and 1930s. The museum collection consists of Lu Xun's manuscripts, letters, personal photographs of his family, woodcuts, and his correspondence with famous writers such as George Bernard Shaw. Lu Xun's grave, which is marked by a memorial statue, is situated in Hongkou Park.

Temple of the Jade Buddha   Also known as the Yu Fo Si, this temple is situated in the northwest section of the city, at the corner of Changshou Road and Jiangmin Road. Built in 1887, it houses a seated white jade Buddha, which was brought from Burma by a Chinese monk in 1881, as well as a rather unusual reclining Buddha. The temple is still used today and is quite noticeable from a distance because of its brilliant saffron-colored walls.

Xi Jiao Park (The Shanghai Zoo)   One of the most popular attractions of the city is the Shanghai Zoo, which has over five hundred species of animals. Situated in an attractive park landscaped with lovely gardens and trees, it is a favorite spot for Chinese family outings.

Workers' Cultural Palace   Situated at the southeast corner of the People's Square, this large entertainment complex, formerly called the Great World (Da Shi Jie), is one of Shanghai's most popular centers for cultural and recreational activities. Facilities provided for the workers include ten theaters where performances of ballet, opera, and drama are occasionally held, several pavilions and exhibition halls, and a number of reading rooms.

Futan University   Founded in 1905, this is one of China's most renowned universities. Long reputed for its excellent academic standing and progressive approaches, it presently has a faculty of over two thousand and offers programs of study in both the sciences and the arts.

Shanghai Workers' Village (Min Hsing or Peng Pu)   If you are interested in the structure and life-style of Chinese workers in urban China it is recommended that you take the opportunity to visit one of the two workers' villages in the suburbs of Shanghai. There you will learn about the social organization and operation of schools, health clinics, industrial factories, stores, and housing within an urban village. Arrangements for visiting one of the urban communes can be made in advance through your guide.

ACCOMMODATION

Peace (Heping) Hotel 20 Nanjing Tung Lu. Phone: 211244.

Located on the waterfront boulevard overlooking the Bund and Huang Po River, this attractive old European hotel offers excellent accommodation. Previously known as the Palace, it retains some of its former grandeur in the bronze-green roof, the brass fittings, and interior decor. The rooms are spacious and comfortable and the services and facilities good. The dining room on the eighth floor affords a spectacular view of the city and river below. Both Western and Chinese food is served, and the meals are excellent. Because of its location near the offices of the Chinese trade corporations, this hotel is very convenient for foreign businessmen and trade delegations as well as tourists.

Jinjiang Hotel Maoming Road. Phone: 534242.

The Jinjiang, another of Shanghai's grand old European hotels, was once part of the French concession and was formerly known as the Cathay Hotel. Situated on Maoming Road near Fuxing Park, today it is usually reserved for foreign guests of the Chinese government. The hotel's facilities include retail shops, a cafe, a post office, and telex services. The hotel dining room, located on the eleventh floor, offers an excellent menu of Chinese and Western cuisine and very pleasant service.

International (Guoji) Hotel 170 Nanjing Road West. Phone: 291010.

The Guoji is an impressive twenty-story hotel across from the Renmin (People's) Park and in the middle of the Nanjing Road shopping district. Formerly known as the Park, this hotel is the favorite of both overseas Chinese and Western visitors. The hotel rooms are spacious and well furnished, and the dining room offers excellent choices of Shanghai cuisine.

Shanghai Mansions 20 Suzhou Road North. Phone: 246260.

From the terrace of the Mansions, which are located at the junction of the Suzhou and Huang Po rivers, visitors may take in some of the best views of Shanghai. The rooms and suites of this seventeen-story hotel are spacious and elegantly furnished. The dining room on the first floor offers a wide selection of good food. A post office, barbershop, and gift store are also located in the hotel.

Overseas Chinese Hotel 104 Nanjing Road West. Phone: 294186.

Located on Nanjing Road near Renmin Park and the shopping district, this hotel is specially reserved for visiting overseas Chinese. The Chinese Travel Services has an office in this hotel for the convenience of foreign visitors.

Mao Ming Hotel, Ruijin Hotel, and *Hongqian Hotel* are three new hotels in Shanghai offering comfortable accommodation.

RESTAURANTS

Being a coastal city, Shanghai is famous for its seafood dishes, especially steamed fresh-water crab (in autumn), eel, and sweet-and-sour river fish. However, Shanghai has a limited number of restaurants that cater to foreign visitors. The best restaurants are those located in the hotels: the International, Peace, and Jinjiang and the Shanghai Mansions. It is possible to arrange special dinner banquets at these hotels. There are a number of other good eating places in the city, but reservations are advised since the capacity of the restaurants is limited.

The following restaurants have a good selection of Shanghai cooking:

Hungyen Restaurant   Fuzhou Road.

Yangzhou Restaurant   Nanjing Road.

Xinya Restaurant   Nanjing Road.

Renmin (People's) Restaurant   Nanjing Road

For those visitors who may want to try the hot, spicy cooking of Sichuan Province, I recommend the *Chengdu Restaurant,* Huai Hai Road, and the *Sichuan Restaurant,* Nanjing Road. In addition, the following two restaurants are also worth a visit:

Guangzhou Restaurant   Nanjing Road.   This restaurant specializes in Cantonese food.

Red House Western Food Restaurant   37 Shaanxi Road South. Phone: 565748.   Here visitors may enjoy a pleasant setting and excellent Western food. The emphasis is on French dishes, including steaks and crêpes suzettes.

Finally, if you want good coffee, cream cake, or ice cream, go to the Peace Hotel. Here, in the eighth-floor dining room, you will find the best coffee in China and excellent creampuffs, chocolate éclairs, and ice cream sundaes.

SHOPPING

Shanghai's main shopping district is located along Nanjing Road, where there are four department stores and numerous specialty shops. The department stores are open seven days a week from 8:00 a.m. to 9:00 p.m. and offer a wide selection of regional products from beautiful silks to local wines.

Number One Department Store   Nanjing Road.   This five-story department store is the biggest store in Shanghai. Formerly known as the Wingon Department Store, it is well stocked with regional and national products, including handicrafts, silks, silk blouses and ties, and cashmere sweaters, all of excellent quality. Here you will also find good supplies of water-color brushes, rice paper, calendars, and notebooks.

Friendship Store   33 Zhongshan Road, E 1.   Located on the Bund, between the Peace Hotel and the Shanghai Mansions, this Friendship Store was formerly the British Consulate. Today the Seaman's Club and the Shanghai Antique (Wen-wu) Store are on the same site. The Friendship Store carries a good selection of silks and cottons, as well as fine linens, tablecloths, hand-embroidered silk blouses, cashmere sweaters, fine jewelry, carvings, and ceramics.

Shanghai Antique (Wen-wu) Store   Zhongshan Road.   Located next to the Friendship Store, this shop sells jade, ivory, and bamboo carvings; old or modern paintings; ceramics; and inkstones.

ENTERTAINMENT

Shanghai Dance School   This is one of China's leading dancing schools and was established in 1960 for the purpose of cultivating and training talented young dancers. Children eleven to twelve years old are usually selected for this school after passing an entrance examination. The full term of training for each student requires six years. The school also organizes the Shanghai Ballet Troupe, which is responsible for professional staging and performances in China as well as in Western countries. In 1977, the Shanghai Ballet Troupe performed the modern ballet *The White Haired Girl* in France and Canada. Foreign visitors may have an opportunity to see one of the ballet's presentations in Shanghai, providing they are performing locally.

Shanghai Puppet Theater   Shanghai is also renowned for its troupe of puppeteers who perform all over the country. So if you have the chance to see a puppet show, don't pass up the opportunity. Usually the puppeteers entertain you with an action-packed drama or modern story such as "Little Red Star" or "The Monkey King," which are great favorites with both the local Chinese and foreign guests. The puppets are about three-quarters life size and are supported by many invisible wires and sticks. Unlike some of the European puppet shows that use recorded voices and music, the Shanghai puppet presentations are accompanied by live sound and light effects, performed by the puppeteers themselves. Since tickets for the puppet theater performances are not sold publicly, you may ask your guide to try and obtain them for you.

Shanghai Opera Theaters   Chinese opera and theater have several distinctive regional differences. Shanghai is well known for its Shaoxing and Fu Qu operatic traditions. The local performances are generally very colorful, melodic, and charming folk plays. If you wish to attend the opera while in Shanghai, you may ask your guide to obtain the tickets for you.

Puppeteers.

SHAOSHAN (Shaoshan)

Hunan Province

Shaoshan, in northwest Xiangtan County in Hunan Province, is 131 kilometers southwest of Changsha and may be easily reached by motor coach or express train. The morning express train from Changsha to Shaoshan usually includes a crowd of local Chinese travelers and foreign visitors. The three-hour ride through the Hunan countryside, past rice paddies, farmers, and their village houses, is a pleasant experience. A Taoist hermitage stands on one of the neighboring peaks. According to legend, the music of "shao" was invented there—hence the name *Shaoshan* ("Mount of Shao").

The main attraction of this small village is that it is Chairman Mao Zedong's birthplace. Mao was born into a middle peasant home in Shaoshan on December 26, 1893. At the time Shaoshan was an isolated farming village surrounded by hills covered with dense pines and cypresses. Mao attended the primary school here and worked hard on the family farm under the rule of a strict father and a loving, tolerant mother. During these impressionable years he learned much about the sufferings and needs of Chinese peasants.

PLACES TO SEE

Mao Zedong's Birthplace   Mao's family home is a Hunan farmhouse built on a hillside and surrounded by trees and rice paddies. In front of the house there is a small pond, which is filled with lovely lotus flowers in summer. Visitors may go through the house, which is maintained as it was when Mao lived there.

Mao Zedong Museum   Located in a modern building near Mao's house, the museum opened in 1967 and contains family photographs, Mao's favorite childhood books, and documentation of his revolutionary activities from 1920 to 1950.

The Old Temple of the Ancestors   This temple to the ancestors of the Mao family has been converted into a memorial hall. It was here that Mao held his first meeting to organize the peasants in Hunan in 1927.

ACCOMMODATION

Shaoshan Guesthouse   This simple two-story hotel has a limited capacity. Thus, arrangements to stay here must be made in advance.

CUISINE AND SHOPPING

Shaoshan Dining Room and Gift Shop   The dining area, which is separated from the guesthouse, is reserved for out-of-town visitors. You can get a delicious but hot Hunan meal of soup, four meat and vegetable dishes, plain rice, fresh watermelon, and tea for just a few dollars. Near the dining hall is a small gift shop where you might find a few Shaoshan crafts.

Shenyang acrobatic show.

SHENYANG (Shenyang)

Liaoning Province

Shenyang, the capital of Liaoning Province, is the largest commercial and industrial city in northeast China and currently supports a population of about three million. It is situated on the north bank of the Han River, a tributary of the Liao River, on a vast plain that was for centuries barren and sparsely populated. In the nineteenth century, however, a wealth of natural resources, of coal, oil, and iron ore, was discovered in the surrounding region, which stimulated the rapid development of Shenyang. The town became an important rail junction when the Trans-Siberian Railway was extended to the coast in 1897 and subsequently a center of contention, for by the end of the nineteenth century both the Japanese and the Russians had vested interests in the rich mineral deposits of the region. When the Chinese finally regained control of the Liaodong Peninsula after World War II, much of the city was rebuilt and expanded.

Today, in addition to being one of China's major steel-producing centers, Shenyang has become a regional base for such industries as metallurgy, chemicals, textiles, food processing, and the manufacturing of machinery and electrical equipment. Shenyang is also the provincial center for culture and education. As well as the university and several technical institutes, the city boasts one of China's most internationally renowned acrobatic companies, which operates its own school and attracts talented acrobats from all over the country.

HISTORY

Shenyang, formerly known as Mukden, was inhabited as early as the Han dynasty (206 B.C.-A.D. 220). No significant development occurred, however, until the time of the Yuan dynasty in the tenth century, when Shenyang became a major trading center for the northern nomadic tribes and herdsmen. By the beginning of the seventeenth century the Manchus had gained complete control of China's northern region, and in 1616 Nuerhachi, founder of the state of Manchuria, set himself up as the first emperor of the Qing dynasty in opposition to the Ming emperor in Beijing. Nuerhachi subsequently established his capital in Shenyang in 1625. In 1644 his successor, Abukai, brought the Ming dynasty to an end by taking Beijing. Thereafter, Shenyang remained the secondary imperial capital of the Qing emperors.

In 1895, following the first war between China and Japan, Manchuria was ceded to the Japanese, who occupied the region until 1945. Shenyang was the center of conflict between the Russians and Chinese during the Boxer Uprising, and from 1933 until the end of the war the city was important as the administrative center of the Japanese state of Manchukuo.

PLACES TO SEE

The Imperial Palace From 1625 until 1644, Shenyang was the imperial capital of the early Qing emperors. The palace, which was completed in 1637, consists of about seventy buildings and several courtyards covering an area of fifty thousand square meters. Although considerably smaller than the palace in Beijing, the Shenyang palace has some of the splendid features characteristic of imperial court architecture, such as the grand entrance flanked by two gilt dragon pillars, the octagonal throne room, and the lacquered green and yellow tile roof. The library, the Wenshu Gallery, once contained a vast collection of books, including one of the prized anthologies of Qianlong (the *Sikuquanshu*) and a voluminous historical work on China. Even though the Qing emperors moved their court to Beijing in 1644, the Shenyang Palace was still maintained as a secondary imperial residence. Collections of ceramics, paintings, carvings, jewelry, and imperial attire are presently displayed in some of the halls.

The Dongling (Eastern Tomb) Situated east of the city near the north bank of the Han River is the tomb of Nuerhachi, the first emperor of the Qing dynasty, who died in 1626, a year after establishing his imperial Manchurian state in Shenyang. He is posthumously known as Tai Zu, the Grand Emperor of the Qing.

The Imperial Tomb, Beiling (Northern Tomb) The tomb of Abukai (1592-1643), son of Nuerhachi and second Qing emperor, is situated north of the city center. Abukai's empress is also buried here. Built in the traditional imperial style of the period, the tomb is located at the end of a long processional path lined with stone sculptures of animals. The tomb is set within a complex consisting of several courtyards, which also contain the Ancestor's Pavilion and the stele pavilion. The site has been restored within the past thirty years and is now surrounded by a lovely park landscaped with trees, gardens, lakes, and pavilions.

Liaoning Exhibition Center   Located in the southern section of Shenyang, this modern Soviet-style building contains a permanent display of the local industrial products.

ACCOMMODATION

Liaoning Guesthouse   Situated on the corner of Zhongshan and Nanjing Roads near the city center and railway station, this lovely old guesthouse is the main accommodation in Shenyang for foreign visitors. The facilities include a shop, post office, and bank. The guesthouse also boasts a fine billiards room.

Liaoning Hotel   This small hotel, which is located near the Beijing park, offers pleasant and comfortable accommodation. Because of its secluded location near the park, it is very peaceful.

CUISINE

One of the popular regional dishes of the northern provinces, particularly during cold weather, is the Chinese hotpot or *huoguo*. The essential base of the *huoguo* consists of a variety of sauces and oils, which are prepared in a Chinese metal pot and heated over a charcoal burner. A selection of seafood and thinly sliced meats, such as mutton, beef, chicken, and pork, is placed in dishes at your table. You cook your own meat and then dip it into a special sauce, if you wish. Following the meat course, vegetables, bean curds, and white bean noodles are cooked in the hotpot, creating a rich and delicious broth at the end. Northern meals such as the *huoguo* are usually accompanied by steamed buns rather than rice. This tasty hotpot may be sampled at either the Nanfang or the Beifang Restaurant; both are located near the Shenyang Railway Station.

SHOPPING

The main shopping district of Shenyang is on Taiyuan Street one block east of the railway station. Here visitors will find a Friendship Store and an antique shop. In the Korean quarter in the southside of the city, one can buy a variety of Korean items, such as Korean ginseng, traditional dresses, and books in Korean. Local handicrafts include ceramics, papercuts, glass wares, and carvings of precious stones, which are available in the local department store.

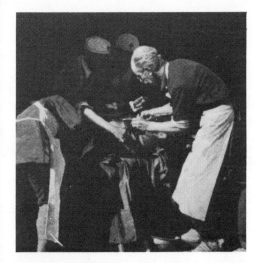

Dr. Norman Bethune.

SHIJIAZHUANG (Shihchiachuang)

Hebei Province

Shijiazhuang, one of northern China's newer cities, is situated east of the Taihang Mountains and bounded by the fertile Hebei Plain to the north, south, and east. Until the beginning of this century it was only a small village of some five or six hundred people. However, with the construction of the railway from north to south, Shijiazhuang became a major junction on the Beijing-Guangzhou line. This in turn stimulated industrial growth. Today Shijiazhuang has a population of approximately 820,000, and as well as being a major textile producer it is a manufacturing center for machinery and chemical and pharmaceutical products. Being the provincial capital of Hebei Province, it is also a center for higher education, having five universities and fifteen vocational schools. Canadian visitors will find Shijiazhuang of particular interest, for it was here that the Candian surgeon Dr. Norman Bethune came in 1938, offering his services to the Communist cause. In honor of his memory, the city's hospital has been named after him, and his tomb lies in the Martyrs' Cemetery to the west of the city.

PLACES TO SEE

Norman Bethune International Peace Hospital   In the 1930s Dr. Norman Bethune came to Shijiazhuang, and, as a contribution to the Communists, he established a hospital to serve members of the People's Liberation Army. As a result of his dedication and innovation, this small, simple, and austere hospital was developed and expanded and now is one of China's model hospitals. Today it has nineteen departments, research and training facilities, and a capacity for eight hundred hospital beds, which serve the military, the local community, and the neighboring communes.

Dr. Norman Bethune Museum   As a tribute to Dr. Bethune's devotion to the Chinese people, this museum is dedicated to preserving and displaying documents and records related to his life and services in China.

The Bethune Mausoleum   In 1952, Dr. Bethune's tomb was moved to the Martyrs' Cemetery in Shijiazhuang, where many of the army cadres and war heroes are also buried. Today, thousands of visitors come to the mausoleum to pay homage to Dr. Bethune, who is honored as a hero of modern China.

Shijiazhuang Cotton Textile Factory   Shijiazhuang is well known for its well-developed textile industry, and a visit to one of the larger factories or mills may be of interest to foreign visitors. The leading cotton textile factory here has 3,900 factory workers, of which 58 percent are female. In addition, this factory offers the workers housing, a health clinic, nursery, and day-care facilities.

ACCOMMODATION

Shijiazhuang Guesthouse   This old guesthouse is located in the southwest quarter of the city. The rooms are simple and clean. The dining room serves excellent food, including a number of local specialty dishes, which are particularly recommended.

Sculpture of Dr. Norman Bethune in museum.

SUZHOU (Soochow)

Jiangsu Province

An old Chinese proverb says: "In heaven there is paradise; on earth there are Suzhou and Hangzhou." For centuries, Suzhou has been renowned for its exceptional scenic beauty. It is often referred to as the "Venice of the East" because of the extensive network of natural waterways and canals that cross the city. In addition, there are many beautiful gardens in Suzhou, which were originally created as private retreats where scholars, artists, and the city's wealthy merchants could enjoy contemplation in tranquillity. Situated on the Yangtze delta in the south of Jiangsu Province, Suzhou is about eighty kilometers from Shanghai and a short distance west of the old Imperial Canal.

苏
州

HISTORY

Historical evidence indicates that a settlement existed on the site of Suzhou for approximately three thousand years, making it one of the oldest towns in the Yangtze Basin. During the sixth century B.C. King He Lu made Suzhou the distinguished capital of his state, the Kingdom of Wu. His tomb is located on Tiger Hill. The city was given its present name a thousand years later during the Sui dynasty. During the late fourteenth century Suzhou became the most prominent center in China for the manufacturing and trading of silk, an industry that had developed in the region during the Tang and Song dynasties. Thus, for a while, Suzhou prospered and was a popular city for the Chinese aristocracy. During the nineteenth century, however, the city fell victim to the Taiping Rebellion and later was made a concession of the Japanese. Although silk is still the most important industry in Suzhou, the city has today become a center for the production of machine tools, precision instruments, electronic equipment, and chemicals. The area surrounding the city is also rich agricultural land, which is suitable for breeding silkworms and growing such crops as rice, tea, and wheat.

PLACES TO SEE

The Cold Mountain Temple (Hanshansi) This temple, which is located to the west of town on a small canal crossed by the old Maple Bridge, was founded in the sixth century A.D. and immortalized by the poet Zhang Ji. It was named after the hermit and Buddhist poet, Han Shan, who lived here with another hermit, Shi Di, for a period during the Tang dynasty (618-907). Surrounding the temple is a brilliant saffron wall, parts of which are covered with foliage. Within the Hanshansi are several small pavilions containing statues of Buddha and his attendants. In the central hall are little statues of the two hermit monks.

The bell tower, which was constructed in the Qing dynasty, contains a reproduction of the original bell that was stolen by the Japanese during World War II. The present temple structure dates from the late Qing dynasty, since the original was destroyed in the Taiping Rebellion.

Tiger Hill (Hu Qiu) This hill, situated about three kilometers northwest of the town, is believed to be the burial site of the King of Wu, He Lu, who founded Suzhou in the sixth century B.C. According to legend, the king's tomb, with all its beautiful treasures, is protected by a giant tiger; hence the name of the hill. The tomb itself has never been unearthed, although in 1956, during restoration work on the pagoda, workers supposedly discovered the secret entrance to the ancient burial chamber. However, because of the instability of the pagoda, further excavation was not pursued.

186   *West Garden (Xi Yuan), Suzhou.*

The most prominent structure on Tiger Hill is the Tiger Pagoda or Yun Yan Si, which is the only surviving building of the original Yunyuan Temple and one of the oldest pagodas in China. Built in A.D. 961, this seven-story octagonal pagoda rises thirty-six meters from the summit and has a considerable list to the southeast. Efforts to restore and reinforce the foundations and structure of the pagoda were undertaken in 1956 and again in 1965. During repairs in 1956, a worker discovered a number of Buddhist treasures, which had been stored for centuries within the brick and stone walls of the structure. The findings included several boxes containing Buddhist sutras, prayer beads, pottery, coins, a mirror, building tools, and several small stone statues. Unfortunately, because of its fragile condition the pagoda is not open to visitors.

By following the path from the entrance gateway to the pagoda, you will encounter several other legendary spots of interest on Tiger Hill. The Stone Where Swords Are Tied, to the right, exhibits a deep crack, which, it is said, was made by the sword of King He Lu. Further along is a pool surrounded by the Thousand Stone Men, so called because the stones were believed to be the sacrificial remains of the King's courtiers and attendants.

Liu Garden   Located one kilometer west of town, this is the largest and most attractively landscaped of the Suzhou gardens. Also known as the Tarrying Garden, it was originally designed in the sixteenth century as part of a country villa owned by the Ming civic official Xu Shitai, who also owned the West Garden across the road. The Liu Garden is divided into two sections, the East and Central Gardens, and covers an area of about three hectares. It was completely rebuilt and opened to the public under its present name in 1876, having survived the ravages of the Taiping, and was again restored in 1954 after many years of neglect. The Central Garden contains a large pond surrounded by trellised walkways and bridges, while the East Garden features several halls set within a landscape of small lakes, artificial hills, and old orchards. Lovely trees, shrubs, and rockeries can be seen through the decorative windows of the halls and covered promenades. Of particular note is the lovely walled garden, which contains some very old miniature trees and potted miniature landscapes. The Chinese were often so taken with a scenic spot that they wanted some reminder of it; consequently, the pots, with their miniature shrubs, trees, lakes, and hills, were traditionally designed as re-creations of the most beautiful landscapes of ancient China.

West Garden (Xi Yuan) and Temple   Located across the road from the Liu Garden, the Xi Yuan was the garden donated to a group of Buddhists by the son of Xu Shitai. The Buddhist temple was built during the Ming dynasty. The present structure, however, dates from the late nineteenth century since the original temple was destroyed during the Taiping Rebellion. The halls contain many statues of Buddha and the Luo Hans (Buddha's disciples). The Hall of the Five Hundred Luo Hans is particularly impressive for its hundreds of statues of devotees.

Plain Man's Politics Garden (Zhou Zheng Yuan)   This attractive garden, which is situated northeast of the center of Suzhou, was originally designed in the sixteenth century as part of the private residence of a retired court censor. Because it is located on marshy ground, much of the area is devoted to small ornamental lakes, ponds, and islets. The Zhou Zheng Yuan is divided into three separate sections, which are landscaped with lovely rockeries, willow trees, lotus ponds, winding bridges, and pavilions. Several of the garden and pavilion walls are decorated with beautifully artistic sculptures and carvings. The Central Garden is the most picturesque of the three gardens. Here the Distant Fragrance Pavilion overlooking the lake offers a pleasant retreat for those who wish to sit awhile and enjoy the tranquillity and seclusion of this attractive setting. The Zhou Zheng Yuan was partially restored in 1949 and was then opened to the public in 1952.

Tiger Hill Pagoda and gardens.

Garden of the Forest of Lions (Shizilin) Originally this beautiful garden formed part of the grounds of a monastery built here in the Yuan dynasty. Designed in 1350, the garden was dedicated to the memory of the monk Zhong Feng, who had at one time lived at "Lion Cliff"; hence the name of this site. Within the garden there are four lakes divided by islets and bridges. Surrounding the lakes are several lovely pavilions and a maze of caves imaginatively incorporated into the rockeries, all of which enhance the beauty of this garden landscape. The most intriguing elements of the lion grove are the unusual rocks, taken from Lake Tai, which vaguely resemble many lions in a variety of postures. Also of interest is the stone boat set in the middle of one of the lakes.

The Suzhou Embroidery Research Institute   Suzhou is one of China's leading centers for embroidery, especially for reversible hand embroidery, in which the subject is so carefully and intricately woven that the identical image appears on both sides of the fabric. This institute supports a large staff of artists and designers who are responsible for developing new designs and techniques to improve the quality of embroidery work. In addition, young artists and apprentices are trained here. If you wish to visit the institute special arrangements should be made in advance through your guide.

The Historical Museum of Suzhou   Located on Xi Bei Street near the Temple of Gratitude (Baoensi), this museum contains a collection of treasures and artifacts dating from the Neolithic era through the Qing dynasty. The exhibits include local carved brickwork, such relics as were found in the Tiger Pagoda, early bronze and iron ware, Song pottery, and silk fabrics.

ACCOMMODATION

Suzhou Grand Hotel   Situated on Youji Road in the southeastern quarter of the town, this lovely old hotel offers reasonably good accommodation and excellent food. The garden surroundings are particularly pleasant and peaceful.

Nanlin Hotel   The newer hotel, which is situated across the road from the Suzhou Grand Hotel, is also very comfortable and reasonably priced. The rooms are spacious and quiet and the dining room offers a good selection of local specialty dishes.

CUISINE

Suzhou has an excellent reputation for its exceptional cuisine. The biggest gastronomic event here is the autumn Crab Feast, which attracts people from all over the surrounding country. The succulent fresh-water crabs, caught in a nearby lake, are usually steamed and served with a special soy and ginger sauce. Other local specialties include seafood, pickled duck, fresh vegetables, and pastries. You may sample these dishes either in your hotel dining room or at a local restaurant such as the Songhelou on Guangqian Road. If you do choose to venture out on your own, you may want to ask your guide to join you to help in ordering the meal.

SHOPPING

In your shopping ventures it is recommended that you visit some of the local shops and the People's Market as well as the Friendship Store. Since Suzhou is renowned for its silks and embroidery works, you will find an excellent selection of these products in most of the local shops. The embroidery, which is done both by hand and by machine, includes crisscross work, petit-point, and a variety of silk and woolen tapestries. Basketry, bamboo artwork, and hardwood furniture are some of the other local crafts of Suzhou. For the art and antique collector, a good selection of interesting old paintings, pottery, jade, inkstones, and seals can be found at the local Wen-wu store.

TAIYUAN (Taiyuan) Shanxi Province

Taiyuan, the capital of Shanxi Province, is located 1,296 meters above sea level at the northern end of the Taiyuan Basin. It may be reached by train from Beijing in thirteen hours. Because the basin is rich in iron ore and coal, Taiyuan developed into an important industrial area in the nineteenth century. It has been the economic, political, and cultural center of Shanxi for centuries.

PLACES TO SEE

Shanxi Provincial Museum Located in an old Taoist temple, this museum contains an interesting collection of stone carvings dating from the Western Han (206 B.C.-A.D. 24) to the Qing dynasty (A.D. 1644-1911), burial pottery and frescoes from Han tombs, and many valuable pieces of Buddhist sculpture.

Chongshansi (Temple Where Goodness Is Worshipped) Built during the Song dynasty (A.D. 960-1280), this temple is in the southeast corner of Taiyuan. The son of the first emperor of the Ming dynasty (A.D. 1368-1644) rebuilt the temple in dedication to his parents. Today the temple is still in use and houses a huge collection of Buddhist sutras.

Other Temples   *The Jinci (Temple of Jin)*, located about twenty-five kilometers southeast of Taiyuan, is the most famous temple in the large complex of temples grouped around the foot of the Xuang Weng Mountains.

The Temple of the Sacred Mother (Sheng Mu Dian) contains a statue of the seated Sacred Mother surrounded by twenty-two life-size terra-cotta statues of ladies-in-waiting, each with different clothing, gestures, and expressions and representing different ages and positions. These statues provide valuable information about the style of the Song period.

ACCOMMODATION

The Yingzi Guesthouse This comfortable hotel is located opposite the Yingzi Park and has a good view of the city.

Bingzhou Hotel The accommodations at this older hotel are poor.

SHOPPING

At the department store you will find a good selection of local crafts as well as *fen jiu*, a famous local wine from Taiyuan. The Friendship Store is situated north of the main square on Wuyi Road.

The No. 1 Carpet Factory, Tianjin.

TIANJIN (Tientsin)   Hebei Province

Tianjin, the capital of Hebei Province, is located about 50 kilometers from the Bohai Gulf and 120 kilometers southeast of Beijing. As the third largest city in China, with a population of 6.2 million people, it is a municipality directly under the central government. Possessing China's largest artificial harbor, Tianjin is a major transportation center for the coastal provinces and Beijing as well as an important international port.

Since 1900, Tianjin has rapidly expanded and become one of China's leading industrial and commercial centers, manufacturing textiles, metals, machinery, chemicals, and rubber. Other products include handicrafts, clay figurines, ceramics, and wood-block prints of New Year pictures made in Yangliuqing, a village fifteen kilometers west of Tianjin. Known as the "Carpet Capital of China," Tianjin is perhaps most famous for its beautiful carpets.

PLACES TO SEE

Park of the Three Lakes   This is one of the most popular spots for visitors because of its scenic surroundings, pavilions, and gardens. Boating is also available for visitors during the spring and summer.

The Second Workers' Cultural Palace   This impressive recreational center, built for the workers in 1954, comprises an area of 300,000 square meters. The indoor facilities include areas for playing sports, performing music, making crafts, and working on scientific projects. Outside there is an artificial lake for swimming, skating, and boating. The center is surrounded by pavilions, bridges, and gardens.

Studio of Clay Sculptor Chang   The Master Chang (1826-1908) was the first to make colored clay figurines in Tianjin. These finely designed figurines, representing characters in Chinese history, opera, and drama, have become a well-known folk art that has been carried on to the fifth generation of the Chang family.

The No. 1 Carpet Factory   A visit to the Tianjin carpet factory, which was established in 1956 by the amalgamation of fifty small and medium-sized carpet plants, can be arranged by your guide if you request a tour in advance. Today, the carpets produced in this factory are shipped to over forty countries.

Nankai University   Founded in 1919, this science and technical university has a small student body of three thousand and is famous for its excellent science programs.

Yangliuqing   Located fifteen kilometers west of Tianjin, this village has been famous for its New Year wood-block prints since the seventeenth century. These colorful prints are used to decorate the windows, doors, and rooms of Chinese homes at the beginning of the New Year and usually stay up all year long.

ACCOMMODATION

Tianjin Grand Hotel   This British-built Victorian hotel, formerly known as Astor House, is located in the old foreign settlement and is used for foreign visitors only when accommodations are scarce.

Haihe Hotel   Formerly the Victoria Hotel, this old-fashioned hotel has comfortable rooms and good food. Both the Haihe Hotel and the Tianjin Grand Hotel are within walking distance of the Friendship Store.

SHOPPING

Yilinge Antique Store   Located at 175 Liaoning Road, this shop offers a good selection of high-quality antique ceramics, paintings, precious stone carvings, seals, bronzes, and calligraphy.

Friendship Store   Visitors will find the best selection of local products and crafts—including hand-loomed carpets, carvings, ceramics, lacquerwares, and papercuts—at the Friendship Store, which is located in Jiefanglu.

Tianjin Kites   The famous artist Wei Yuantai makes kites in various shapes, designs, and colors. They make wonderful gifts for children.

Painting and calligraphy by Ming artist Shen Zhou (1427-1509).

TURPAN (Turfan)

Xinjiang Uygur Autonomous Region

Turpan, a desert oasis in the Turpan Basin, is situated about two hundred kilometers southeast of Urumqi in Xinjiang Uygur Autonomous Region. The Turpan Basin, which covers an area of fifty thousand square kilometers deep in the Tianshan Mountains, is, at 154 meters below sea level, the lowest dry depression in the world. With mountains, gorges, deserts, sand dunes, and verdant oases, it possesses some of the most spectacular natural scenery in China. This region is also rich in mineral resources, most of which can be found in the lake occupying the center of the basin.

Historically, Turpan was a significant center of commerce, culture, and religion. It was particularly important as the crossroad on the northern and southern Silk Road and for centuries attracted scholars, explorers, and adventurers from the West. Several other cities, such as Gaochang and Jiaohe, arose and flourished here through the centuries, but today most of them are merely deserted ruins. In addition, there are many ancient tombs and Buddhist caves in the Turpan Basin, which are of special interest to archaeologists and historians. The area is populated primarily by the Uighurs, who are devout Moslems. The Han and Hui peoples make up the rest of the population here.

Turpan is also renowned as the hottest spot in China, its midsummer temperatures often reaching 50° C. Since the city is not supported by any substantial river and gets almost no rainfall, it is dependent on subterranean channels and wells for most of its water supply (drinking water is taken from a small river nearby). This ancient manmade irrigation system, the *Karez*, as it is called, was built hundreds of years ago and extends over a vast area from the base of the mountains to the surrounding plains. Consequently the area is agriculturally productive, yeilding exceptionally good crops of long-fiber cotton, grain, and fruit. Turpan is particularly noted for its grapes and Hami melons, which have been grown here in abundance for centuries. The varieties of grapes cultivated here include the sweet red grape, the green grape, the Kashgar grape, and the famous white seedless grape. The latter is usually sundried, producing the very popular Xinjiang raisin. Grape vines, trellises, and vineyards abound, providing shade during the dry hot summer. Because of the great heat the farmers of this area work only at dawn and dusk, withdrawing to cool cellars dug out of the earth during the day.

PLACES TO SEE

The Ancient City of Gaochang   Situated southwest of Turpan, these ruins are all that remain of the old city of Gaochang. Founded in the first century A.D. under the Han dynasty (206 B.C.-A.D. 220), it flourished for over fifteen hundred years as one of the great centers surrounding the junction of the northern and southern Silk Road. From the fourth through the seventh centuries Gaochang was an independent state, after which it became a provincial capital under the Tang dynasty (A.D. 618-907). It was again taken as an independent kingdom in the tenth century, this time by the Uighurs. It is believed that Gaochang was finally abandoned several hundred years ago when its water supply dried up.

As a result of the arid climate in the Turpan Basin the city remains are in a remarkably good state of preservation. The existing ruins indicate that Gaochang was built according to a traditional city plan found in several other ancient Chinese cities, such as Beijing. Covering about two square kilometers, it consists of an inner and outer city and palace, all of which are encompassed by a thick tamped-earth wall with twelve gates. Gaochang also possesses some old temples and a Persian-style monastery that dates from the fifth century A.D. Among the temple remains there are some interesting Buddhist statues and frescoes, which are of particular interest to archaeologists. Other ruins include cave dwellings and workshops. Northwest of Gaochang are four hundred tombs dating from 273 to 772.

Jiaohe (Yar Kotho)   This ancient city, also deserted and in ruins, is situated on the edge of two dry riverbeds just west of Turpan. Its name, which means "Confluence of the *Yars* or Streams," indicates that Jiaohe was once one of the green oases of the region. Although smaller than Gaochang, it too has a large wall, which is still intact. In addition, several ancient tombs have been discovered here.

The Turpan Grape Commune   This commune, which is located in the center of the region south of the Flaming Mountains, produces an abundance of cereals, cotton, and fruit. The sunny, hot, and dry weather here is particularly excellent for grapes, which are grown on trellises covering the pathways. Visitors will be served some of the commune's best fruit and grapes after a tour of the surrounding farmland.

The Turpan Bazzaar   This is an open market that offers a variety of local fresh and dried fruit, cottons, silks, embroidery, and local crafts.

ACCOMMODATION

Visitors staying in Turpan are accommodated in a "caravanserai" where rooms are very simple yet clean. Because the guesthouse has thick brick walls and vaulted ceilings, it is pleasantly cool.

Women of Xinjiang.

URUMQI (Urumchi)

Xinjiang Uygur Autonomous Region

Urumqi is the capital of Xinjiang Uygur Autonomous Region. The city is about 3,270 kilometers from Beijing, or a five-hour flight.

Comprising 16 percent of the total land area, Xinjiang is the largest region in the country. Located in northwestern China, it is bordered by Mongolia, the Soviet Union, Afghanistan, Pakistan, and India. Of its total population of 11 million, the majority are Uighurs, a Central Asian people of colorful costumes and cultural traditions. Other prominent minority residents are the Han, Kazakhs, Hui, and Mongolians.

Xinjiang manufactures steel, oil, sugar, chemicals, and tractors. Its most famous oil field is at Karamai, near Urumqi. Xinjiang's major crops are cotton and wheat, as well as maize, sorghum, millet, and various fruits. Although the province's mineral sources are largely undeveloped, Hetian (Khotan) in Xinjiang is a famous source of jade. There are eight universities, including two medical colleges, in Xinjiang.

PLACES TO SEE

Lao-Min City Located west of Urumqi, this town was originally a division of the Qing dynasty. Today it is known for its agricultural institute. The local specialties, mutton and assorted wheat cakes, can be bought at street stands.

The People's Park This park, located on the west bank of the Urumqi River, has a scenic lake, bridges, and lovely pavilions surrounded by gardens.

The People's Theater Since ancient times, Xinjiang has been known as the "Land of Songs and Dances." The music and dances of the Uighurs are regularly performed at the theater, which is constructed in the neoclassical Russian style.

Urumqi Carpet Factory Visitors may make arrangements to see the carpet factory and watch how carpets are made on big framed looms.

乌鲁木齐

Tianchi (Lake of Heaven) Located about one hundred kilometers northeast of Urumqi, the Tianchi is almost two thousand meters above sea level, halfway up to the misty Bogda Feng (Peak of God). In summer, the meadow is green and the snow-capped mountains cast their images on the crystal clear water. Boat tours on the lake can be arranged.

Commune in Baiyangge (Valley of the White Poplars) This horse-breeding commune is a three hour drive from Urumqi. Here the Kazakhs, who are both skillful horse breeders and excellent horsemen, demonstrate their riding skills for visitors. Then guests are invited into the *yurts* (felt tents about eight meters in diameter used as living units) to eat fermented mare's milk, sour-milk bread, hard cheese, and boiled mutton.

ACCOMMODATION

Urumqi Guesthouse This fairly comfortable hotel was originally built for Russian consultants. The dining room serves both traditional Chinese food and the local specialties, boiled mutton and lamb kebabs. The menu is quite limited.

SHOPPING

Visitors may find good buys in carpets at the local stores. Furs and hides are inexpensive, but the selection is not great. Colorful hats, embroidered vests, leather boots, and jewelry are good choices.

Vine-shaded path, Urumqi.

Wuhan Iron and Steel Company.

WUHAN (Wuhan) Hubei Province

Wuhan, the capital of Hubei Province, is really three towns—Hankou, Hanyang, and Wuchang—combined into one. Situated at the confluence of the Han and Yangtze rivers, Wuhan was founded in the third century as the capital of the state of Wu and has been an important city in Hubei Province through the centuries.

Hankou was a fishing village until the mid-nineteenth century, when foreign firms began establishing offices there as a result of the Treaty of Nanjing (1861). After the railroad was built in the early 1900s, Hankou rapidly became an important industrial city. Hanyang was founded during the Sui dynasty (A.D. 581-618) and became a center for political reform at the end of the nineteenth century. The oldest of the three municipalities, Wuchang was also the cradle of the Communist revolution; in 1911 the first battle of the revolution was won there, and later the Central Institute of the Peasant Movement was established in Wuchang. In 1957 the building of the Yangtze River Bridge made Wuhan the center of transportation, industry, agriculture, and trade.

PLACES TO SEE

Hankou   Tourist attractions in Hankou include the Handicrafts Display Center, Sun Yat-sen (Chungshan) Park, the Institute of Medicine, and the Wuhan Zoo.

Hanyang Lotus Lake (Lienhua Hu)   This is a small but charming lake near the Yangtze River Bridge. The area around the lake was once a suburb for retired officials.

Hanyang Tortoise Hill (Kueishan)   This is one of the very few sizeable hills in Wuhan. Visitors may see pavilions, caverns, and a former monastery here.

Workers' Cultural Palace—Hanyang   Located in a park containing the Terrace of the Ancient Lute, the palace may be of interest to visitors.

Hubei Provincial Museum (Hubei Buowuguan)—Wuchang   This museum records the historical development of the province and displays art treasures from recent archaeological finds in the area. The exhibit includes a collection of pottery dating from the Three Kingdoms dynasty (A.D. 220-265) to the Qing dynasty (A.D. 1644-1911) found in the tombs around Wuhan.

Snake Hill (Sheshan)—Wuchang   The highest point in Wuchang, Snake Hill offers an excellent view of the "three cities."

The Central Institute of the Peasant Movement   Located in the northwest corner of Wuchang, the institute was founded to train and organize the peasants. Mao Zedong was the director in 1927. Today the institute is used as a middle school, but Mao's former living quarters and some classrooms have been preserved and are open to the public.

East Lake (Donghu)—Wuchang   This lovely lake in Wuchang is surrounded by a park that contains many gazebos and pavilions, including a pavilion dedicated to the ancient patriotic poet Qu Yuan.

Educational Institutions   Wuhan has several institutions of higher education, including the Physical Education Institute, the Survey and Cartography College, the Central China Teachers College, and the Minorities Institute. Wuhan University is especially popular with tourists.

ACCOMMODATION

The Victor Hotel (Shenli Fandian)   This older hotel is located on Shenli Road in the former French sector of Hankou. The rooms are spacious and comfortable, and the food is good.

The Wuhan Hotel   Because this hotel is located across from the Friendship Store on Jiefang Road, it is convenient for shopping.

CUISINE

Visitors may want to try some of the local specialties, including fresh fish and wild duck from East Lake and meats and vegetables flavored with chili. All of the local cuisine can be ordered at your hotel dining room.

WUXI (Wusih) Jiangsu Province

The town of Wuxi in Jiangsu Province is a popular scenic resort on the Tai Hu (Great Lake). Situated in the lower Yangtze Valley on the Grand Canal, it is a major transportation junction and can easily be reached by train from Shanghai, 120 kilometers to the southeast. The name *Wuxi* means "Without Tin." This refers to the local Xishan tin mine that was discovered in the Zhou dynasty (1122-770 B.C.) and exhausted in the third century A.D. under the Han dynasty.

The area surrounding Wuxi was inhabited as early as the Shang dynasty (1766-1122 B.C.). However, the town was not officially founded until the Han dynasty (206 B.C.-A.D. 220), at which time it became a regional state capital. Even with the building of the Grand Canal, which was completed in A.D. 610, the town did not expand to any great extent. Rather, it remained a relatively small market town, of no historical significance, well into this century.

Apart from silk, which has been produced here for over fifteen hundred years, Wuxi had developed very little industry prior to the 1930s. Since then, the town has rapidly developed and, with a population of 700,000, it is now a manufacturing center for high technology equipment. Its industrial output includes precision tools, electronic components, diesel engines, and a variety of machinery. In addition, the silk factories, which were established in the nineteenth century, have been extensively renovated and expanded. Conse-quently, the overall production of silk now includes weaving, dyeing, and printing as well as separating and spinning. There are also several light industrial goods and folk arts and crafts produced here, the most celebrated of which are the Huishan pottery figurines.

Wuxi is known as the "Land of Fish and Rice." The mild climate, abundant rainfall, and rich fertile land make excellent conditions for growing rice and cotton and breeding fish and silkworms, the principal market products cultivated in the Wuxi communes.

There are relatively few historical sites in Wuxi. The main attractions therefore are the lake and the beautifully landscaped parks and gardens.

PLACES TO SEE

Tai Hu Boat Trip   The Tai Hu is one of the five largest fresh-water lakes in China. Surrounded by low green hills and fed by four rivers, it covers an area of about 2,250 square kilometers and contains over ninety islands. A boat trip, which usually takes a few hours either in the morning or in the afternoon, offers a spectacular view of the Tai Hu and some of the lakeshore islands. Square-sailed fishing boats passing through the mists evoke an atmosphere often depicted in traditional Chinese landscape painting. During your excursion the boat will pass by Three Hill Island and then stop at the Yuantouzhu or Turtle Head. This latter island, so called because its shape resembles the head of a turtle, is located between a smaller lake, the Li Hu, and the Tai Hu near the northeastern shore. Although referred to as an island, the Yuantouzhu is actually a peninsula and is connected to the shore by the Baojie Bridge. The island features several lovely walkways, gardens, pavilions, and teahouses. On the headland, near the lighthouse, is a rock bearing the engraved characters of the island's name. From the summit of the Yuantouzhu you can get a magnificent panoramic view of the lake and surrounding hills.

Plum Garden (Meiyuan)   This garden, which is situated on a hill west of the town, is noted for its many beautiful plum trees; hence its name. In the spring the slopes are a mass of white blossoms, while in autumn the garden abounds with fragrant sweet osmanthus flowers. The resulting specialty, honeyed plums flavored with osmanthus blossoms, is considered a great delicacy of Wuxi.

Huishan Clay Figurine Workshop   Wuxi is renowned for its clay statuettes, which have been produced here since the Ming dynasty (A.D. 1368-1644). Using the special black clay from the Huishan, the local artists combined their unique style and technique to create miniature theatrical and operatic characters. Gradually the designs were expanded. Today a diversity of pottery pieces and figures are produced, depicting modern as well as traditional themes. In this workshop, you may observe craftsmen doing two types of clay work: the molded gypsum objects, which are plain and practical in style; and the traditional hand-shaped figurines, which are modeled in a variety of lively and expressive postures. Some of the most delightful examples of this Huishan folk art are the miniature Chinese figures of children of the minority nationalities. A small shop is located within the factory, where visitors may buy some of the clay figurines.

Li Garden   Located on the north shore of the Li Hu, this classical Chinese garden is known for its lovely ornamental landscape. It features a variety of trees and rare flowers, which are set within a picturesque arrangement of ponds, arched bridges, promenades, pavilions, and rockeries. A covered walkway, with windows carved out in the shape of flowers, leads to the miniature pagoda and the midlake pavilion.

Xihui Park This park is situated between the Xi and Hui hills on the western outskirts of Wuxi. The Dragon Light Pagoda at the summit of the Xishan dates from the Ming dynasty (A.D. 1368-1644) and commands an excellent view of the lake and town. It was from this hill that tin was mined during the first century A.D. Atop the Huishan are the remains of a temple that was built in A.D. 420. The Huishan Spring at the base of this hill has been renowned for centuries for the purity of its water. Believed to be one of the oldest springs in China, it was made famous by a ninth century writer who praised the spring for producing the most excellent water for making tea. The Xihui Park also contains the Jichang Garden, which was built in the early sixteenth century for a retired court scholar of the Ming dynasty. Situated between the Xishan and Huishan, it features the traditional winding stream and pond surrounded by galleries, pavilions, and unusual rockeries. One gets the impression that this small walled garden is much larger than it really is. This is an illusion created by the clever design, which suggests that the exterior hills and landscape are incorporated as part of the garden. The rest of the park is pleasantly landscaped and contains several teahouses.

ACCOMMODATION

While there are four hotels in Wuxi—the Chaoyang, the Wuxi, the Tai Hu, and the Li Hu—most foreign visitors usually stay at the lakeside Tai Hu or Li Hu Hotel.

Tai Hu Hotel This hotel, which is situated on the northeast shore of the lake, offers very pleasant accommodation within an attractive garden setting. The rooms are modern, spacious, and air-conditioned, and the services and facilities include a post and telegraph office, a retail shop, and a dining room. The latter serves excellent meals, including many of the local specialty dishes.

Li Hu Hotel Located south of the Tai Hu Hotel near the Baojie Bridge, this hotel overlooks the smaller lake Li Hu. The accommodation is much the same as in the Tai Hu Hotel, with modern and comfortable rooms and facilities and a good restaurant.

CUISINE

The local specialties of Wuxi include fresh seafood such as crisp eel, crab, and shrimp, braised spare-ribs, and fresh fruits such as plums and local watermelon. Providing you can speak the language or have your guide accompany you, it can be an adventure to try some of the local restaurants. However, as most of these do not cater to foreigners, it is probably best to sample the local cuisine at your hotel dining room.

SHOPPING

In addition to the Huishan clay figurines you will find a good selection of local handicrafts and products such as silk and silk items, linen embroidery, and Yixing pottery in the Wuxi stores.

Return Hall of Chen Jiageng, Xiamen.

XIAMEN (Amoy) <small>Fujian Province</small>

Xiamen, a famous port on the west coast of Xiamen Island, lies between the People's Republic of China and Taiwan on the southern coast of Fujian Province. Since 1956, the island has been connected to the mainland by a wide, five-kilometer-long causeway that is used for trains, motor vehicles, and pedestrians.

Since 1949, Xiamen has been gradually rebuilt and modernized. About three hundred manufacturing industries export textiles, food, chemicals, and marine products to seventy-four countries all over the world. Its cod-liver oil, canned fruit, and photographic and marine products are particularly well known.

Xiamen's scenic location also makes it a popular tourist resort and a beautiful place to live. This subtropical city is the home of many returned overseas Chinese, who make up about half of its 200,000 people.

HISTORY

Xiamen Island has had a long and romantic history. Because of its shape, which resembles a flying egret, Xiamen has been called the Island of the Egret, and at one time the island was indeed inhabited solely by birds.

Besides having been a commercial port for centuries, the island was once the stronghold of the patriotic Ming general Zheng Chenggong, who fought the Dutch across the Taiwan Strait during the seventeenth century. Zheng Chenggong also held the Formosa Strait for many years, fighting against the Qing rulers.

Following the Opium War, the 1842 Treaty of Nanjing brought Westerners to the island after Xiamen was declared an open port. The European
presence on Gulangyu Island off Xiamen introduced bars, opium dens, and
brothels into the area, as well as trade, but left Xiamen itself poor until the
founding of the People's Republic in 1949.

PLACES TO SEE

Ten Thousand Stone Park   Located in the northeastern part of Xiamen,
this formerly barren, rocky hill is now a lovely park, renowned for its historical
relics and its tropical and subtropical trees and flowers. It also features a lake,
with a palm-covered island, and several lotus flower ponds, which are
surrounded by bamboo-lined paths, cedar trees, and green lawns. Situated at the
entrance is the Xiamen Martyrs' Monument.

South Pu Tuo Temple   One of China's famous ancient monasteries, the
South Pu Tuo Temple was built during the Five Dynasties period (A.D.
907-960) at the foot of Wulao Peak. The temple survived damage during the
Ming dynasty (A.D. 1368-1644) and was rebuilt during the Qing dynasty (A.D.
1644-1911). Since 1949, the temple has been renovated and is now preserved as
a historical monument for public display.

South Pu Tuo was built in the southern Fujian style. Carved flowers,
dragons, and figures adorn the beams and eaves of the main hall. Three
lacquered Buddhas, each one over three meters high, and a seated Guanyin
(Goddess of Mercy), are the main attractions of the temple. The eight-meter-
high Hall of Compassion, an octagonal wooden building with a three-tiered
roof decorated with flying dragons, stands next to the temple. Visitors may
sample the temple's famous vegetarian cuisine, which was developed by the
monks of the South Pu Tuo Temple.

Xiamen University   Situated on a peninsula southeast of Wulao Hill, this
well-known university owes much of its fine reputation to the work of Chen
Jiageng, an overseas Chinese who did much to promote cultural exchange and
education here. It has ten departments, thirty specializations, and two scientific
research institutes.

Overseas Chinese Museum   This museum, which was founded in 1959,
contains collections of bronzes, pottery, and handicrafts dating from the Ming
and Qing dynasties. In addition, the museum also has a photo exhibition
showing the lifestyles of overseas Chinese around the world.

Gulangyu Island   Situated south of Xiamen, this island is also a part of the
city and at one time was held by foreign concessions. Also known as the
"Garden on the Sea," Gulangyu is a pleasantly quiet and picturesque spot,
abounding in beautiful flowers, which bloom all year round. The highest point
of the island is Sunshine Peak atop Longtou Hill. Here one can see the remains
of the platform and castle from which the famous Ming general, Zheng
Chenggong, oversaw the training of his naval troops. Below is the long soft
sandy beach. Gulangyu is also renowned for its lovely music. During the
evening you can always hear the sound of voices and instruments, and
frequently there are concerts and festivals.

Bell Tower, Xi'an.

XI'AN (SIAN) Shaanxi Province

Xi'an, the capital of Shaanxi Province in northwest China, is one of the most ancient cities in the country. At one time it was renowned as the largest and most splendid imperial city in the world and, over a period of some two thousand years, it was the national capital of eleven dynasties. Situated in a fertile valley between the Wei River, a tributary of the Huang He, and the Shaanxi Plateau to the north and the Qinling Mountains to the south, it has long been an important political, commercial, cultural, and transportation center. Today, with a population of two and a half million, it has become one of China's model inland industrial centers, producing chemicals, textiles, fertilizers, plastics, machinery, and electrical equipment. In addition, Xi'an is surrounded by rich irrigated agricultural land, which yields a variety of crops, the most important being cotton and wheat. This magnificent historical city possesses a wealth of interesting archaeological sites. It can be reached by air or rail from Beijing, which is 900 kilometers directly northwest (by rail the distance is somewhat longer at 1,165 kilometers), or from Shanghai, which is 1,500 kilometers to the southeast.

HISTORY

Xi'an is considered to be one of the cradles of Chinese civilization. Evidence from the excavations at Banpo Village in the suburbs of the city indicates that the surrounding Wei Valley was inhabited by the Yangshao culture as early as 6000 B.C. Some five thousand years later several kings of the Zhou dynasty (1122-770 B.C.) established their various capitals just a few kilometers north of the present-day site.

Xi'an, however, was not officially founded as a national capital until the third century B.C., when China was unified under the emperor Qin Shi Huang Di (259-210 B.C.). At this time the city was enlarged and a palace was begun south of the existing settlement. The capital subsequently fell to the Hans (206 B.C.-A.D. 220), who destroyed the former imperial residences and moved the capital once again to the north. Xi'an was then known as Chang'An and developed as a major commercial and cultural center at the eastern end of the Silk Route.

Xi'an then declined in importance until it was revived again at its present site in the sixth century A.D. under the Sui dynasty (A.D. 589-618). Thereafter the city flourished until the fall of the Tang dynasty (A.D. 618-907). Throughout this latter period Xi'an was a magnificent imperial capital unparalleled anywhere in the rest of Asia. With a population of over a million it attracted foreign merchants, scholars, and ambassadors from as far away as Europe.

Although Xi'an was never to regain its former glory, it was chosen as the site of the imperial palace of a son of Emperor Hong Wu in the early Ming dynasty (A.D. 1368-1644). During this period Xi'an was rebuilt on a more modest scale. Under the Qing dynasty (A.D. 1644-1911) the city became a strategic military fortress of the Manchus. Xi'an nevertheless remained a relatively isolated provincial city until this century, experiencing very little of the revolutionary unrest of the 1920s and 1930s, with the exception of the "Xi'an Incident" of 1936. This particular episode involved Chiang Kaishek who, while visiting the city, was arrested by a local warlord and forced to make an agreement with the Communists that they would lay their differences aside and join forces to fight the Japanese.

Since the 1930s, Xi'an has developed quite dramatically as a result of the government's concerted attempts to modernize and industrialize the city.

PLACES TO SEE

Shaanxi Provincial Museum   This museum, which was formerly a Confucian temple, is situated in the southern part of the walled city. Its exceptionally fine collection includes artifacts from the ancient Neolithic period through the Ming dynasty. For further information about the Shaanxi Museum, refer to the section entitled "Major Museums of China."

Banpo Village and Museum   The eight-thousand-year-old Neolithic village of Banpo, which is located just east of Xi'an, was discovered during construction work in 1953. In addition to the village site, 30,000 square meters of which is under a protective roof, visitors can see the ancient artifacts and archaeological remains that were unearthed during subsequent excavations. This museum is discussed in further detail in the section entitled "Major Museums of China."

Huaqing Hot Springs (Huaqing Gong)   For centuries these lovely hot springs in the Lishan Hills to the east of Xi'an were popular with the kings and emperors of ancient China. From the eighth century B.C. through the eighth century A.D. many imperial residences and resort palaces were built around the springs, the last of which was the pleasure palace Huaqing Gong, built for the Tang emperor Xuan Zong. With the fall of the Tang dynasty, this palace and many of the other imperial buildings were abandoned and destroyed. However, in the tenth century a Taoist monastery was constructed from the ruins of the Huaqing Gong.

Since the beginning of this century the springs, which have an average temperature of 40° C, have been used as health spas. It was at the Huaqing Hot Springs that Chiang Kaishek was staying when he was captured and arrested in 1936. Today the hot springs, which are surrounded by beautiful gardens and pavilions, are open to the public and attract visitors from all over the country.

Qin Shi Huang Di Tomb   The surrounding valley and hills to the north and east of Xi'an, stretching as far as the Huang He, abound with the remains of ancient capital sites, palaces, and tombs from the Zhou through Tang dynasties. Although they are of great archaeological interest, the most impressive site is the third century B.C. tomb of Emperor Qin, first emperor of unifed China, which was discovered in 1974. This spectacular tomb is situated about thirty kilometers to the east of Xi'an. The museum on location contains many of the treasures and relics unearthed during recent excavations. This museum is also mentioned in further detail in the section entitled "Major Museums of China."

Art Center of Huxian Peasant Paintings   The town of Huxian, which is located southwest of Xi'an, is renowned as a center of peasant painting. This particular genre of Chinese art, which emerged in the 1950s, was created by a group of local amateur painters who were inspired to give artistic expression to the communal life of rural China. Perceiving their daily activities, the land, and the people in simple terms, they are known for their bold, colorful paintings that are somewhat idealized portraits of modern rural China. The tradition of Huxian peasant painting is still active, with many of the artists' works being exhibited internationally.

Bell Tower   This tower, which is situated in the center of Xi'an, was rebuilt on its present site in 1384, during Ming reconstruction of the city. Originally designed to hold a large bell, the thirty-six-meter structure consists of a two-story wooden structure set on a broad square brick base. Restored in the eighteenth century, many of its fittings and decorative motifs date from the late Qing period. While the bell is no longer in place in the tower, the building still serves as a historical landmark of the city. From the second floor balcony one can get an excellent view of the city. The Drum Tower, just to the west, is of similar design and also dates from the Ming dynasty.

Big Wild Goose Pagoda (Dayan Ta)   In A.D. 647, the Tang emperor Gao Zong had the Temple of Great Goodwill built on the site of a former temple of the Sui dynasty. The pagoda, which dates from A.D. 652, was then built to house the large collection of Buddhist sutras that had been brought from India and translated into Chinese by the famous pilgrim monk Xuang Zang. Thereafter the pagoda was renowned as a symbol of Buddhism and attracted poets, scholars, and disciples from all over Asia. Many left their mark here in the form of engraved stone steles and tablets, which can be seen on both the interior and the exterior of the pagoda.

Three-color glazed pottery of the Tang dynasty, Xi'an.

Shortly after being built, however, the five-story brick structure fractured, and, in the process of restoration, two additional stories were constructed above the existing pagoda. Over the centuries it was destroyed and rebuilt several times. The present pagoda, which stands sixty-four meters high, dates from the Ming dynasty, although many of the tablets are from the original Tang pagoda.

When the ancient imperial capital extended over a much larger area during the Tang period, the temple and pagoda were part of the city. Today, however, they stand several kilometers south of the walled city. The summit of the pagoda, reached by a winding staircase, commands a magnificent view of the city and surrounding valley.

Small Wild Goose Pagoda (Xiaoyan Ta)   This pagoda, which is located just outside the South Gate (Nanpilu) of Xi'an, was formerly part of the seventh century Buddhist Daqingfu Temple. Built in A.D. 706 to house the Buddhist texts brought from India by the monk Yi Jing, the pagoda originally stood fifteen stories high. However, over the past twelve hundred years it has suffered structural damages as a result of many earthquakes. The most severe earthquake, in 1555, created a large fracture, which caused the two upper stories to collapse. The original pagoda still stands, and although it has been restored, it remains a thirteen-story structure. Today it is surrounded by an attractive garden.

ACCOMMODATION

People's Hotel (Renmin Tasha)   This large austere complex, located on Dongxin Street northeast of the city, is currently the only hotel in Xi'an for foreign guests. The rooms are spacious yet simple, and the dining room food ordinary and plain. The hotel facilities include a post office, bank, barber shop, and retail gift shop.

RESTAURANTS

Xi'an Fan Zhuang (Xi'an Restaurant) This modern restaurant is situated on Dongda Street in the new city square of Xi'an. It offers a broad selection of northern Chinese dishes, many of which are reputed to have been passed down from the Han and Tang dynasties. Its specialties include Callabash chicken, stewed quail, fish braised in milk soup, black moss with egg, assorted peacock dishes, and a wide variety of steamed dumplings and fried buns.

SHOPPING

Local handicrafts include shell and feather paintings, carved lacquerware, enamelware, basketry and wickerwork, pottery, stone rubbings, and cotton products. These items can be found in the department store and the shops on Dong Dajie Street. In addition Xi'an's local Wen-wu Store offers a good selection of antiques.

Qin Shi Huang Di Tomb.

Pottery figurines excavated from the tomb.

Harvest time, Xining.

XINING (Sining) Qinghai Province

Xining, which means "Peace of the West," is the capital and main agricultural center of mountainous Qinghai Province. Situated east of the Koko Nor (Blue Sea) in the upper Huang He River Basin, it can be easily reached by air, road, or rail from Langzhou in Gansu Province to the east. While hardy crops such as wheat are grown in this northern province, it is primarily a livestock-breeding region. The communes surrounding Xining are noted for breeding the highly prized Qinghai horses. Xining is also renowned for its exceptionally fine wools. A small provincial city, Xining is best seen on a day trip from Langzhou.

PLACES TO SEE

Taur Si Temple This huge Buddhist compound is situated about twenty-five kilometers from Xining. Also known as the Jinta Si (Golden Brick Temple), this mountain sanctuary dates from A.D. 1560 of the Ming dynasty and contains approximately one thousand temples and halls.

Qutan Temple Located east of Xining near the town of Ledu, this temple dates from the Hong Wu period (1368-1399) of the Ming dynasty. The largest of the four main halls is the Long Gao Dian. Built in 1427 it contains two large bronze incense burners, which were imperial gifts presented by Emperor Xuande. On the veranda of the Jin Gang Dian Hall are four statues of Buddha. The temple was restored as early as 1644 during the Qianlong period.

Wool Factory and Horse-breeding Commune Visitors may enjoy a tour of these centers, which can be arranged through your tour guide.

ACCOMMODATION

If visitors decide to stay in Xining they may be accommodated at the Xining Guesthouse, a small yet hospitable hotel in the center of town.

YAN'AN (Yenan)   Shaanxi Province

Yan'an, which is located about 270 kilometers north of Xi'an in Shaanxi Province, is renowned for its recent historical and political importance as the stronghold of the early Communist Party. Today, it is primarily an agriculturally based market center, supporting a population of about 60,000. Surrounded by terraced hills on the banks of the Yan River, Yan'an is somewhat isolated and can only be reached by plane from either Xi'an to the south or from Taiyuan to the northeast. The principal sites of interest here are those which are associated with the revolution and Communist occupation.

It was in Yan'an that the Communist Eighth Route Army, led by Mao Zedong, ended their two-and-a-half-year Long March in 1936. From then until 1947, the town was the headquarters of the Communist Party. During this period the Communist leaders redeveloped their former policies and strategies in the form of the Yan'an Legacy, which won them the support of the rural peasantry.

The Red Army eventually gathered some fifty thousand additional volunteers as a result of Communist campaigns directed from Yan'an. Despite the Nationalists' persistence in bombing the town throughout this period, the Communists managed to sustain their political and military strength, holding on to this natural fortress until forced out in 1947.

PLACES TO SEE

Museum of the Revolution   This large museum contains a historical exhibition of the revolutionary activities of the "Yan'an Period" (1936-1947). In addition to the displays, there are several statues of Mao Zedong and his colleagues Zhu De and Zhou Enlai.

Residence and Headquarters of the Communist Party   During the ten years in which the Communists occupied Yan'an, Mao Zedong and many of the leaders were forced to move their accommodation and headquarters as a result of Nationalist bomb attacks. Quite often they sought refuge in the surrounding hills along with the local residents. Visitors today may visit the caves where they stayed, which are situated at Fenghuang Hill, Wangjiaping, Yangjialing, and Zaoyuan. In addition, one can see the replica of the original Assembly Hall at Wangjiaping where the Party Congress was held in 1945.

Baota (Precious Pagoda)   Originally this pagoda formed part of a temple that was built in the tenth century of the Song dynasty. The Baota is also the symbol of Yan'an and is visible from all points in the town.

ACCOMMODATION

Yan'an Hotel   This hotel, the only one in town serving foreign visitors, offers very plain and simple accommodation.

YANGTZE GORGES
(Yangtze Gorges) Sichuan Province

The three famous gorges of the Yangtze River—the Chutang, Wuhsia, and the Xiling gorges—encompass an area of 189 kilometers between Chongqing, Sichuan Province, and Wuhan, Hubei Province. Visitors may take one of the cruises through these magnificent gorges, where spectacular mountains tower over the turbulent water. Each of the "East is Red" steamers accommodates approximately eight hundred passengers. There are five classes; foreigners are usually put into a second class cabin. Each steamer has two dining rooms and, on the top deck, a lounge.

The trip downriver, from Chongqing to Wuhan, takes two and a half days, while the trip upriver, from Wuhan to Chongqing, takes three days. The cruise usually starts early in the morning, the boat slipping past junks, sampans, freighters, and villages located high on the banks. On the second day of the downstream cruise, the boat reaches the first gorge, Chutang, where the rocky walls rise sharply to heights of five hundred meters. Next comes Wuhsia, a magnificent thirty-five kilometer-long gorge surrounded by twelve peaks with such mystical names as Witches' Mountain, Flying Phoenix, Ascending Clouds, Precious Stone Castle, and Fairy Peak. The third gorge, Xiling, is famous for its spectacular scenery and spiky reefs. The steamer stops at several villages along the way, where you might want to buy some local handicrafts, fruit, wine, or tea.

If you are on a prearranged CP Air group tour that includes the Yangtze River cruise, you can simply enjoy the spectacular scenery without worrying about the details of arranging the trip. If you are traveling privately with a small group or on your own, you must make reservations for the cruise through the China International Travel Services.

YANGZHOU (Yangchow)

Jiangsu Province

Yangzhou is located in northern Jiangsu Province on the north bank of the Yangtze River near its confluence with the Grand Canal. Although it is a transportation center, Yangzhou has very little industry. With a population of 280,000, the city covers an area of sixty-seven square kilometers.

Yangzhou was an important port in ancient China. The Grand Canal, which is 1,782 kilometers long and links North and South China, was built by Emperor Yang Di during the Sui dynasty (A.D. 581-618). During this period, Yangzhou was known as Jiangdu, the "River Capital."

Visitors may see relics of the famous poets Li Bai, Ouyang Xiu, and Su Shi in Yangzhou. Because of its scenic beauty, Yangzhou has always attracted artists and was the home of the famous Qing painters, the "Eight Eccentrics of Yangzhou." Marco Polo served as an official here during the Yuan dynasty (1280-1368). Behao Aldin, an Arabian missionary, preached Islamism here in the late Southern Song dynasty (1127-1279) and was buried here in Yangzhou.

PLACES TO SEE

The Less West Lake   Yangzhou is renowned for its parks and gardens. The Less West Lake, which is located in a park at the northern end of the city, was dredged during the Sui (581-618) and Tang dynasties (618-907) and is one of the most attractive and serene spots in Yangzhou. The park also contains a lovely temple and a bridge dating from the eighteenth century.

Wenfeng Pagoda   Situated by the Grand Canal, this ancient landmark is a lovely sight by moonlight.

Jian Zhen Memorial Hall   Jian Zhen was an outstanding Buddhist monk of the Tang dynasty who crossed the sea to Japan and promoted cultural exchange between China and Japan. Born in Yangzhou, he was highly respected both in Japan and China for his efforts, and in 1974 a memorial hall was built in Yangzhou to honor him. The main hall is designed in the style of the chief hall of the Toshodai Temple of Nara in Japan. Today there are special exchanges between Yangzhou and Nara in memory of Jian Zhen.

He Yuan Garden   Visitors will enjoy the He Yuan's beautiful Tai Hu rockeries and romantic pavilions.

SHOPPING

Yangzhou is well known for its arts and crafts, especially its woodcarvings, wooden combs, papercuts, and paintings. The local stores are a good source of carvings, pottery, and inlaid woodwork. Antique collectors might find some surprises in the local Wen-wu Store.

Bowl from the Yixing Pottery Studio.

YIXING (Yising) Jiangsu Province

Yixing is situated in Jiangsu Province about fourteen kilometers west of the Tai Hu (Lake Tai) in one of China's richest areas, the "Land of Fish and Rice." The city, which was founded during the Han dynasty (206 B.C.-A.D. 220), has been famous for centuries for its reddish brown pottery. Scholars, poets, and tea drinkers alike have praised the Yixing teapots for their excellent quality. In addition, Yixing is renowned for its two karst caverns, which make it one of the popular sidetrips on the tour of the Grand Canal.

PLACES TO SEE

Shanjuan Caverns It is said that these fantastic caves were named after the poet Shanjuan, who moved south from the Huang He River valley some four thousand years ago to live in seclusion here. Covering an area of about five thousand square meters, they consist of several individual caverns—the upper, middle, lower, and water caverns.

Just inside the entrance to the middle cavern is the enormous seven-meter-high stalagmite called the "Foundation Pillar," which was formed over many thousands of years. Here one can also see numerous ancient inscriptions carved on the inner walls, the earliest of which is a poem written by a scholar of the sixth century A.D. Beyond this the cave opens up onto a large rock chamber, the Lion and Elephant Arena, so called because of the two rocks on either side of the chamber, which resemble an elephant and a lion.

Passing through the misty upper cavern with its unusually shaped stalactites, the passageway narrows into a winding tunnel that leads down to the lower cavern. As you descend the stone stairs you will hear the sounds of waves, wind and thunder, war drums, and galloping horses. This phenomenon is a result of the acoustics of the tunnel, which modify the different sounds and intonations of the waterfall as it crashes down the wall at the end of the tunnel. Signaling each change in sound is a gate; thus, in descending into the lower cavern you will pass through the Breaker, Wind and Thunder, War Drum, and Ten Thousand Horses Gates. The narrow 180-meter-long lower cavern has many interesting stalactites. The spring rising from a pool in this cavern falls to the water cavern below, where visitors can explore further by rowboat.

Zhanggong Caverns These caverns are named after Zhang Guolao, one of the Eight Immortals of Taoism, who allegedly made the Zhanggong Caverns his shrine. Although considerably smaller than the Shangjuan Caverns, these seventy-two adjoining caves appear much larger. Unique rock and stalactite and stalagmite formations are characteristic of the caves. At the top of the spiral staircase leading from the first cavern is the Hall of the Sea God, which contains two great pillarlike stalagmites as well as many large rocks suspended from the ceiling. These fantastic forms are reflected in the beautifully clear and mirrorlike pool at the center of the cavern.

Many smaller caves branch off from the Hall of the Sea God, several of which are associated with their own legends and fables. Mazelike, often narrow passages weave in between the caves. Visitors may find the Chessboard Cavern particularly interesting. Hanging from the ceiling here is a large square boulder etched with lines, making it look like a giant chessboard. According to the legend, this is where the gods once gathered to play chess.

The steep flight of steps outside the Zhanggong Caverns takes you to the summit of the mountain, where an inscription from the twelfth century reads *Hai Nei Qi Guan*, or "Wonder of the World."

Visitors are warned that the temperature inside these caverns is considerably cooler than the outside temperature—sometimes as low as ten degrees below zero.

Yixing Pottery Kilns Situated in the village of Dingshu, just south of Yixing, these kilns are still in use today, producing the attractive reddish brown pottery with its natural rich colors and unique designs for which Yixing is famous. Visitors may enjoy a visit to the kilns, where one can see the traditional wares being made.

Yixing Pottery Factory.

ZHENGZHOU (Chengchow)

Henan Province

Zhengzhou, the capital of Henan Province, is situated south of the Huang He River, on the western border of the North China Plain. With the building of the railways in the early part of this century, it became a major junction of the north-south Beijing-Guangzhou line, and the east-west Long-Hai line. Since 1950 Zhengzhou has undergone tremendous development and today, with a population of 1.7 million, it is one of North China's major industrial and agricultural centers. Its industries, which are closely linked to its agricultural production, include food processing and refining and the manufacturing of farm equipment, fertilizers, insecticides, and textiles. The major crops grown in this area are wheat, cotton, and rice.

During expansion and construction of Zhengzhou in 1955, the remains of an ancient Shang capital, dating back some three thousand years, were discovered here. However, although Zhengzhou is one of the oldest cities in China, it never attained prominence in subsequent centuries, at least not until the end of the late nineteenth century.

The city's modern history is marked by labor unrest and several disastrous incidents. It was here, in 1923, that the railway workers staged a major strike, which was quickly, yet violently, suppressed by the local warlord. Later, during the Sino-Japanese war, the Nationalists, in the interests of preventing the Japanese from advancing on Zhengzhou, dammed the Huang He River to the northeast of the city. This caused severe flooding and the loss of many lives. Finally, Zhengzhou suffered a great deal of damage at the height of the 1948-1949 war between the Communists and Nationalists.

Today Zhengzhou serves as a fine example of modern redevelopment in China. In general, however, the city offers very little of interest to foreign visitors.

PLACES TO SEE

Henan Provincial Museum This museum contains a collection of ancient treasures and relics from the Neolithic period and early dynasties, which were found in the province of Henan. There is also a section devoted to the modern history of the province with an exhibition recording contemporary events and revolutionary activities such as the railway strike of 1923. For further detail see the section entitled "Major Museums of China."

Factories and Mills Visitors are invited to take a tour of the local communes, factories, and schools, where one can see the great extent to which Zhengzhou has been modernized. The textile mills are particularly impressive and are considered to be some of the most technologically advanced in the country.

ACCOMMODATION

Zhengzhou Hotel This Soviet-style hotel is located near the airport on Jinshui Road. Although it is an impressive-looking hotel, the accommodation is somewhat below standard.

RESTAURANTS

Jinshui Restaurant Overlooking the Jinshui River in the People's Park near the city center, this restaurant specializes in river fish.

Bronze vessel of the Zhou dynasty, Henan Museum, Zhengzhou.

ZHOUKOUDIAN (Chukoudian)

Hebei Province

Located fifty kilometers southwest of Beijing, Zhoukoudian is famous as the home of Peking Man. In 1929 the Chinese anthropologist Pei Wenzhong and his team discovered the well-preserved skull of a primitive man at Dragon Bone Hill near Zhoukoudian. They determined that the ape-man lived about 500,000 years ago and named him *Homo erectus Pekinensis*, or Peking Man.

Dragon Bone Hill is the site of the cave where Peking Man lived and hunted with his primitive weapons. Located on the northern slope of Dragon Bone Hill, the cave is estimated to have been about 140 meters by 40 meters and was filled with stratified deposits 40 meters thick. The presence of ashes in these deposits shows that Peking Man used fire. Further up the hill is the site of the cave where Upper Cave Man (*Homo sapiens*) lived.

In 1953 a museum was established near the cave site. It includes an exhibition hall and the remains of the cave home of Peking Man. A tour to the museum may be arranged with the curator through your China Travel Services guide.

217

Acknowledgments— Charts and Maps

The tables on pages 18, 236-237, 238-239, and 242-243 are reprinted from *China Sights and Insights* by permission of the publisher, Howard Lo. The maps on pages 81 and 246-255 are reprinted with permission of the New World Press, Beijing, and the map of the People's Republic of China is reproduced courtesy of Ditu Chubanshe of Beijing. Special thanks to Wanda Chu for typing the Chinese characters in the glossary.

APPENDIX

Useful Chinese Vocabulary

GENERAL

Hello!	Nǐ hǎo!	你好.
How are you?	Nǐ hǎo ma?	你好嗎?
I am fine, thank you.	Wǒ hěn hǎo, xièxiè nǐ.	我很好，謝謝你
Welcome.	Huānying.	歡迎.
Good morning.	Zǎoann.	早安.
Good evening.	Wǎnann.	晚安.
Goodbye.	Zàijiàn.	再見.
Please.	Qǐng.	請
Thanks. Thank you.	Xièxie. Xièxie nǐ.	謝謝！ 謝謝你.
No thank you.	Bú shi xièxiè.	不是，謝謝
Excuse me. (I am sorry.)	Duì bù qǐ.	對不起.
Do you speak English?	Nǐ jiǎng yīngyǔ ma?	你講英文嗎?
Is there an interpreter?	Yǒurén fānyi ma?	有人翻譯嗎?
I don't understand.	Wǒ tīng bù dǒng.	我聽不懂。
My name is ...	Wǒ xìng ...	我姓····
What is your name?	Guìxìng?	貴姓?
This is my first trip to China.	Wǒ dìyīci lái Zhōngguó.	我第一次來中國
I am a Canadian.	Wǒ shi Jiānádàrén.	我是加拿大人.

I am an American.	Wǒ shì Měiguórén.	我是美國人.
Very good, excellent	Hěn hǎo	很好.
Friend	Péngyǒu	朋友
Guest	Kèren	客人
Friendship	Yǒuyì	友誼.
Holiday	Fàngjià	放假
Yes	Shì	是
No	Bú shì	不是
Surely	Yídìng	一定.
What is this?	Zhè shì shénme?	這是甚麼?
Where is the washroom?	Cìsuǒ zài nàr?	廁所在那裏?
... men's?	Nán	男廁所在那裏?
... women's?	Nǚ	女廁所在那裏?
May I take a photograph?	Wǒ kéyǐ zhào xiàng ma?	我可以照相嗎?

HOTEL

Hotel	Lǚguǎn	旅館
Guesthouse	Bīnguǎn	賓館
Room	Fángjiān	房間
Floor	Lóu	樓
Bedroom	Wòshì	臥室
Bath	Xǐzǎo	洗澡

vel	Máojīn	毛巾
p	Féizào	肥皂
let	Cìsuǒ	廁所
let paper	Wèishēng zhǐ	衛生紙
ndry	Xǐyī	洗衣
el desk	Fúwu zhàn	服務站
vator	Diàntī	電梯
stairs	Lóushàng	樓上
wnstairs	Lóuxia	樓下
endant	Fúwùyúan	服務員
ling Room	Cāntīng	餐廳
ir salon	Lǐfà diàn	理髮店
here is the dining room?	Cāntīng zài nǎr?	餐廳在那兒？
here is the hotel shop?	Xiǎomàibù zài nǎr?	小賣部在那兒？
is room is fine.	Zhège fangjiān hǎo.	這個房間好
ase write it down.	Qǐng xiěxià lǎi.	請寫下來
ase come in.	Qǐng jìnlái.	請進來
ase wait a moment.	Qǐng děng yi huǐ.	請等一會
ase bring me ...	Qǐng gēi wǒ ...	請給我
some cold water.	liángkāi shuǐ.	涼開水
some boiled water.	kāi shuǐ.	開水

221

English	Pinyin	Chinese
some tea.	yìdiǎr chá.	有茶嗎？
I want to have my hair done.	Wǒ yào lǐ fà.	我要理髮

TRANSPORTATION

English	Pinyin	Chinese
Plane	Fēijī	飛　機
Airport	Fēijīcháng	飛機場
Train	Huǒchē	火　車
Bus	Gōnggòng qìchē	公共汽車
Taxi	Chūzū chē	出租車
Luggage	Xíngli	行　李
Ticket	Piào	票
Passport	Huò zhào	護照
Embassy	Dàshǐguǎn	大使館
Entrance	Rù kǒu	入口
Exit	Chū kǒu	出口
North	Bei	北
South	Nan	南
East	Dong	東
West	Xi	西
Where is the train station?	Huǒchē zhàn zài nǎr?	火車站在那兒
Please call a taxi.	Qǐng tí wǒ jiàochuzūchē.	請替我叫出租
How much is it?	Duō shǎo qián?	多少錢？

Where is the CAAC Airline ticket office?	Mín hóng jú zài nǎr?	民航在那兒？

TELECOMMUNICATIONS AND POSTAL SERVICES

Post office	Yóu zhèng jú	郵政局
Telegraph office	Diànbào jú	電報局
Telephone	Diànhuà	電話
Stamp	Yóupiào	郵票
Postcard	Mínxìnpiēn	明信片
Envelope	Xìnfēng	信封
Letter	Xìn	信
Air mail letter	Hǎng kōng xìn	航空信
I need to buy some stamps.	Wǒ yào mǎi yóupiào.	我要買郵票
Where is the letter box?	Xìntǒng zài nǎr?	郵筒在那裏
I want to make a long-distance telephone call.	Wǒ yào dǎ chángtú diànhuà.	我要打長途電話
I want to send an express telegram.	Wǒ yào dǎ jí diànpāo.	我要打緊急電話

RESTAURANT AND DINING

Restaurant	Fàngguan	飯館
Water	Shǔ	水
Tea	Chá	茶
Coffee	Kāfēr	咖啡
Milk	Niúnǎi	牛奶

Soft drink	Qìshuǐ	汽水
Mineral water	Quánshuǐ	礦水
Fruit juice	Guǒzizhī	果子汁
Beer	Píjiǔ	啤酒
White wine	Báijiǔ	白酒
Red wine	Hóngjiǔ	紅酒
Breakfast	Zǎofàn	早飯
Lunch	Wǔfàn	午飯
Dinner	Wānfàn	晚飯
Hot	Rìde	熱
Cold	Liángde	冷
Spicy	Làde	辣
Chinese food	Zhōngcān	中菜
Western food	Xìcān	西菜
Fruit	Shuǐ guǒ	水果
Vegetable	Sūcài	蔬菜
Rice	Fàn	飯
Ice cubes	Bīng kuài	冰
Duck	Yā	鴨
Chicken	Jī	鷄
Pork	Zhǔròu	猪肉
Beef	Niúròu	牛肉
Seafood	Hǎiwèi	海味

Menu	Càidān	菜單
Egg	Jīdàn	鷄蛋
Cook	Chúshī	羹（食）
Cheers!	Gānbēi	乾杯
Tasty food	Càihǎo chī	菜好吃
I like Chinese food.	Wǒ xǐhuān chī Zhōngguó cài.	我喜歡吃中國菜
I don't like too hot-peppery food.	Wǒ bù xǐhuān chī tài làde.	我不喜歡吃太辣
Please recommend a restaurant.	Qǐng jièshao yíge fàngguan.	請你介紹一個餐館
Please recommend a few good dishes.	Qǐng jièshao jǐyàng hǎo cài.	請你介紹一些好菜
I enjoyed the meal.	Cài hěn hǎo chī.	菜很好吃
Drink to our friendship.	Wèi wǒmende yǒuyi gān bēi.	爲我們的友誼乾杯
Please make up the bill.	Qǐng suànzhàng.	請算帳
Where is the restaurant?	Fànguàn zài nǎr?	飯館在那兒？
Please bring ...	Qǐng lái ...	請拿····
I do not like ...	Wǒ bú xǐhuān chī ...	我不喜歡吃···。
Chopsticks	Kuàizi	筷子
Glass	Bēizi	杯子

HEALTH CARE

Sick	Sōn bìng	生病
Doctor	Yīshēng	醫生

Hospital	Yīyuàn	醫院
Headache	Tóutòng	頭痛
Fever	Fāshāo	發燒
Medicine	Yào	藥
Common cold	Shāngfēng	傷風
Temperature	Tǐwēn	體溫
Headache pill	Tóutòng yào	頭痛藥
Injection	Dǎzhēn	打針
Medical treatment	Yīliáo	醫療
Stomach ache	Dǒutòng	肚痛
I am sick.	Wǒ sōn bìng.	我生病
I want to rest.	Wǒ yào xiuxi.	我要休息
I want to see a doctor.	Wǒ yào kàn yīshēng.	我要看醫生
I want to take some medicine.	Wǒ yào chī yào.	我要吃藥
Cold	Lěng	冷
Tired	Lèi	累
Bleeding	Lùxiè	流血

SHOPPING

Salesperson	Shòuhuòyuán	售貨員
Bookstore	Shūdiàn	書店
Arts and crafts	Yìshū pǐn	藝術品
Antique	Gǔtóng	古董

226

lk	Szezhǒu	絲綢
eramics	Taozǎo	陶瓷
ory	Xiàngyā	象牙
de	Yǔ	玉
ainting	Huà	畫
amboo	Zhùzi	竹子
riting paper	Xiě zi zhì	寫字紙
garettes	Yān	煙
ay I have a receipt?	Qíng gěi wǒ fapiao?	請給我發票？
opping	Mǎi dōngxi	買東西
ess	Yīfu	衣服
eater	Máoyī	毛衣
at	Dàyī	大衣
ousers	Kùzi	袵子
t	Maòzi	帽子
oes	Xiézi	鞋子
ket	Shàngyī	上衣
ks	Wàze	襪子
teries	Diàn chí	電池
m	Jiaojuàn	膠卷
w much is it?	Duōshǎo qían?	多少錢？
ant to buy ...	Wǒ yào mǎi ...	我要買⋯

English	Pinyin	Chinese
I will take this.	Wǒ yào zhège.	我要這個
Too big	Tài dà	太大
Too small	Tài xiǎo	太小
What size is it?	Duō dà?	多大？
Red	Hóng	紅
Yellow	Huáng	黃
Blue	Lán	藍
White	Bái	白
Black	Hēi	黑
Green	Lü	綠
Pink	Fěnhóng	粉紅
Gray	Huī	灰
This kind is too expensive.	Zhè zhǒng tài gūi.	這種太貴
This kind is inexpensive.	Zhè zhǒng piányi.	這種便宜
This is fine.	Zhè zhǒng hen hao.	這種很好
May I try it on?	Kěyi shiyishi ma?	可以試一試嗎？
I like this one.	Wǒ xǐhuàn zhège.	我喜歡這個

NUMBERS

English	Pinyin	Chinese
Zero	Ling	零
One	Yī	一
Two	Er	二

Three	Sān	三
Four	Sì	四
Five	Wǔ	五
Six	Liù	六
Seven	Qī	七
Eight	Bā	八
Nine	Jiǔ	九
Ten	Shí	十
One hundred	Yībǎi	一百
Two hundred	Èrbǎi	二百
Five hundred	Wǔbǎi	五百
One thousand	Yīqiān	一千
Three thousand	Sānqiān	三千
Ten thousand	Yīwǎn	一萬

DAYS OF THE WEEK

Monday	Xīngqī yī	星期一
Tuesday	Xīngqī èr	星期二
Wednesday	Xīngqī sān	星期三
Thursday	Xīngqī sì	星期四
Friday	Xīngqī wǔ	星期五
Saturday	Xīngqī liù	星期六
Sunday	Xīngqī rì	星期日

Morning	Shàngwǔ	上午
Afternoon	Xiàwǔ	下午
Evening	Wǎnshàng	晚上
Noon	Zhōngwǔ	中午
Day	Tiān	天
Today	Jīngtiān	今天
Tomorrow	Míngtiān	明天

TIME AND MONTHS OF THE YEAR

Two o'clock	Liǎng diǎn	兩點
Six o'clock	Liù diǎn	六點
Eight o'clock	Bā diǎn	八點
Quarter to eight	Ba diǎn shǎo yī kè	八點少一刻
Quarter past six	Liù diǎn yī kè	六點一刻
January	Yī yuè	一月
February	Èr yuè	二月
March	Sān yuè	三月
April	Sì yuè	四月
May	Wǔ yuè	五月
June	Liù yuè	六月
July	Qí yuè	七月
August	Bā yuè	八月

September	Jiǔ yuè	九月
October	Shí yuè	十月
November	Shí yī yuè	十一月
December	Shí èr yuè	十二月

MONEY

Ten cents	Shí fēn	十分
Fifty cents	Wǔ shí fēn	五十分
One dollar	Yī yüan	一元
Five dollars	Wǔ yüan	五元
Twenty-two dollars	Èr shí èr yüan	二十二元
One hundred dollars	Yī bǎi yüan	一百元

NATIONS

Canada	Jiānádà	加拿大
United States	Méiguó	美國
Great Britain	Yīngguó	英國
West Germany	Xīdeguó	西德
France	Fǎguó	法 國
Italy	Yìdàlì	意大利
Spain	Xībānyá	西班牙
Sweden	Ruìdiǎn	瑞 典

Norway	Nuówēi	挪威
Mexico	Mòxigē	墨西哥
Japan	Rìbĕn	日 本
Russia	Sūlián	蘇聯

BUSINESS AND TRADE

I am in China on business.	Wŏ shì lai Zhōnggōng yŏu shāngyè.	我是來中 做生意
Report	Bàobào	報告
Product	Chéngpĭn	成品
Office	Bàngōngshì	辦公室
Engineer	Gōngchēngshī	工程師
Industry	Gŏngyè	工業
Machine	Jīxiè	機械
Factory	Gòngchăng	工廠

For Further Reading

The following books and periodicals can be found in the public library or the library of your local college or university.

SOCIAL AND POLITICAL BACKGROUND

Chang, P.H. *Power and Policy in China.* University Park. Pennsylvania State University Press, 1976.

Chen, Jack. *A Year in Upper Felicity: Life in a Chinese Village during the Cultural Revolution.* New York: Macmillan, 1973.

Committee of Concerned Asian Scholars. *China: Inside the People's Republic.* New York: Bantam Books, 1972.

Coye, M.J., and Livingston, J. *China Yesterday and Today.* New York: Bantam Books, 1975.

Curtin, K. *Women in China.* New York: Pathfinder Press, 1975.

Fairbank, J.K. *The United States and China.* 3rd ed., rev. Cambridge, Mass: Harvard University Press, 1972.

Galbraith, J.K. *A China Passage.* Boston: Houghton Mifflin, 1973.

Han, Suyin. "Reflection on Social Change." *Bulletin of the Atomic Scientists* 22 (1966): 80-83.

Hinton, W. *Fanshan: A Documentary of a Revolution in a Chinese Village.* New York: Vintage Books, 1966.

McCullough, C. *Stranger in China.* New York: William Morrow, 1973.

Milton, D., and Milton, N.D. *The Wind Will Not Subside: Years in Revolutionary China, 1964-1969.* New York: Pantheon Books, 1976.

Needham, J. *The Grand Titration: Science and Society in East and West.* London: Allen and Unwin, 1969.

Salisbury, H.E. *To Peking—And Beyond.* Toronto: Fitzhenry & Whiteside, 1973.

Sidel, R. *Women and Child Care in China.* New York: Penguin Books, 1973.

Snow, E. *Red Star over China* New York: Vintage Books, 1971.

Terrill, R. *Flowers on an Iron Tree: Five Cities of China.* Boston: Little, Brown, 1975.

Tuchman, B.W. *Notes from China* New York: Collier Books, 1972.

BUSINESS AND TRADE IN CHINA

China Business Review (bimonthly magazine). The National Council for US-China Trade, Washington, D.C., 20036.

Far Eastern Economic Review (weekly publication in Hong Kong.)

Mobius, J.M.   *Trading with China*   New York: Arco Books, 1973.

Neilan, E., and Smith, C.R.   *The Future of the China Market.*   Washington, D.C. : American Enterprise Institute for Public Policy Research, 1974.

EDUCATION, RELIGION, AND PHILOSOPHY

Beijing Review (weekly magazine).   Beijing.

Chai, C., and Chai, W.   *The Changing Society of China.*   New York: New American Library, 1969.

China Reconstructs (monthly magazine).   Beijing.

China Pictorial (quarterly magazine).   Beijing.

China—A Geographical Sketch.   Beijing: Foreign Languages Press, 1974.

Chinese Literature (monthly magazine).   Beijing.

Co-operative Medical Service Is Fine.   Beijing: Foreign Languages Press, 1978.

Fifteen Cities in China.   Beijing: *China Reconstructs* Magazine, 1980.

Gottschang, Karen Turner.   *China Bound: A Handbook for American Students, Researchers and Teachers.*   Washington, D.C. : U.S.-China Education Clearinghouse, The Committee on Scholarly Communication with the People's Republic of China and the National Association for Foreign Student Affairs, May 1981.

Mao Zedong.   *Four Essays on Philosophy.*   Beijing, 1968.

———————.   *Quotations From Chairman Mao Tse-tung (Mao's Red Book),* 1972.

———————.   *Mao Tse-tung Poems.*   Beijing: Foreign Languages Press, 1976.

———————.   *Selected Works of Mao Tse-tung.*   Beijing: Foreign Languages Press, 1961-77.

New China's First Quarter-Century.   Beijing: Foreign Languages Press, 1975.

Wen-wu (monthly archaeological magazine in Chinese).   Beijing.

Women in China (monthly magazine).   Beijing.

CHINESE ART AND ARCHAEOLOGY

d'Argence, Rene-Yvon.   *Avery Brundage Collection of Chinese Jades.*   New York: Kodansha International, 1972.

Chinese Arts and Crafts.   Beijing: Foreign Languages Press, 1973.

Feng, Xian-Ming, and Leung, Sophia M.R.   "Thirty Years of Archaeological Study on Chinese Ceramics." *Arts of Asia,* Vol.12, No. 3, 1982.

Leung, Sophia M.R.   "Chinese Paintings in the Imperial Palace Collection." *Arts of Asia,* Vol. 6, No. 6, 1976.

———————   "Cultural Treasures of Xi'an and Shanghai." *Arts of Asia,* Vol. 6, No. 4, 1976.

—————————. "Displays in the Forbidden City." *Arts of Asia,* Vol. 8, No. 6, 1978.

—————————. "A Visit to the Canton Museum." *Arts of Asia,* Vol. 9, No. 5, 1979.

—————————. "A Visit to Chingtechen." *Arts of Asia,* Vol. 10, No. 2, 1980.

Murck, A., and Fong, W. *A Chinese Garden Court.* New York: The Metropolitan Museum of Art, 1980.

Smith, B., and Weng, W. *China: A History in Art.* New York: Doubleday, 1972.

Sullivan, M., *The Arts of China.* Berkeley: University of California Press, 1977.

The Exhibition of Archaeological Finds of the People's Republic of China. London: George Rainbird, 1973.

Treasures from the Bronze Age of China. New York: The Metropolitan Museum of Art, Ballantine Books, 1980.

Valenstein, S.G. *A Handbook of Chinese Ceramics.* New York: The Metropolitan Museum of Art, 1975.

HEALTH CARE

Chabot, H.T.J. "The Chinese System of Health Care: An Enquiry into Public Health in the People's Republic of China." *Tropical and Geographical Medicine* 28 (1976): 87-134.

Cheng, T.; Axelrod, L.; and Leaf, A. "Medical Education and Practice in the People's Republic of China." *Annals of Internal Medicine* 83 (November 1975): 716-724.

Chin, H.K. "A Barefoot Doctor Describes His Work." *China Reconstructs* 25 (1976): 7-11.

Horne, J.S. *Away with All Pests—An English Surgeon in People's China: 1954-1969.* New York: Monthly Review Press, 1969.

Leung, S.M.R.; Miller, M.H.; and Leung, S.W. "Chinese Approach to Mental Health Services." *Canadian Psychiatric Association Journal* 23 (1978): 354-360.

Leung, S.M.R. "Mental Health Home Care Program in the Communes of the People's Republic of China." *Journal of Psychiatric Treatment and Evaluation* 3 (1981): 53-58.

Sidel, V.W., and Sidel, R. "The Delivery of Medical Care in China." *Scientific American* 230 (April 1974): 19-27.

ADDRESSES OF THE CHINA INTERNATIONAL TRAVEL SERVICE (LUXINGSHE)

HEAD OFFICE: 6 East Changan Avenue, Beijing
Cable Address: LUXINGSHE BEIJING
Telephone: 551031
Telex: 22350 CITSH CN

BRANCH OFFICES

CITY	ADDRESS	PHONE	CABLE ADDRESS
Beijing	2 East Qianmen Avenue	757181, 755374	BEIJING 5861
Changchun	2 Stalin Avenue	9119	
Changsha	130 Wuixi Road, Sanxingjie	22250	
Chengdu	Jingjiang Hotel	5914	
Chongqing	People's Auditorium, Renmin Road	51449	
Dalian	56 Fenglin Street	25103	
Guangzhou	179 Huanshi Road	32648	GUANGZHOU 1954
Guilin	14 North Ronhu Road	3870, 3628	
Hangzhou	10 Baochu Road	22921	
Harbin	124 Dazhi Street, Nangang District	33001, 31441	HARBIN 1954
Hefei	Jianghuai Hotel Changjiang Road	2221, 2227	
Jinan	372 Jingsan Road	35351	
Jiujiang	Nanhu Guesthouse	4015	
Kunming	West Huashan Road	2192 ext. 362	
Luoyang	Friendship Guesthouse	7006 ext. 701	
Lushan	443 Hedong Road	2497	
Nanjing	313 North Zhongshan Road	85153	
Nanning	Xinmin Road	2042, 4793	
Qingdao	9 Nanhai Road	28877	
Shanghai	59 Xianggang Road	217200	SHANGHAI 1954

Shenyang	Nanzhan	34653	
Shijiazhuang	Weiming Road	8962, 9622	
Suzhou	115 Friendship Road	5931, 2593	
Tianjin	55 Chongqing Road	34831	
Wuhan	195 Zhongshan Avenue, Hankou	25018	HANKOU 1962
Wuxi	7 Xinshan Road	5469	
Xi'an	Renmin Mansion	21191	
Xiamen	444 Zhongshan Road, Xiamen	4286, 2729	XIAMEN 3330

MAJOR HOTELS IN CHINA

CITY	HOTEL	ADDRESS	PHONE
Beijing	Beijing Hotel	East Chang'an Ave.	552231
	Minzu (Nationalities) Hotel	West Chang'an Ave.	668541
	Qianmen Hotel	Yongan Road	338731
	Youyi (Friendship) Hotel	Haidian Road	890621
	Xingqiao Hotel	Dongjiaomin Lane	557731
	Yanjing Hotel		
Changchun	Changchun Hotel	128 Changchun	26772
	Chunyi Hotel	2 Stalin Blvd.	38495
Changsha	Hunan Hotel	Yingbin Road	26331
	Xiangjiang Hotel	Zhongshan Road	26263
Chengdu	Jinjiang Hotel	South Renmin Road	4481
Chongqing	Chongqing Hotel	Minsheng Road	53158
	Renmin Hotel	Renmin Road	53421
Dalian	Bangchuidao Hotel	Bangchuidao	25131
Dalian Hotel	3 Zhongshan Road		23111
Guangzhou	Baiyun Hotel	Huanshi Road	67700
	Dongfang Hotel	North Renmin Road	69900
	Guangzhou Hotel	Haizhu Square	61556
	Liuhua Hotel	North Renmin Road	68800
Guilin	Lijiang Hotel	North Shanhu Road	2881
	Ronghu Hotel	North Ronghu Road	3150
Hangzhou	Hangzhou Hotel	2 North Huanhu Road	22921
	Huagang Hotel	Xishan Road	24881
	Liutong Hotel	Santaishan, Xihu	26356
	Xiling Hotel	North Huanhu Road	22921
	Zhejiang Hotel	Xidingjiashan, Xihu	24483
Harbin	Guoji Hotel	124 Dazhi Street	31431
Jilin	Dongguan Hotel	Songjiang Road	3555
	Xiguan Hotel	661 Songjiang Road	5645
Jinan	Jinan Hotel	372 Jingsan Road	35351
	Nanjiao Hotel	Nanjiao	23931
Kunming	Kunming Hotel	122 East Dongfeng Road	2240
	Xiyuan Hotel	Xiyuan	9969
Nanchang	Jiangxi Hotel	Bayi Dadao	
Nanjing	Dingshan Hotel	90 Chaha'er Road	85931

	Nanjing Hotel	259 North Zhongshan	34121
	Shuangmenlou Hotel	38 Shuangmenlou	85535
Qingdao	Huiquan Hotel	Nanhai Road	
	Zhanqiao Hotel	31 Taiping Road	27402
Shanghai	Hengshan Hotel	534 Hengshan Road	377050
	Heping (Peace) Hotel	20 East Nanjing Road	211244
	Jinjiang Hotel	59 South Maomin Road	534242
	Jing'an Hotel	370 Huanshan Road	563050
	Shanghai Mansion	20 North Suzhou Road	246260
Shenyang	Liaoning Hotel	27, Sec. 2, Zhongshan Road	32641
Suzhou	Suzhou Hotel	Youyi Road	4646
	Nanlin Hotel	Youyi Road	4441
Taiyuan	Bingzhou Hotel	Yingze Dajie	25924
	Jinci Hotel	Jinci Nanjiao	29941
	Yingze Hotel	Yingze Dajie	23211
Tianjin	Tianjin Hotel	219 North Jeifand Road	32493
	Youyi (Friendship)	Shengli Road	35663
Wuhan	Jianghan Hotel	211 Shengli Street Hankou	23998
	Shengli Hotel	Shenli Street Hankou	22531
	Xuangong Hotel	45 Jianghanyi Road Hankou	24404
Wuxi	Hubin Hotel	Liyuan	
	Taihu Hotel	Huanhu Road	3931
Xi'an	Renmin Hotel	Dongxin Street	25111
	Shaanxi Hotel	Zhangbagou, Nanjiao	23831
Zhengzhou	Zhongzhou Hotel	Jinshuihe Road	4938

HEAD OFFICES OF CHINA'S FOREIGN TRADE CORPORATIONS

China National Cereals, Oils, and Foodstuffs Import and Export Corporation:
> 82 Tung An Men Street, Beijing, PRC
> Cable: CEROILFOOD BEIJING
> Telex: 22281 CEROF CN or 22111 CEROF CN

China National Native Produce and Animal By-Products Import and Export Corporation:
> 82 Tung An Men Street, Beijing, PRC
> Cable: CHINATUHSU BEIJING
> Telex: 22283 TUSHU CN

China National Textiles Import and Export Corporation:
> 82 Tung An Men Street, Beijing, PRC
> Cable: CHINATEX BEIJING
> Telex: 22280 CNTEX CN

China National Light Industrial Products Import and Export Corporation:
> 82 Tung An Men Street, Beijing, PRC
> Cable: INDUSTRY BEIJING
> Telex: 22282 LIGHT CN

China National Arts and Crafts Import and Export Corporation:
> 82 Tung An Men Street, Beijing, PRC
> Cable: ARTCHINA BEIJING
> Telex: 22155 CNART CN

China National Chemicals Import and Export Corporation:
> Erh Li Kou, Hsi Chiao, Beijing, PRC
> Cable: SINOCHEM BEIJING
> Telex: 22243 CHEMI CN

China National Machinery and Equipment Export Corporation:
> 12 Fu Xing Men Wai Street, Beijing, PRC
> Cable: EQUIPEX BEIJING

China National Metals and Minerals Import and Export Corporation:
> Erh Li Kou, Hsi Chiao, Beijing, PRC
> Cable: MINMETALS BEIJING
> Telex: 22241 MIMET CN

China National Complete Plant Export Corporation:
> An Ting Men Wai, Beijing, PRC
> Cable: COMPLANT BEIJING

China National Machinery Import and Export Corporation:
> Erh Li Kou, Hsi Chiao, Beijing, PRC
> Cable: MACHIMPEX BEIJING
> Telex: 22242 CMIEC CN

China National Technical Import Corporation:
> Erh Li Kou, Hsi Chiao, Beijing, PRC
> Cable: TECAIMPORT BEIJING

Telex: 22244 CNTIC CN

China National Foreign Trade Transportation Corporation:
Erh Li Kou, Hsi Chiao, Beijing, PRC
Cable: SINOTRANS BEIJING
Telex: 22153 TRANS CN
22154 TRANS CN
22265 TRANS CN

China National Chartering Corporation:
Erh Li Kou, Hsi Chiao, Beijing, PRC
Cable: ZHONGZU BEIJING
Telex: 22153 TRANS CN
22154 TRANS CN
22265 TRANS CN

China Ocean Shipping Company:
6 Tung Chang An Street, Beijing, PRC
Cable: COSCO BEIJING
Telex: 22264 CPC PK

Guozi Shudian (newspapers and periodicals in Chinese and foreign languages):
P.O. Box 399, Beijing, PRC
Cable: GUOZI BEIJING

China Film Distribution and Exhibition Corporation:
25 Hsin Wai Street, Beijing, PRC
Cable: SOUTHFILM BEIJING

China Stamp Company:
28 Tung An Men Street, Beijing, PRC
Cable: CHINASTAMP BEIJING

The People's Insurance Company of China:
P.O. Box 2149, Beijing, PRC
Cable: 42001 BEIJING
Telex: 22102 PICC

Bank of China:
17 Hsi Chiao Ming Hsiang, Beijing, PRC
Cable: HOCHUNGKUO BEIJING

Chinese Export Commodities Fair:
Guangzhou
Cable: CECFA GUANGZHOU

China's Foreign Trade
4 Tai Ping Chiao Street, Beijng, PRC
Cable: COMTRADE BEIJING

FOREIGN CURRENCIES AND
TRAVELER'S CHECKS (T/C) ACCEPTED IN CHINA

Foreign Currencies:
Australian Dollar (A$), Austrian Schilling (Sch), Belgian Franc (BF), Canadian Dollar (Can$), Danish Krone (DKr), West German Mark (DM), French Franc (FF), Japanese Yen (Y), Malaysian Dollar (M$), Dutch Guilder (FL), Norwegian Krone (NKr), Singapore Dollar (S$), Swedish Krona (SKr), Swiss Franc (SF), Pound Sterling (£), US Dollar (US$), and Hong Kong Dollar (HK$).

TRAVELER'S CHECKS AND INTERNATIONAL BANK DRAFTS

Rafidain Bank, Baghdad, Iraq	US$, £	T/C
Arab Bank Limited, Amman, Jordan	US$, £	T/C
The National Bank of Australia Ltd., Melbourne, Australia	A$	T/C
Bank of New South Wales, Sydney, Australia	A$	T/C
The Rural & Industries Bank of Western Australia, Perth, Australia	A$	T/C
Australia & New Zealand Banking Group Ltd.	£, A$	T/C
Commonwealth Trading Bank of Australia, Sydney, Australia	£, A$	T/C
The Mitsui Bank Ltd., Tokyo	Y	T/C
The Bank of Tokyo Ltd., Tokyo	Y, US$	T/C
The Sumitomo Bank Ltd., Tokyo	Y	T/C
The Fuji Bank Ltd., Tokyo	Y	T/C
Barclays Bank International Ltd., London	£, US$	T/C
Lloyds Bank Ltd., London	£	T/C
Standard Chartered Bank Ltd., London	£, US$	T/C
The Royal Bank of Scotland Ltd., London	£	T/C
Grindlays Bank Ltd., London	£	T/C
Midland Bank Ltd., London	£	T/C
National Westminster Bank Ltd., London	£	T/C
Thomas Cook & Son Ltd., London	£, US$, Can$, A$	T/C
The Hong Kong & Shanghai Banking Corp., Hong Kong	HK$	T/C
Deutsche Genossenshcaftsbank Frankfurt, Berlin	Standard DM	T/C
Baden-Wurttembergische Bank, Stuttgart	Standard DM	T/C
Bankhaus H. Aufhauser, Munchen	Standard DM	T/C
Bank fur Gemeinwirtschaft, Frankfurt	Standard DM	T/C
Bayerische Hypotheken-und-Wechsel Bank, Munchen	Standard DM	T/C
Bayerische Vereinsbank, Munchen	Standard DM	T/C
Berliner Bank, Berlin	Standard DM	T/C
Berliner Handels-und-Frankfurter Bank, Frankfurt, Berlin	Standard DM	T/C
Bankhaus Burgardt & Brockelschen, Dortmund	Standard DM	T/C
Commerzbank, Dusseldorf, Frankfurt,		

Hamburg	Standard DM	T/C
Deutsche Bank, Frankfurt, Dusseldorf	Standard DM	T/C
Deutsche Girozentrale-Deutsche		
Kommunalbank, Frankfurt, Berlin	Standard DM	T/C
Deutsche Verkenes-Kredit-Bank, Frankfurt	Standard DM	T/C
Deutsche Unionbank, Frankfurt	Standard DM	T/C
Dresdner Bank, Frankfurt	Standard DM	T/C
Bankhaus Hallibaum, Maier & Co.,		
Hannover	Standard DM	T/C
Handels-und-Privatbank, Koln	Standard DM	T/C
Lubeck Commerzbank, Lubeck	Standard DM	T/C
Hauck (Georg) & Sohn, Frankfurt	Standard DM	T/C
Bankhaus Martens & Weyhausen, Bremen	Standard DM	T/C
Merck, Finck & Co., Munchen, Dusseldorf,		
Frankfurt	Standard DM	T/C
National Bank, Essen	Standard DM	T/C
Bankhaus Neelmeyer, Bremen	Standard DM	T/C
Nikolaus Bank Hannover, Brunswick		
(Braunschweig), Gotingen	Standard DM	T/C
Oldenburgische Landesbank, Oldenburg	Standard DM	T/C
Reuschel & Co., Munchen	Standard DM	T/C
Karl Schmidt Bankgeschaft, Hof	Standard DM	T/C
Vereins-und-Westbank, Hamburg	Standard DM	T/C
M.M. Warburg-Brinckmann, Wirtz & Co.,		
Hamburg	Standard DM	T/C
Westfalenbank, Bochum	Standard DM	T/C
Banque Nationale de Paris, Paris	FF	T/C
Societe Generale, Paris	FF	T/C
Credit Lyonnais, Paris	FF	T/C
Swiss Bankers Travellers Cheque Center,		
Borne	SF	T/C
Banque de Bruxelles, Brussels	BF	T/C
Societe Generale de Banque, Brussels	BF	T/C
Algemene Bank Nederland N.V.,		
Amsterdam	FL	T/C
Amsterdam-Rotterdam Bank N.V.,		
Amsterdam	FL	T/C
Nederlandsche Middenstandsbank N.V.,		
Amsterdam	FL	T/C
Norwegian Travellers Cheque	NKr	T/C
Citicorp, New York	US$	T/C
Bank of America, San Francisco	US$	T/C
Manufacturers Hanover Trust Co.,	US Int.	T/C
New York	Money Order	
Chase Manhattan Bank, New York	US$	T/C
American Express Co., New York	US$, Can$, SF,	T/C
	£, DM, FF, Y	
First National Bank of Chicago, Illinois	US$	T/C
Republic National Bank of Dallas, Texas	US$	T/C
The Royal Bank of Canada, Montreal	Can$, US$, World	T/C
	Money Order	

FOREIGN DIPLOMATIC OFFICES IN BEIJNG

COUNTRY	ADDRESS	PHONE
Australia	15 Tungchimenwai	522331
Austria	5 Xiashui Street South Jianguomenwai	522061
Belgium	6 Sanlitun Road	521736
Canada	10 Sanlitun Road	521475
Denmark	1 Fifth Avenue East Sanlitun	522431
East Germany	3 Fourth Avenue East Sanlitun	521631
Federal Republic of Germany	5 Tungchimenwai	522161
Finland	30 Kwanghua Road	521753
France	3 Third Avenue East Sanlitun	521331
Greece	19 Kwanghua Road	521391
Ireland	3 Ritan Road East	522691
Italy	2 Second Avenue East Sanlitun	522131
Japan	7 Ritan Road Jianguomenwai	522361
Mexico	5 Fifth Avenue East Sanlitun	521731
Netherlands	10 Fourth Avenue East Sanlitun	521731
New Zealand	1 Second Avenue East Ritan Park	522731
Nigeria	2 Fifth Avenue East Sanlitun	523631
Norway	1 First Avenue East	522261
Peru	Ste. 2 Diplomatic Office Building	522178
Russia	4 North Central Avenue Tungchimenwai	522051
Spain	9 Sanlitun Road	523520
Sweden	3 Tungchimenwai	523331
Switzerland	3 Fifth Avenue East Sanlitun	522831
United Kingdom	11 Kwanghua Road	521961
United States	17 Kwanghua Road	522033

Maps of the Major Cities

Beijing
Changsha
Guangzhou
Guilin
Hangzhou
Nanjing
Shanghai
Suzhou
Wuhan
Wuxi

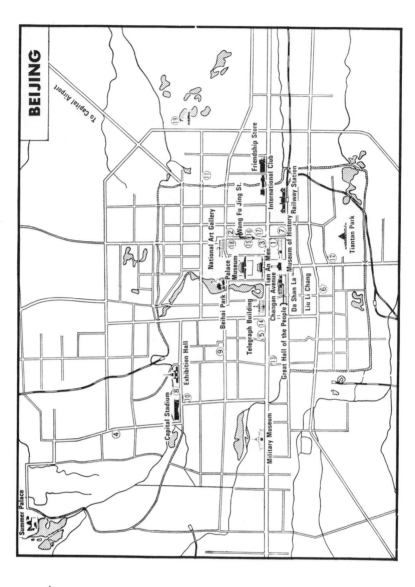

BEIJING

To Capital Airport

Summer Palace

Capital Stadium

Exhibition Hall

Military Museum

Telegraph Building

Beihai Park

Palace Museum

National Art Gallery

Wang Fu Jing St.

Tian An Men

Changan Avenue

Great Hall of the People

Da Shan La

Liu Li Chang

Museum of History

Railway Station

International Club

Friendship Store

Tiantan Park

1 Head Office of China International Travel Service
2 International Travel Service Branch
3 Beijing Hotel
4 Friendship Hotel
5 Minzu Hotel
6 Qianmen Hotel
7 Xinqiao Hotel
8 Beijing Zoo
9 Lu Xun Museum
10 Planetarium
11 Workers' Gymnasium
12 Museum of Natural History
13 TV Building
14 Nationalities Cultural Palace
15 Department Store
16 Dongfeng Bazaar
17 Arts and Crafts Store
18 Wai Wen Book Store
19 Agricultural Exhibition Hall

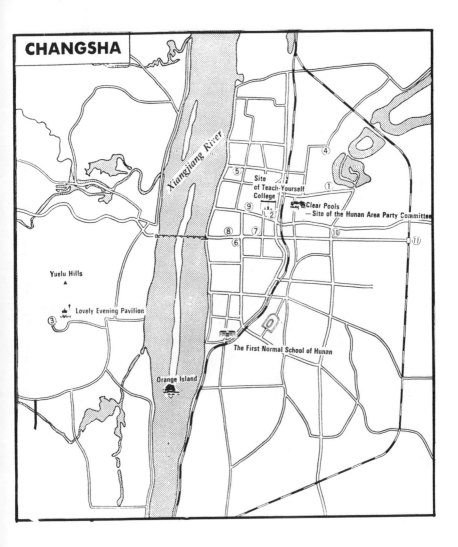

CHANGSHA

Xiangjiang River

Site of Teach-Yourself College

Clear Pools
— Site of the Hunan Area Party Committee

Yuelu Hills

Lovely Evening Pavilion

The First Normal School of Hunan

Orange Island

1 Hunan Hotel
2 Xiangjiang Hotel
3 Yunlu Palace
4 Hunan Provincial Museum
5 Workers' Cultural Palace
6 Arts and Crafts Store
7 Wai Wen Book Store

8 May 1st Department Store
9 Zhongshan Road Department Store
10 Shaoshan Road Department Store
11 Railway Station

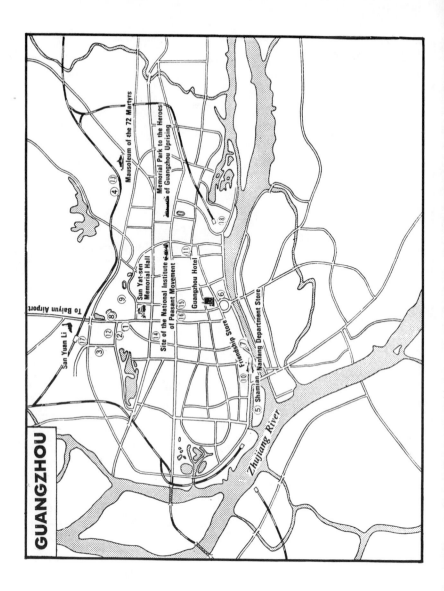

GUANGZHOU

- San Yuan Li
- To Baiyun Airport
- Mausoleum of the 72 Martyrs
- Memorial Park to the Heroes of Guangzhou Uprising
- Sun Yat-sen Memorial Hall
- Site of the National Institute of Peasant Movement
- Guangzhou Hotel
- Friendship Store
- Shamian
- Nanfang Department Store
- Zhujiang River

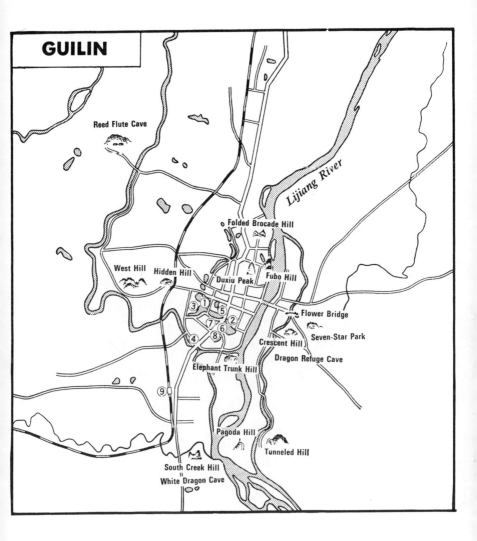

GUILIN

Reed Flute Cave

Lijiang River

Folded Brocade Hill

West Hill Hidden Hill

Duxiu Peak Fubo Hill

Flower Bridge

Seven-Star Park

Crescent Hill

Dragon Refuge Cave

Elephant Trunk Hill

Pagoda Hill

Tunneled Hill

South Creek Hill
White Dragon Cave

1 International Travel Service
  Branch
2 Lijiang Hotel
3 Banyan Lake Hotel
4 Guilin Hotel

5 Friendship Store
6 Wai Wen Book Store
7 Antique Shop
8 Department Store
9 Railway Station

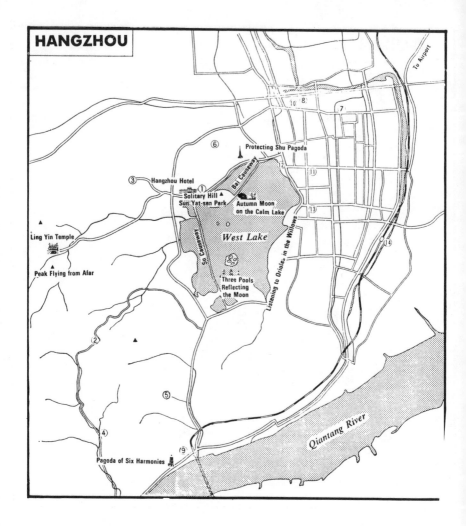

HANGZHOU

To Airport

Protecting Shu Pagoda

Bai Causeway

Hangzhou Hotel

Solitary Hill
Sun Yat-sen Park

Autumn Moon
on the Calm Lake

West Lake

Su Causeway

Ling Yin Temple

Peak Flying from Afar

Three Pools
Reflecting
the Moon

Listening to Orioles in the Willows

Pagoda of Six Harmonies

Qiantang River

1 Xileng Hotel
2 Dragon Well
3 Jade Fountain
4 Nine Creeks
5 Tiger Spring
6 Yellow Dragon Cave
7 Gymnasium
8 Provincial Exhibition Hall

9 Exhibition Hall of the Deeds
of Martyr Cai Yongxiang
10 Friendship Store
11 Arts and Crafts Store
12 Wai Wen Book Store
13 Department Store
14 Railway Station

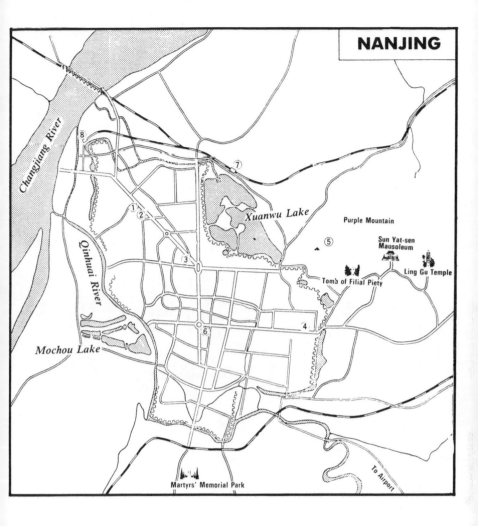

NANJING

Changjiang River

Qinhuai River

Mochou Lake

Xuanwu Lake

Purple Mountain

Sun Yat-sen Mausoleum

Ling Gu Temple

Tomb of Filial Piety

Martyrs' Memorial Park

To Airport

1 International Travel Service
  Branch

2 Nanjing Hotel

3 Drum Tower

4 Nanjing Museum

5 Observatory

6 People's Bazaar

7 Railway Station

8 West Railway Station

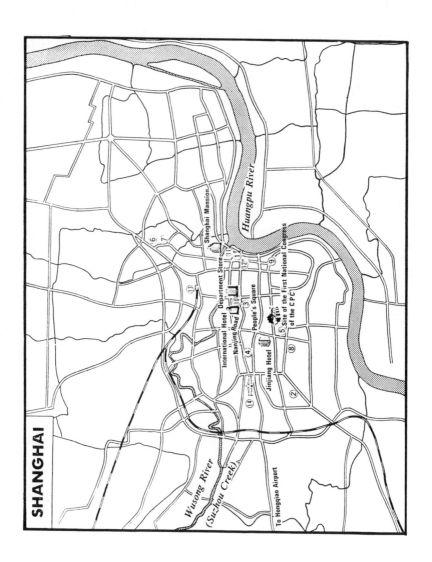

SHANGHAI

Huangpu River

Shanghai Mansion

Department Store

International Hotel

Nanjing Road

People's Square

Jinjiang Hotel

Site of the First National Congress of the C P C

Wusong River
(Suzhou Creek)

To Hongqiao Airport

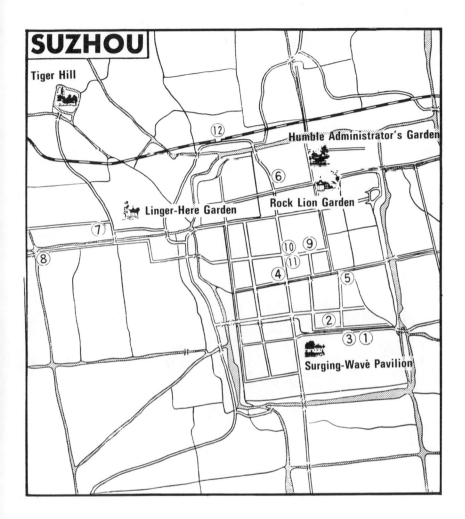

SUZHOU

Tiger Hill

⑫

Humble Administrator's Garden

⑥

Linger-Here Garden

Rock Lion Garden

⑦

⑧

⑩ ⑨

⑪

④

⑤

②

③ ①

Surging-Wave Pavilion

1 International Travel Service
  Branch
2 Nanlin Hotel
3 Wangshi Garden
4 Yiyuan Garden
5 Twin Pagodas
6 North Temple Pagoda

7 West Garden
8 Han Shan Temple
9 Friendship Store
10 Wai Wen Book Store
11 People's Bazaar Arts and
   Crafts Store
12 Railway Station

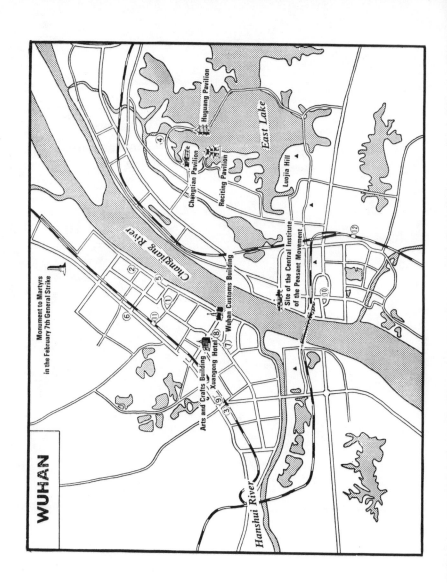

WUHAN

Monument to Martyrs in the February 7th General Strike

Changjiang River

Hanshui River

East Lake

Huguang Pavilion

Chengtian Pavilion

Reciting Pavilion

Luojia Hill

Wuhan Customs Building

Arts and Crafts Building

Xuangong Hotel

Site of the Central Institute of the Peasant Movement

1 Jianghan Hotel
2 Shengli Hotel
3 Wuhan Hotel
4 Monument to the Nine Heroines
5 Monument to the Battle Against Flood in 1954
6 Friendship Store
7 Arts and Crafts Store
8 Wai Wen Book Store
9 Wuhan Bazaar
10 Wuchang Department Store
11 Hankou Railway Station
12 Wuchang Railway Station

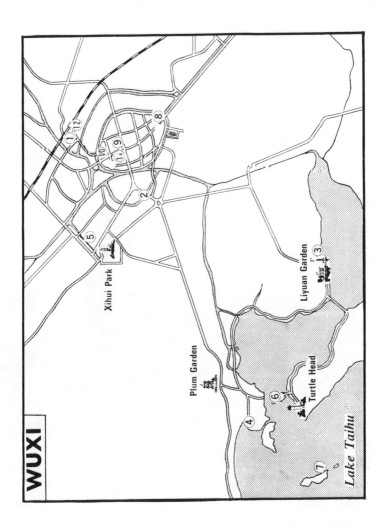

WUXI

Xihui Park

Plum Garden

Liyuan Garden

Turtle Head

Lake Taihu

1 International Travel Service Branch
2 Wuxi Hotel
3 Lihu Hotel
4 Taihu Hotel
5 Huishan Clay Figurine Factory
6 Worker's Sanatorium
7 Three-hill Island
8 Friendship Store
9 Antique Shop
10 First Department Store
11 Dongfanghong Bazaar
12 Railway Station

Lhasa, Xizang Autonomous Region (Tibet).

INDEX